The Novels of
ALEX MILLER

The Novels of
ALEX MILLER
An Introduction

Edited by Robert Dixon

LONDON AND NEW YORK

First published 1912 by Allen & Unwin

Published 2020 by Routledge
2 Park Square, Milton Park, Abingdon, Oxon OX14 4RN
605 Third Avenue, New York, NY 10017

Routledge is an imprint of the Taylor & Francis Group, an informa business

Introduction and selection copyright © Robert Dixon 2012
Copyright © in individual contributions retained by authors

All rights reserved. No part of this book may be reprinted or reproduced or utilised in any form or by any electronic, mechanical, or other means, now known or hereafter invented, including photocopying and recording, or in any information storage or retrieval system, without permission in writing from the publishers.

Notice:
Product or corporate names may be trademarks or registered trademarks, and are used only for identification and explanation without intent to infringe.

Cataloguing-in-Publication details are available
from the National Library of Australia
www.trove.nla.gov.au

Internal design by Brittany Britten
Set in 11/16 pt Minion by Post Pre-press Group, Australia

ISBN-13: 9781742378640 (pbk)

CONTENTS

Acknowledgements — vii
Chronology — viii

Disestablished Worlds: — 1
An Introduction to the Novels of Alex Miller
    Robert Dixon

1. **The Mask of Fiction:** A Memoir — 29
    Alex Miller

2. **Alex Miller and Leo Tolstoy:** — 42
Australian Storytelling in a European Tradition
    Brenda Walker

3. **'My Memory Has a Mind of Its Own':** — 55
Watching the Climbers on the Mountain and
The Tivington Nott
    Peter Pierce

4. **Alex Miller:** — 66
Migrant Writer
    Ingeborg van Teeseling

5. **The Presence of Absence in** *The Sitters* — 78
    Ronald A Sharp

6. **Like/Unlike:** — 89
Portraiture, Similitude and the Craft of Words in *The Sitters*
    Brigitta Olubas

7. **An Artist in the Family:** — 101
Reconfigurations of Romantic Paradigms in *Prochownik's Dream*
    Adrian Caesar

8. Representing 'the Other' in the Fiction of Alex Miller 114
    Elizabeth Webby

9. Continental Heartlands and Alex Miller's Geosophical Imaginary 125
    Elizabeth McMahon

10. Personal Perspectives on the Central Queensland Novels 139
    Frank Budby, Elizabeth Hatte and Anita Heiss

11. The Frontier Wars: 156
    History and Fiction in *Journey to the Stone Country* and *Landscape of Farewell*
    Shirley Walker

12. Old Testament Prophets, New Testament Saviours: 170
    Reading Retribution and Forgiveness Towards Whiteness in *Journey to the Stone Country*
    Liliana Zavaglia

13. Dougald's Goat: 187
    Alex Miller and the Species Barrier
    David Brooks

14. The Ruin of Time and the Temporality of Belonging: 201
    Journey to the Stone Country and *Landscape of Farewell*
    Brigid Rooney

15. Trusting the Words: 217
    Reflections on *Landscape of Farewell*
    Raimond Gaita

16. 'Bright Treasures of Perception': 231
    Writing Art and Painting Words in *Autumn Laing*
    Geordie Williamson

Further Reading 245
Contributors 249
Index 254

ACKNOWLEDGEMENTS

This book had its origins in a symposium on 'The Novels of Alex Miller' hosted by Australian Literature at the University of Sydney on 13–14 May 2011. Brenda Walker's chapter, 'Alex Miller and Leo Tolstoy: Australian Storytelling in a European Tradition', was originally presented on the evening of 13 May as the 2011 Herbert Blaiklock Memorial Lecture. I want to thank Alex Miller for his generous and tactful engagement with the project; Stephanie Miller for her assistance in preparing the Chronology and photographic illustrations, and her transcription of Chapter 11, 'Personal Perspectives on the Central Queensland Novels'; Frank Budby, Liz Hatte and Anita Heiss for their memorable involvement in the symposium; Geordie Williamson for his fine essay on what was, at the time of writing, a novel still in press; Melpomene Dixon, Georgina Loveridge, Stephen Mansfield and Liliana Zavaglia for various kinds of research, editorial and administrative assistance; and finally Elizabeth Weiss and Siobhán Cantrill at Allen & Unwin, and Ali Lavau, for their commitment to publishing a book of literary criticism and appreciation.

CHRONOLOGY

1936 Birth of Alexander McPhee Miller, 27 December, to Winifred Mary Millar (née Croft) and Alexander McPhee Millar. (The surname Miller is incorrectly entered into the records.) Lives at 32 Cumberland Street, London SW1 with parents and one sibling, Kathy.
1938 Moves with parents and two siblings, Kathy and Ruth, to 101 Pendragon Road, Downham, SE6.
1948 Birth of brother, Ross.
1951 Leaves home and works as a farm labourer in Somerset.
1952 Travels alone to Australia.
Works as a farm hand near Gympie; as a stockman at Goathlands Station near Springsure; then as a ringer on Augustus Downs in the Gulf of Carpentaria.
1957 Works in New Zealand breaking in horses.
1958 Arrives in Melbourne.
Meets Max Kelly, historian, who encourages Alex to go to university.
1959 Begins evening study to gain entry to university.
Meets Max and Ruth Blatt. Max becomes a close friend and mentor.
1961 Marries Anne Neil, social worker and artist in her later life. They separate for the last time in 1970 and divorce in 1983. Anne remains a close friend until her death in 2004.
1965 Completes Bachelor of Arts in history and English, University of Melbourne. Travels to Italy for three months and returns to England for one year, where he works for the Japanese Trade Commission.

1966   Works as research officer, Department of External Territories then Department of Trade and Industry, Canberra.
1969   Purchases farm at Araluen. Raises beef cattle while writing novels.
1974   Sells farm and travels to Paris to write and to learn French.
1975   Publishes 'Comrade Pawel' in *Meanjin* and meets Jim Davidson, historian and editor of *Meanjin*.
Meets lifelong partner Stephanie Pullin.
Completes Diploma of Education and commences teaching humanities at Brunswick Technical School. Develops a close friendship with Alan O'Hoy, art teacher, artist, art collector and the inspiration for Lang Tzu in *The Ancestor Game*.
1977   Travels to England with Stephanie.
1978   Returns to Melbourne for performance of *Kitty Howard* by the Melbourne Theatre Company.
Birth of Alex and Stephanie's son, Ross.
1980   Works as emergency humanities teacher.
Moves with Stephanie and Ross to Port Melbourne, their home for the next twenty-one years.
Founds Anthill Theatre with Jean-Pierre Mignon and ex-Pram Factory people. Meets playwright and novelist Ray Mooney.
1981   Performance of *Exiles* at Anthill.
1982   Encouraged by the poet Kris Hemensley, Alex abandons the theatre and returns to novel writing.
Begins teaching English at Glenroy Technical School.
1983   Marries Stephanie in Melbourne with his parents present.
1984   Death of Alex's father.
Negotiates half-time teaching position at Glenroy Technical School. Works on *The Tivington Nott*.
1986   Teaches professional writing half-time, Holmesglen College of TAFE. Meets Peter Davis, writer and photographer, and Liz Hatte, teacher and archaeologist.
1987   Visits Shanghai and Hangzhou with Stephanie and Ross while writing *The Ancestor Game*. Meets Ouyang Yu, poet and novelist.
1988   Publishes *Watching the Climbers on the Mountain*.

1989 Publishes *The Tivington Nott*.
Birth of Alex and Stephanie's daughter, Kate.
1990 Meets Barrett Reid, poet, and Paul Carter, writer and intellectual, at the Braille Award for *The Tivington Nott*. Is invited to Barrie Reid's home at Heide. At Heide he meets the artist Rick Amor and later sits for a portrait by Amor.
1992 Publishes *The Ancestor Game*.
1993 Receives his first major awards for *The Ancestor Game*: the Miles Franklin Literary Award, the Commonwealth Writers' Prize and the Barbara Ramsden Award.
Travels to London for a private audience with the Queen, then on to Toronto and New York for literary festivals.
1994 Death of Alex's mother.
Invited to teach creative writing at La Trobe University.
1995 Publishes *The Sitters*. Visits Tunisia and Rome for work on *Conditions of Faith*.
1997 Visits Liz Hatte in Townsville and meets Col McLennan, the models for Bo and Annabelle in *Journey to the Stone Country*.
2000 Publishes *Conditions of Faith* and begins an ongoing relationship with Allen & Unwin.
Spends six weeks in Paris with Stephanie and family.
Travels from Townsville to Mount Coolon with Liz Hatte and Col McLennan, elder of the Jangga. Meets Frank Budby, elder of the Barada, at Nebo. The friendships that follow lead to the novels *Journey to the Stone Country* and *Landscape of Farewell*.
2001 Wins the Christina Stead Prize for Fiction in the New South Wales Premier's Literary Awards for *Conditions of Faith*.
Awarded the Centenary Medal.
Moves from Port Melbourne to Castlemaine with Stephanie and Kate.
2002 Publishes *Journey to the Stone Country*.
Opens *Sanctuary* at Herring Island, an exhibition of work by artists Lyndell Brown, Charles Green and Patrick Pound. This experience informs the novel *Prochownik's Dream*.

	Begins an important literary friendship with the biographer Hazel Rowley.
2003	Wins second Miles Franklin Literary Award for *Journey to the Stone Country*.
2005	Publishes *Prochownik's Dream*.
	Meets writer, academic and Aboriginal activist Anita Heiss at an Australian literature conference in Hamburg.
2007	Publishes *Landscape of Farewell*.
2008	Travels to Beijing to accept the 2008 Weishanhu Award for Best Foreign Novel in the 21st Century from the People's Literature Publishing House in China for *Landscape of Farewell*.
	Awarded the Manning Clark House National Cultural Award for an outstanding contribution to the quality of Australian cultural life.
2009	Publishes *Lovesong*.
2010	Travels to Kilkenny in Ireland and to Scotland with Stephanie, visits London and while there finds the voice for Autumn in *Autumn Laing*.
2011	Wins the *Age* Fiction Award, the *Age* Book of the Year and the Christina Stead Prize for Fiction in the New South Wales Premier's Literary Awards, as well as the People's Choice Award, for *Lovesong*.
	Symposium on 'The Novels of Alex Miller', University of Sydney, 13–14 May.
	Publishes his tenth novel, *Autumn Laing*.
	In late 2011 Alex learned of the extraordinary coincidence that his great-great-aunt Jane Miller was married in Castlemaine in 1871—the country town where Alex lives with his wife Stephanie—and that Jane Miller died in South Yarra in 1900. It now seems Alex has several generations of family connections in Castlemaine and Melbourne.
	Until he received this information, Alex believed himself to be the sole representative of his family's line in Australia.

DISESTABLISHED WORLDS:
An Introduction to the Novels of Alex Miller

ROBERT DIXON

CRITIC AND NOVELIST BRENDA Walker begins her essay in this volume by suggesting that 'Alex Miller may be Australia's greatest living writer' (42). The purpose of *The Novels of Alex Miller* is to begin the work of testing that claim. Miller has now published ten novels. He has won the Miles Franklin Literary Award (twice), the Commonwealth Writers' Prize and the New South Wales Premier's Literary Award; his novels have been warmly embraced by Australian readers and translated into other languages, most notably into Chinese; and in 2001 he was awarded the Centenary Medal. Surprisingly, though, for a writer of this stature, there has yet been no major study of his life and work. One reason for this may simply be the reluctance of Australian publishers to take on serious, evaluative works of literary criticism: it has been many years now since the *Oxford Australian Writers* and the *UQP Australian Authors* series were wound up, and one consequence has been that an entire generation of Australian writers, including Miller, has not been accorded the critical appreciation that was routinely given to our major writers prior to the late 1980s.

A second reason may be that Miller has come upon us relatively quickly as a major writer. His first novel, *Watching the Climbers on the Mountain*, was published as recently as the Bicentennial year, 1988. Major national and international recognition came with the publication of his third novel, *The*

Ancestor Game, in 1992. As I write in August 2011, that is only nineteen years ago, yet Miller's tenth novel, *Autumn Laing*, is now in press and due for publication in October 2011. This is an extraordinary rate of production—on average, a major novel every two years—although, as we will see, Miller's commitment to the vocation of writing was made early, and the novels were sometimes long in gestation. His novels are by and large accessible to the general reading public yet manifestly of high literary seriousness—substantial, technically masterly and assured, intricately interconnected, and of great imaginative, intellectual and ethical weight.

A third reason may be that Miller's novels have often drawn upon and imaginatively transformed the details of his own life and the lives of his friends in ways that we are only now beginning to understand. We might recall how much our understanding of Patrick White, for example, was enhanced by the publication of his own memoir, *Flaws in the Glass*, in 1981, and by David Marr's biography and edition of the letters in 1991 and 1994. No wonder, then, that Australian readers and critics are still coming to terms with Miller's body of work. *The Novels of Alex Miller* has been designed to provide foundational information about Miller's life and the sources of his art that will further help readers to appreciate the richness and complexity of his achievement in fiction: to that end, it includes a memoir, 'The Mask of Fiction', freshly written for this collection, a chronology, a selection of photographs, and a series of essays in which nineteen contributors—including leading academic critics, novelists, writers and literary journalists—begin the work of exploring Miller's achievement across the entire range of his novels, from *Watching the Climbers on the Mountain* (1988) to *Autumn Laing* (2011).

Alexander McPhee Miller was born in London on 27 December 1936, the son of a Scottish father and an Irish mother. The family lived initially at 32 Cumberland Street, London SW1, and in 1938 moved to 101 Pendragon Road in the Downham council estate in Bromley SE6. His mother, Winifred, had been in private service before her marriage to his father, Alexander McPhee. His father was a cook at Crockford's Club and later at the Grosvenor Hotel in London. There were three other children: sisters Kathy and Ruth, and brother Ross. Miller has said that it was made 'very clear' to him that the family were not part of England's 'ruling culture', and that this made it difficult for him to find 'meaning and purpose' in his early life (Van Teeseling, interview). His sense of unsettlement was perhaps exacerbated by the effects of the war on his father's personality and behaviour, to which Miller refers discreetly in a number of essays and interviews. Increasingly estranged from his family and with no strong feelings of belonging to local or national communities, Miller sensed the need to get away, and at the age of fifteen he left school in London to work as a farm labourer on Exmoor in Somerset. There is an echo here—or perhaps it is an inverted echo, given their different family backgrounds and expatriate directions—of the young Patrick White, who at the same age also felt himself to be 'a stranger in my own country' (*Flaws*, 46). At this time, as he explains in 'The Mask of Fiction', Miller was shown a collection of black and white photographs of the Australian outback, the work—as he would learn many years later—of Sidney Nolan. These images had an intense impact on his burgeoning artistic sensibility and led him to formulate a plan of escape from the austerity of post-war Britain by emigration to a new country that he was coming to see in near-mythical terms. In *The Ancestor Game*, the young Lang Tzu, who is establishing the grounds of his own freedom by severing his ties with his ancestors, is advised to 'Long for something you can't name . . . and call it Australia' (259). Despite Miller's sense of displacement, this image of place as a site of almost utopian possibility would recur in the novels that began to germinate in his memory and imagination from this time. It is what Bill Ashcroft, drawing on the utopian philosophy of Ernst Bloch, describes as '*Heimat*', 'that "home" that we all sense but have never experienced', and which is fundamental to literature's role in producing those moments of 'anticipatory illumination' by which we begin to imagine a different world ('Australian Transnation', 1).

Miller arrived in Australia alone in 1952 at the age of sixteen. It was to be his 'land of fresh beginnings', and he immediately hitchhiked north from Sydney in search of Nolan's outback. Despite the uncertainties of his childhood, photographs taken at this time show a young man whose physical strength and youthful grace are suggestive of an inner strength: a growing sense of purpose and self-presence. For the next six years he would work in a variety of rural jobs, initially as a farm hand near Gympie in southeast Queensland, then as a stockman at Goathlands Station near Springsure in Queensland's Central Highlands, and later as a ringer on Augustus Downs, a cattle station in the Gulf of Carpentaria. In 1957 there was a spell as a horse breaker in New Zealand. He recalls that the dramatic escarpments of the Central Queensland ranges were not quite Nolan's outback, 'but I fell in love with the country', and when he returned to it as a successful writer in 2000, it would inspire the settings of his Central Queensland novels, *Journey to the Stone Country* (2002) and *Landscape of Farewell* (2007).

Miller 'came out of the bush' when he was twenty-one, arriving in Melbourne in 1958. Recognising his artistic and intellectual aspirations, a group of friends—including Polish Jewish émigrés Max and Ruth Blatt, and the historian Max Kelly—encouraged him to undertake the evening studies that would allow him to qualify for university entrance. Miller was an arts student at the University of Melbourne in the early 1960s, graduating in 1965 with majors in history and English. At this time he met Anne Neil, a social worker and painter, whom he married in 1961. The marriage failed, but after their final separation in 1970 and until her death from a stroke in 2004, Anne remained a close friend to Miller and his second wife, Stephanie. After graduation, Miller spent some months travelling in Italy and returned to England, where he worked for the Japanese Trade Commission and began to heal the breach with his first family. Returning to Australia in 1966, he worked as a research officer for the Department of External Territories and then for the Department of Trade and Industry in Canberra, but in 1969 he left the public service and bought a farm in the Araluen Valley west of Goulburn, where he raised beef cattle and began his apprenticeship as a novelist.

Miller has said that while he had been a storyteller from early childhood, it took many years before he found his 'authentic material' ('Waxing', 24). A key to this process was the wise counsel of his friend, Max Blatt, whom Miller recalls as 'a central European intellectual of the kind JP Stern and WG Sebald write about with such beautiful nostalgic elegance' ('Waxing', 25). Max interpreted European literature and philosophy to him in a way that he had not encountered at university, and helped him find his vocation as a writer. At Araluen, between 1969 and 1974, Miller wrote three manuscripts which he describes as his 'pre-novels' ('Waxing', 25). Max would come up to visit by train from Melbourne, staying for a week at a time. On one such visit, Miller presented him with a 400-page novel in manuscript, which Max read through the day and into the early evening. Miller recalls: 'I was woken by the thump of the 400 pages landing beside my head. I sprang up. Max was lighting a cigarette. With a mixture of disappointment, frustration and regret, he said, "Why don't you write about something you *love*?"' ('Waxing', 25). And then an exchange took place between the two men that resonates throughout Miller's mature novels. That night, Max Blatt told Miller the story of his own escape from an anti-Semitic attack in Poland at the beginning of the war: 'He told me the simple bones of the story in a few sentences. I did not sleep that night but wrote the story in detail and in the morning I gave it to him to read ... When he finished reading it, he said with feeling, "You could have been there", and embraced me' ('Waxing', 25). The result was Miller's first published piece of fiction, the short story 'Comrade Pawel' (1975), which is set in Poland in 1939. This sharing of a personal story foreshadows the way Steven Muir, in *The Ancestor Game*, reworks Gertrude Spiess's own fictionalisation of her father's diaries; it foreshadows the way the artist's memory is reinvigorated by his encounter with Jessica Keal in *The Sitters*, and again when Toni Powlett first speaks of his father's death to Marina Golding in *Prochownik's Dream* (2005); it prefigures Professor Max Otto's writing up of Dougald Gnapun's account of his ancestor's military leadership in *Landscape of Farewell*; and it is echoed nearly forty years later in the novelist's appropriation of John Patterner's story in *Lovesong* (2009). In recalling this foundational moment with Max Blatt, Miller asks, 'Why did I believe, and why do I still believe, that this story was mine? What made it mine?' ('Waxing', 25).

There is much here that illuminates the novelist's craft and preoccupations. These include, as Peter Pierce remarked in a pioneering article on Miller, the essential 'solitariness' of the writer who nonetheless enters into deeply empathic engagements with other people and other cultures; the sharing of a private experience or place or event that triggers the memory and imagination of both teller and listener; and the simultaneously imaginative and ethical nature of both interpersonal engagements, and the equally intimate acts of writing and reading: 'He told me the story so that I would understand … anti-Semitism' and 'I took him to mean … that my account of the events that happened to him … conveyed the truth of his experience' ('Waxing', 25). Miller therefore shares with Jacques Derrida a concern with the ethics of friendship as a force for our own becoming, which nonetheless honours the essential difference of the other person. And he shares with Martha Nussbaum a belief that the novel is peerless among modern forms of communication for dealing with the affective and ethical dimension of human relationships, both intimate and social. Writing, Miller has said, is his way of 'locating connections' in what has otherwise been a life characterised by a series of disconnections—'plural selves, worlds and cultures' ('The Mask of Fiction', 30). Those three 'pre-novels' had been too self-absorbed to interest a publisher. The exchange with Max Blatt and the writing of 'Comrade Pawel', however, awakened the relationship between the self and the other that is not only a hallmark of Miller's novels, but also of his mode of writing as an imaginative and ethical practice. As he puts it so simply and directly, 'In this preoccupation with the self I was mistaken, and it was not until I ceased writing directly about myself and began to write imaginatively of the people and the places most dear to me that my writing began to … gain me a readership' ('The Mask of Fiction').

After the sale of the Araluen property in 1974, and following a period in Paris, Miller moved back to Melbourne where he completed a Diploma of Education and began a new career as a humanities teacher at Brunswick Technical School. He there developed a close friendship with Alan O'Hoy, an art teacher, artist and art collector who would be the inspiration for Lang Tzu in *The Ancestor Game*. Also in 1975, Miller met Stephanie Pullin, whom he married in 1983. In 'The Mask of Fiction', he confesses that meeting Stephanie and creating their family finally made sense of his life (30): their son Ross was born in 1978 and their daughter Kate in 1989. In 1980, the family moved to Port Melbourne, where they lived for the next twenty-one years until the move to Castlemaine in central Victoria in 2001.

During the late 1970s and early 1980s, Miller was active in Melbourne theatre circles and focused on writing plays. *Kitty Howard* was performed by the Melbourne Theatre Company in 1978, and in 1980 he co-founded the Anthill Theatre with Jean-Pierre Mignon and others from the Pram Factory.

His play *Exiles* was performed there the following year. In 1982, encouraged by the poet Kris Hemensley, Miller abandoned the theatre and returned to novel writing. Supporting himself and his young family by a series of teaching positions—full-time at Glenroy Technical School from 1982 and then half-time from 1984, and half-time at Holmesglen College of TAFE from 1986—Miller set about making the difficult transition to being a professional writer. He was working on a large manuscript that would become his first two published novels, *Watching the Climbers on the Mountain* and *The Tivington Nott*. They were originally conceived as a single work drawing on Miller's experience as a farm hand on Exmoor, his subsequent emigration to Australia, and his years in Central Queensland and the Gulf of Carpentaria. It was to be called *Jimmy Diamond*, in memory of an Aboriginal ringer with whom he had worked in the Gulf Country in the mid 1950s. As he explains in 'The Mask of Fiction', 'this book was going to bridge the two lives, the two worlds, and their apparently unconnected realities' (32), but when he reached the end of the Exmoor section, he realised that the first novel had emerged from his re-creative imagination whole and complete. It was a novel about English rural life, and Miller was unable to find a publisher for it in Australia, and so the second novel to be written, *Watching the Climbers on the Mountain*, which is set in Central Queensland, was published first, in Sydney in 1988. The Exmoor novel, *The Tivington Nott*, was published in London in 1989. In these first two novels, we find in their earliest form many of the themes of Miller's later work. As Brenda Walker observes, *The Tivington Nott* 'is centrally concerned with the situation of the outsider' (48); it is 'a meditation on issues of territory and intrusion' (49). And despite their different settings, their shared gestation is readily apparent in the many structural and thematic connections between them. As Peter Pierce says of *Watching the Climbers on the Mountain*, 'a hemisphere away, but we are again with a closed rural community, as in *The Tivington Nott*, one that is about to be disrupted by an outsider' (59).

Miller was now in his early fifties, and in drawing upon his earlier experiences for fiction, he has said that he felt like an archaeologist who had only just begun to excavate 'a buried city of great complexity' ('This Is How', 30). Those metaphors he uses to describe the original project of *Jimmy Diamond*—the novel as a bridge between lives, between worlds, between 'apparently unconnected realities'—appear casual enough, but as we get to know Miller's work and become accustomed to his voice, we learn that he never utters a lightly considered phrase. Typically, these are leitmotifs that signal his lifelong aesthetic and ethical preoccupations; they are meant to reveal to us the profound interconnections between his novels, whose architecture is indeed, we come to see, like some 'buried city of great complexity'. In *Watching the Climbers on the Mountain*, for example, Ward Rankin's library anticipates the library at Ranna in *Journey to the Stone Country*, while Ida Rankin's climbing of Mount Mooloolong as a young girl gives her a 'sacred place' and a private story that she will later share with the young stockman, Robert Crofts, anticipating the sharing of places and stories in the later novels. Typically for Miller, these are acts of both giving and taking, of love and betrayal, of guilt and redemption. They include Huang's journey with his daughter Lien to the shrine of their ancestors in *The Ancestor Game*, Bo Rennie and Annabelle Beck's plan, later abandoned, to travel together to the ritual sites of the old people in *Journey to the Stone Country*, and Max Otto and Dougald Gnapun's journey to find the burial site of his ancestor, the warrior Gnapun, in *Landscape of Farewell*. These recurring patterns and motifs between the early and late works signal that Miller's novels are part of a continuing and connected project that demands synoptic reading.

Miller's third novel, *The Ancestor Game*, brought national and international recognition. In 1993, it won the Miles Franklin Literary Award, the Commonwealth Writers' Prize and the Barbara Ramsden Award, and he was feted at literary events in Australia, Canada, the United States and the United Kingdom, where he was granted a private audience with the Queen. The seed of that novel lay in another friendship, in this case with the artist Alan O'Hoy, whom Miller had met while teaching at Brunswick Tech in the mid 1970s. It began as an impulse to honour the life of his Chinese-Australian friend, whose suicide is evoked subtly by Lang Tzu's unexplained disappearance in the final pages of the novel. While writing it in 1987, Miller also visited Shanghai and Hangzhou, and his understanding of Chinese history and culture was deepened by a number of people, including Professor Bao Chien-hsing of the Shanghai Foreign Language Institute, the painter Yehching, Nicholas Jose, who was then cultural attaché at the Australian Embassy in Beijing, and the writer Ouyang Yu. The novel is dedicated to Max and Ruth Blatt, and its cover features the painting *Celestial Lane* (1989) by Rick Amor, whom Miller had met at Heide, the home of the poet Barrett Reid, in 1990.

Miller writes in 'The Mask of Fiction' that *The Ancestor Game* was 'my attempt to make sense of my friend's life and death, to see his alienation from his community and culture as something of exceptional value' (33). At the heart of the novel is Miller's conviction that the modern artist is an exile in his own country. This is conveyed by the book's introductory citation from Kierkegaard: 'Our age has lost all the substantial categories of family, state and race. It must leave the individual entirely to himself, so that in a stricter sense he becomes his own creator.' *The Ancestor Game* begins with Melbourne writer Steven Muir returning briefly to England, where he remains estranged from his mother and unreconciled to the memory of his father. Back in Melbourne in 1976—the year of Mao's death—he is writing a book called *The Chronicle of the Fengs*, and is drawn into friendships with Lang Tzu, an art teacher, artist and collector, and Lang's friend, the artist and writer Gertrude Spiess. Gertrude's father, August Spiess, was an expatriate German doctor working in the international community in Shanghai in the 1920s and 1930s, who delivered Lang and became his tutor, later accompanying him to Melbourne when he was sent abroad by his wealthy industrialist father, CH Feng, to avoid the Japanese invasion of China in 1937. As Elizabeth Webby observes, these themes of dislocation and diaspora, and also the manner of the novel's construction, built up through a nested series of perspectives on the stories of the Feng and Spiess families across several generations and in several locations, make it one of Miller's most postmodern works (117).

Each of the traditional cultures described in *The Ancestor Game*, including those of Germany, China, and both Anglo and Indigenous Australia, has been severed from the apparent plenitude of its past by the globalising forces of colonialism, war and commerce. In China in 1927, Lang is born into 'a disintegrating world' (290). The forces at play are represented by his (traditional) maternal inheritance—his grandfather's crumbling home in Hangzhou and his vocation as a scholar and literary painter—and his (modern) paternal inheritance—his father's house in Shanghai, which 'mimics' European styles and expresses Feng's 'commitment to internationalism' (29). Lang's conflicted relation to these historical forces is expressed by the trauma of his breech birth and the asymmetrical features of his damaged face. In choosing to destroy Huang's ancient book of the ancestors, Lang cuts the taproot of tradition and from this point he must live as a modern person, 'at home while travelling' (193). Yet there is no simple division here between past and present, between tradition and modernity, for what appears to be the authenticity of the past is often an effect of nostalgia and retrospection. Lang's fall into modernity is not simply caused by his destruction of a still-living, authentic culture, since the past has already been subject to change—as is evident in the earlier events, including the First Opium Wars and the Victorian gold rush of the 1850s, which caused his paternal great-grandfather, the first Feng, to live between worlds, with families in both Melbourne and Amoy.

This massive canvas of cultural dislocation provides a rich context for Miller's reflections on the nature of fiction and the artistic sensibility. As Huang attempts to fend off the modern world by undertaking a pilgrimage to the tomb of his ancestors, Lang is destroying the book of the ancestors and accepting 'the precious gift of dimorphism' (193). Like his tutor, Dr Spiess, Lang is a traveller, a pilgrim, an extraterritorial, a prodigal son: 'Lang Tzu; two characters which in Mandarin signify the son who goes away' (116). Spiess helps him to see that this condition of becoming, and not the illusory timelessness of his grandfather's house, is the true legacy of the modern artist: 'Art belongs to no nation. Art is the displaced. It is not validated by nationality' (260). As a son who also went away, Miller's own biographical displacement is visibly braided into his fictionalisation of Alan O'Hoy's story.

In Spiess's diaries, Miller pursues a series of associations between the colonist, the invader, the parasite and the artist that are among his central preoccupations as a writer. On his visit to Huang's home in 1927, Spiess is dressed in a fur coat and served ceremonial meals, likening his appearance to 'a lava of one of their famous silkworms ... waiting to be fed my due apportionment of mulberry leaves' (119). Realising that as a foreign invader he presents a theatrical spectacle to the resentful Chinese servants, he speculates on the etymological link between 'lava' and 'mask': 'in Latin it signifies a mask or spectre whose true form is hidden, a form yet to be revealed ... It was but a short step from this ... to the full-blown idea of the fantastic and motley character of the masque itself' (120). As an invader, Spiess is like the writer who hides behind what Miller tellingly calls 'The Mask of Fiction', partly for the purposes of storytelling, partly so that he can plunder the stories of others, and partly to mask his own metamorphosis.

These associations are developed further when Steven comes upon the work table of Lang's Melbourne relative, Victoria Feng, also a writer, in a gazebo in the grounds of Coppin Grove. The gazebo has a military origin: it is a place of vantage where one keeps a look out for the enemy. Steven's discovery of the gazebo is a fable about the artist both as an observer and as an invader in the homeland of the other. As he approaches, he parts 'the tremulous mask of aspen leaves' that shields it from observation, and realises that he has become a parasite: 'I had found my way there ... by the instinctive homing intuitions of a true parasite ... I was delighted by the extension of my metaphor, of myself as a parasite, as "one who eats at the table of another"' (153–4). Earlier, this metaphor is rendered literal when Steven is given access to the palimpsest of Lang's family archive, which is piled upon and beneath the dining table at Coppin Grove: 'Occupying the centre of this room was a mahogany table of magisterial proportions ... Completely covering the ample surface of the table, to a depth of half a metre or more, was a disordered heap of unstretched oils and watercolours and sketches and books and catalogues and other marginalia ... a collection, a hoard' (66). Steven's parasitic relation to his material is paralleled in Gertrude and Victoria's own, earlier plundering of their ancestors' stories. Like Steven Muir—and Alex Miller—Victoria writes 'with a desire to make the material of her scrutiny her own, to possess it by means of the location of herself at its centre. She enters it by degrees. She insinuates herself' (159).

The idea that the artist is an 'extraterritorial' is explored in Spiess's reflections on the imaginary landscapes of the painter Claude Lorrain, who was himself neither German, French nor Italian. Nor was he a mapmaker (274) because his landscapes are imaginary places that anyone can inhabit by imagination rather than by right of citizenship. The international settlement at Shanghai is just such a Claudian landscape and Spiess sees himself as one of its 'extraterritorials', 'beings not from present reality', 'inhabitants of a

No-land' (93). In such phrases, Miller appears to celebrate extraterritoriality, and has spoken positively of the ambiguities bestowed on artists and writers by cultural displacement ('The Mask of Fiction', 32). This is certainly the fate that Lang chooses. Having violated his grandfather's study, he plays the ancestor game, a process of self-invention in which he is free to make up the rules as he goes along. If art is beyond nation, then Lang has no place in China, but Spiess suggests that he may find a home in Australia: 'You are literally un-familiar here. But in Australia, which is I believe a kind of phantom country lying invisibly somewhere between the West and the East, you may find a few of your own displaced and hybrid kind to welcome you' (260). As a place of exile and migration, Miller's Australia therefore anticipates the postmodern condition from the moment of its foundation. The painting to which Elizabeth Webby refers in her chapter—once owned by Alan O'Hoy and now in the Art Gallery of Ballarat—is of a Chinaman, an Irishman and an Aborigine—corresponding to Miller's characters Feng, Nunan and Dorset—each of whom is forcibly liberated from his ancestral ties. Miller might therefore be seen as espousing ideas of hybridity, diaspora and indeterminacy that were popular in postcolonial and postmodern theory in the 1980s. Yet these ideas at play in Spiess's diaries are also subject to narrative irony. The extraterritorial is not, after all, immune from reality—as Dorset discovers when he is killed by white settlers—and the colonist or invader is locked in a two-way relation of power with the other, its host—as Spiess discovers when he is attacked by a mob of Chinese workers and is then forced to witness their torture and execution in a Shanghai police cell. 'For twenty blissful years,' Spiess writes, 'I had lived as if the condition of extraterritoriality were a kind of literary conceit' (268).

The Sitters (1995) was the next in a sequence of Miller's novels, including *The Ancestor Game* and *Prochownik's Dream*, that together constitute one of the most sustained examples of ekphrasis (or writing about art) in Australian literature. Miller once had aspirations to be a painter, and has many connections with the art world among his family and friends. Like the unnamed artist's father in *The Sitters*, Miller's father was an amateur watercolourist. His first wife, Anne Neil, was a painter, and there are a number of painters among his Melbourne friends, including Alan O'Hoy and Rick Amor. The studio practices described in these novels—including Lindner's Gallery in *The Ancestor Game* and Toni Powlett's studio in *Prochownik's Dream*—are informed by Miller's knowledge of Rick Amor's studio, while the friendship with Reid provided a link with the legendary period at Heide, and with Sidney Nolan whose work, as we have seen, Miller has long admired.

In *The Sitters*, Miller continues to explore the issues of ethics and aesthetics initiated in *The Ancestor Game*. Ronald Sharp argues that it is a novel that 'foregrounds the connections between literary and visual art, between a novelist creating a character and a painter creating a portrait' (78). *The Sitters* also exemplifies Miller's view that 'The novel . . . is always the story of the isolated self seeking to transcend its isolation by becoming the other' ('Chasing', 6). Brigitta Olubas gets to the heart of these matters in her discussion, drawing on Veronica Brady's original review, of the artist's first charged encounter with Jessica Keal: 'It points us to the real subject, a ceremonious introspection, at once profoundly intimate and yet paradoxically impersonal, as the artist pursues her in himself and himself in her through labyrinthine ways of memory as well as of the unfolding of ambiguous relationships' (92). The artist's quest for understanding of himself through the practice of portraiture is made all the more poignant when it is revealed, finally, that Jessica Keal is absent, having died before the commencement of the present narrative. There are affinities here with Maurice Blanchot's concern with the intimate relation between writing and death, or writing and absence, as both Sharp and Olubas demonstrate. In retrospect, the presence of this absence can be felt in the novel's powerful opening sentences: 'When I was old and could no longer hope for new friendships, one of the saddest episodes of my life began to come back to me and to offer me the greatest joy. Under the influence of this memory, revisiting me in its new guise, I was able to paint again . . . And that is what she gave me, Jessica Keal, the subject of this altered memory' (1).

In *Prochownik's Dream*, Miller explores the roles of friendship and collaboration in the creation of art, but also, as Adrian Caesar argues, its potentially damaging effects on friendships and families. 'We are all collaborators,' Marina Golding says to Toni Powlett. 'All of us. None of us does this completely on our own' (156). When Toni is reluctant to give Marina his drawing of her she realises, 'You did it for yourself, not for me' (55), and when he looks at an earlier sketch, made while he was a student, he is aware of 'the trace of himself at the edge of the drawing' (67). This echoes the artist's initial refusal, in *The Sitters*, to let Jessica Keal see his portrait of her, which Olubas recognises as 'a dispute over ownership of the likeness' (97). Collaboration, then, is central to Miller's thinking about artistic practice and yet, as his comparison of the artist to an invader and a parasite suggests, that word has darker meanings in the sense of betrayal of one's friends and family, either by destroying something that belongs to them or through complicity with outsiders. These positive and negative meanings are explored together in the complex knot of collaborations that link the Schwartz/Golding and Powlett/Prochownik families. The collaboration between Robert Schwartz, who is an academic and writes essays for *Art and Text*, and his partner Marina Golding, is one in which he provides the theories and subjects that she then realises in paint. Marina's instinctive sense of Robert's constraint of her creativity is one contributing factor leading to her collaboration, in a very different way, with Toni Powlett, Robert's former student, which bristles with Oedipal motives. But as Caesar astutely observes, it is the transformation of 'human mystery' and the 'libidinous energy' of relationships that make art, not academic theories (104). Like Steven Muir, Toni Powlett rediscovers his artistic energies by 'insinuating' himself into Robert and Marina's lives, drawing parasitically on the tensions that hold them together and push them apart as a couple: he 'mines their intimacies' (132). Toni's studio, like Victoria's gazebo at Coppin Grove, is set apart from his own family home, a place from which to look out for the enemy—in one sense his wife, Teresa, whose dedication to their domestic life supports Toni's professional career, making her, too, a collaborator, but at the same time preventing her from being his muse. One register of the novel's language, relating art to war and the hunt, reveals the moral ambivalence of these energies that produce art, perhaps recalling Patrick White's idea of the artist as a vivisector.

With the publication of *Conditions of Faith* in 2000, Miller moved from Penguin, who had published both *The Ancestor Game* and *The Sitters*, to Allen & Unwin, where he began what has been an ongoing relationship with publisher Annette Barlow. The novel had an unusually difficult birth, as Miller explains in 'The Mask of Fiction', having been interrupted by his work on *The*

Sitters. Its inspiration was a diary of his mother's that came into his possession after her death, which allowed him to imagine her hopes and aspirations as a young woman. In 1995, while researching the novel, Miller also visited Tunisia and Rome. As always, behind the mask of fiction, the novelist was looking not only into the life of another person, but 'chiastically', as Brigid Rooney puts it, into the life of the self: 'While I wrote,' he recalls, 'I did so with my love of my mother foremost in my mind masking the deeper impulse to tell my own story, indeed to conflate her story and my own' (34).

Like Lang Tzu, Miller's young Australian heroine, Emily Stanton, embraces her future by divesting herself of a series of possible identities laid out for her in advance. Her challenge, like Lang's in playing the ancestor game, is to reinvent 'the conditions of faith' under which she can conduct a meaningful life after the old absolutes of home, family, patriarchy, religious faith and national identity have been abandoned. While Spiess describes Lang's condition as 'dimorphic', Emily's might be thought of as 'cosmopolitan' in the sense that Amanda Anderson uses the term: that is, 'the capacious inclusion of multiple forms of affiliation, disaffiliation, and reaffiliation, simultaneously insisting on the need for informing principles of self-reflexivity, critique, and common humanity' (*The Powers of Distance*, 30–1).

The events of the novel unfold across a single year, 1923, during which Emily not only marries, moves from Melbourne to Paris with her husband Georges and gives birth to a daughter, but also gives birth to a new self, fashioned in response to new and exotic cultures. The beginnings of this reaffiliation lie in her friendship with Antoine Carpeaux, a homosexual friend of Georges's, who introduces her to modes of living beyond her inherited ideas of home and family, and to cultures and ways of life that carry her beyond her own nation and the Anglophone world in which it remains embedded. It is this ability to create convincing characters from a wide range of different periods and cultures that has earned Miller his well-deserved reputation for sympathetic characterisation. Emily writes to her father, 'I could not imagine meeting such a man in Melbourne' (58–9). Antoine's father was a French landowner in Tunisia, and during Emily's difficult pregnancy, while Georges is preoccupied with his work in Paris, he takes Emily to convalesce at Sidi bou-Saïd, his family's home near the ancient Roman amphitheatre at Carthage. Here, Emily discovers an intellectual vocation in reinterpreting the life of the early Christian martyr, Perpetua. This project of cross-cultural research is gifted to her by her new friends, who invite her to enter into and interpret their worlds. The tokens of this invitation are Perpetua's medallion, given to her by Antoine, an edition of Perpetua's journal, given to her by the archaeologist Hakim el-Ouedi, and the academic career given to her by her mentor, the American scholar Dr Olive Kallen.

Emily's interest in Perpetua's story is cosmopolitan in the sense of being a compulsion to think and feel beyond the nation, but it is also deeply personal and therefore compromised. The invader, as we have seen in Miller's earlier novels, is always deeply involved with those whose territory he enters. Just as Spiess had wrongly believed that his extraterritoriality made him immune to the lives of the Chinese, so Emily is an engaged observer: Perpetua's struggle with the Catholic church parallels her own struggle to accept her unwanted pregnancy to a Catholic priest. Far from seeing this as a handicap, however, Hakim is alert to the importance of a scholar's intimate engagement with their material. Foreshadowing the collaboration between Dougald Gnapun and Max Otto in *Landscape of Farewell*, Hakim and his colleague, Ahmed, have approached her because they hope that this foreign woman might open up a new and empowering interpretation of their nation's history: 'Give her the book, [Ahmed] told me. She's a young married woman and is to have a child soon ... Ahmed ... thought you might see something in [Perpetua's] situation that we don't see' (178). Although Hakim pays tribute to the British ideal of disinterested scholarship (207), the reality is that all involved in the struggle for interpretation of Perpetua's story are compromised by conflicts of interest. Emily wishes to be 'an independent scholar' but this cannot be achieved without the generous and liberating gifts of her French, Tunisian and American friends. Her intellectual vocation is at once grounded in her own condition while aspiring to be universal; it is personally motivated but requires sympathy for other cultures; it strives for objectivity and scholarly rigour while being complicit with a number of incompatible interests—religious, ethnic, national and personal. In that regard she resembles the novelist.

Miller had 'come out of the bush' when he moved to Melbourne in 1958, and it was not until the late 1980s, when he began *Watching the Climbers on the Mountain*, that he began to draw deeply on that period of his life in writing fiction. Even then, he would again set the Queensland material aside for a number of years while he worked with the very different subject matter of *The Ancestor Game*, *The Sitters* and *Conditions of Faith*. The delay was perhaps more significant than it seemed, revealing a profound personal disconnection between his present and past lives that corresponded to an equally profound series of disconnections in Australian history and in the contemporary public sphere. 'For more than twenty years,' he recalls in 'The Mask of Fiction', 'I thought my Queensland days would never be part of my life again' (31). Although Miller felt this to be a personal and perhaps unusual experience, in reality it was symptomatic of Australia's dissociation from its frontier history at this time. In 1983, I had myself moved from Sydney via Perth to Far North Queensland, where I first met the historian Henry Reynolds at James Cook University in Townsville. I well remember the extraordinary impact of the region's climate and landscape, and the palpable sense of its colonial history, and so I understood immediately when Reynolds told me that he could never have begun the research that led to his seminal book, *The Other Side of the Frontier* (1981), had he not moved to Townsville from Hobart some years earlier. Miller's apparently autobiographical sense of disconnection between his regional and metropolitan experience, the amnesia that seemed to separate these two times and places in his life in Australia, were in fact symptomatic of the time. As a novelist, he was about to commence a major and distinctive new phase of his career, working now in the late 1990s to bring these two parts of the Australian experience together in fiction in a way that would be as significant as the books that Reynolds was writing at much the same time: *This Whispering in Our Hearts*, for example, appeared in 1998.

The opportunity for Miller to bridge the two hemispheres of his experience came about once again through a gift of friendship and the sharing of personal stories. Miller had first met Liz Hatte when they were both working at Holmesglen TAFE in 1986. While he made the transition to full-time writing, she left teaching to study archaeology, eventually returning to her home in Townsville, where she established Northern Archaeological Consultancies, a company that specialises in reports on prior Indigenous occupation for mining companies and government instrumentalities. When Miller visited her in Townsville in 1997, he met her partner, Col McLennan, a Jangga elder who in his youth had been a ringer in Central Queensland. Miller recalls, 'it was the first time I had spoken with a ringer from the old days . . . A vital connection was made for me through Col and his story between the two worlds of my early years in North Queensland and my subsequent university and writing life in Melbourne' (00). In 2000, Miller returned to Townsville, and McLennan took him to the country of his people, the Jangga, and to meet his old droving partner, Frank Budby, a Barada elder from Nebo. Liz Hatte, Col McLennan and Frank Budby were the inspiration for Annabelle Beck, Bo Rennie and Dougald Gnapun in Miller's Central Queensland novels, *Journey to the Stone Country* and *Landscape of Farewell*. Miller says of *Journey to the Stone Country*, which in 2003 won him his second Miles Franklin Literary Award, 'It is a reflection of my own realities and the realities of those friends, heightened, simplified and transmuted into the organic whole of story' (00).

Just as Miller's first two novels were initially conceived as a single larger work, *Jimmy Diamond*, so the Central Queensland novels first emerged in his thinking as a Reconciliation Trilogy, with a third, projected novel to be called *The Departure* (Miller, email, 2006). At the dark inner core of both *Journey to the Stone Country* and *Landscape of Farewell* is the persistence of violence in human history, especially the frontier violence of colonial Australia: in the first novel, a massacre of Aboriginal men, women and children by the first generation of white settlers in Central Queensland, and in the second, a massacre of white settlers by Aboriginal people. As Shirley Walker says, 'Miller is nothing if not even-handed' (00). In 'The Mask of Fiction', Miller explains that the distinctive purpose of *Landscape of Farewell* emerged during a visit to Hamburg in 2005, when he began to seek ways of connecting the frontier massacres in Australia with his childhood memories of the Holocaust. As a young schoolboy in London, he had seen the terrible newsreels recording the entry of Allied troops into the death camps of Belsen and Buchenwald, and 'A sense of guilt-by-association was inescapable' (00). At Springsure in the mid 1950s, Miller had first heard accounts of the massacre at Cullin-la-Ringo Station in 1861, in which a large group of settlers was killed by Aborigines. Inspired by his meeting in Hamburg with Indigenous writer Anita Heiss—the model for Professor Vita McLelland in the novel—he began to sketch 'lines of intersection' between these traumatic events, hoping to see 'how they fitted together into a whole, not an Australian or a European whole, but a human whole' (37). The heroism of Gnapun the warrior, the leader and strategist of the Cullin-la-Ringo massacre, was also a way of celebrating the contemporary leadership of Frank Budby, whom Miller describes as 'a quiet, unassuming and deeply intelligent man', who 'rescued his people from the depredations of white culture' (36). The genesis of these two important and closely linked novels is recalled here both in Miller's memoir, 'The Mask of Fiction', and in 'Personal Perspectives on the Central Queensland Novels', the transcript of a panel session with Frank Budby, Liz Hatte and Anita Heiss at the University of Sydney symposium, The Novels of Alex Miller, on 14 May 2011.

These are the biographical sources of the Central Queensland novels, but as we have seen, they also have links to broader developments in the public life of Australia at this time. *Journey to the Stone Country* and *Landscape of Farewell* were partly a response, in ways that we are still coming to understand, to the controversial issues associated with race politics in Australia in the 1980s and 1990s. Liliana Zavaglia reminds us that 'apology and the admission of the Aboriginal dead into the pages of white history have been difficult prospects for Australians' (174). Miller first met Liz Hatte on the eve of the Bicentenary of European 'settlement' in 1988, which sparked criticism from Indigenous leaders and calls for land rights, sovereignty and a treaty. In 1992 the High Court of Australia delivered its *Mabo* decision, which gave a basis in law for claims to native title, dispelling the legal fiction of *terra nullius*. In 1997, the year Miller first visited Hatte in Townsville, the Human Rights and Equal Opportunity Commission's report, *Bringing Them Home: Report of the National Inquiry into the Separation of Aboriginal and Torres Strait Islander Children from Their Families*, was tabled in Federal Parliament, though it was not until 13 February 2008 that Prime Minister Kevin Rudd offered a formal apology in the parliament to members of the Stolen Generations. The intervening years of the Howard Liberal–National coalition government saw what Stuart McIntyre and Anna Clarke called 'the History Wars', whose battles ranged from Keith Windschuttle's polemic, *The Fabrication of Aboriginal History* (2002), to historian Inga Clendinnen's 2006 essay,

The History Question, in which she criticised novelist Kate Grenville for her depiction of frontier conflict in *The Secret River* (2005), and her apparent claim that fiction could deal with such issues more insightfully than history. Miller's Central Queensland novels were also written in this charged political context, and at a time of intense debate about the relationships between history and fiction, and fiction and politics. Understanding their complex relation to this intensely contested period in Australian public life is one of the most difficult challenges confronting his readers.

During the 1990s and early 2000s, Miller's long-standing interest in ethics therefore became increasingly focalised through concrete issues and debates about social justice in Australia. For Brigid Rooney, the later novels are at once more accessible and more 'nationally oriented' (202). When a novelist engages in this way with issues of moment in the public sphere, it is easy for readers to see their work reductively, as if it were simply 'about' those social issues or directly reflective of particular opinions held by commentators such as journalists, politicians, historians or public intellectuals. But this would be to do Miller a grave injustice, and it is not how the contributors to this book have chosen to read him. Rooney reminds us that in using fiction to address debates about colonisation and social justice, Aboriginal dispossession, and the push for and frustration of reconciliation at this time, Miller attracted both a broader readership but also strong criticism from some quarters, especially postcolonial critics (203). At its most extreme, this criticism reads the Central Queensland novels as examples of 'sorry' literature, accusing Miller of romanticising his Indigenous characters and projecting onto them a register of 'new-age wish fulfilment'. If, as she suggests, the acknowledgement of Indigenous collaborators in *Landscape of Farewell* has worked to deflect critical objections otherwise levelled at *Journey to the Stone Country* (203), then the personal testimonies by Miller, Frank Budby and Liz Hatte included in this book may be caught up in this complex interaction between the novels and their reception. Yet the essays on these novels by Shirley Walker, Liliana Zavaglia, Brigid Rooney, David Brooks and Raimond Gaita, each in its different way, read Miller's novels as absorbing these issues deeply into their own fabric of self-reflection. These are emphatically not what have been called 'sorry' novels, but complex ethical meditations that reflect upon both the wish for reconciliation and the series of barriers and recuperations that deny them what Zavaglia, quoting Dominick LaCapra, calls the 'facile uplift' of easy atonement. These complex issues are incorporated into the novels themselves, and make them ethically challenging, equivocal and unresolved. This is partly achieved by the way Miller opens the novels up to opposing voices—Bo Rennie *and* Les Marra, Grandma Rennie *and* Panya—but also by the way he is always prepared, as Ronald Sharp observes, to risk interrupting the ostensible realism and accessibility of his narrative and descriptive surface to complex phenomenological and ethical effects (80). As Rooney puts it, 'Miller's prose works to slow down hasty or precipitate reading'; his attention to matters of style and composition 'inherent in self-consciously literary works, are deeply constitutive of the fullest range of meanings in play' (205). These novels both 'seem aware of, and work within' ethical contradictions, never quite resolving them but foregrounding the question, for their most attentive readers, of ethical living.

Miller wrote important essays at this time dealing with the relations between history and fiction, between the novel and 'truth'. 'Written in Our Hearts', published in the *Weekend Australian* of 16–17 December 2006, does not refer directly to the attacks on Grenville, but is clearly shaped by the context of the History Wars. Miller points out that he majored in history at university in the 1960s and that he remains an avid reader of history. Yet despite the fact that the Commonwealth Writers' Prize judges wrote that *The Ancestor Game* 'takes the historical novel to new frontiers', Miller insists, 'I make no claim to have written an historical novel' (8). Referring directly to a recent exchange in the History Wars between Robert Manne and Andrew Bolt, he cites with approval Manne's claim that 'History is based on documents and eyewitness accounts', immediately going on to say that 'the novelist has a different task' (8). For Miller, the novel is still 'a cultural project' (8), but one that uses the resources of story, memory and the imagination to examine the 'interior life'. Quoting Murray Bail, he suggests that 'novels arise out of the shortcomings of history'. In so far as Miller does engage with contemporary realities, then, he does so through the resources of memory and the empathic imagination, through the sharing and imaginative transformation of his and others memories in a way that they recognise to be 'true'. These ideas go back, of course, to the initial exchange with Max Blatt at Araluen. He concludes by distancing himself from the kinds of claims Grenville was taken to have made for the novel, saying, 'I know of no novelist who claims to write history or who wishes to "nudge the historian from the path"' (9). The real test of the novel's success is not whether it can be verified by reference to documents but 'whether the people we write about are able to celebrate in our work the truth they know of themselves' (9). And that, as we have seen repeatedly in Miller's work, involves the empathic imagination and the sharing of story.

This coincides precisely with the account Miller gives of the genesis of the Central Queensland novels in 'The Mask of Fiction': 'My own displacement from one side of the world to the other, my loss of culture and home, is dealt with silently in my empathy with the displacement and dispossession of the book's principal characters, black and white' (35). The word 'silently' here carries a great weight, since for Miller these books are not just about the displacement of their Indigenous characters—they are equally about the sense of personal and cultural displacement of the authorial consciousness that allows the stories of these *other* displaced people to be realised sympathetically in story. Like the landscapes of Claude Lorrain described in *The Ancestor Game*, Miller's Central Queensland is not a 'map' in the sense of being literally 'true', but the novelistic evocation of 'a disintegrating world'.

There is a moment in *Journey to the Stone Country* that illustrates this particularly well. Near the end of their journey together, Bo takes Annabelle to the ghost town of Mount Coolon. At the Mount Coolon Picture Palace, they enter the ruined building and discover the rusting remains of the machine that projected the dreams of their youth. Bo recalls his love for the John Wayne western, *True Grit*, and the way he modelled himself as a young man on the Hollywood star. The ruined cinema is compared to the inside of an abandoned ship, suggesting the opening scene of *Conditions of Faith*, in which Emily Stanton swims away from her family towards the ominous silhouette of a shipwreck in Port Phillip Bay. Despite the obvious fact that he is an Indigenous character, Bo Rennie is not just Miller's romanticised version of the noble savage, as some postcolonial critics claim, but one of his many versions of a person displaced from home and tradition by the effects of global modernity. They include Robert Crofts, Lang Tzu, August Spiess,

Emily Stanton and Sabiha—and of course Max Blatt and Miller himself. To recall an image from *Prochownik's Dream*, the artist is always visible 'at the edge' of his compositions. It is this shared sense of displacement, Miller suggests elsewhere, that makes Australia 'postmodern': 'In Australia . . . we have found ourselves to be the inhabitants of a disestablished world in which the dominant cultural experience is that of displacement' ('Modern, European and Novel', 42).

In another essay from this period, 'Sweet Water', published in the *Bulletin* in 2003–04, Miller speaks of the value of the novel in dealing with social issues. Perhaps alluding to criticisms of *The Secret River* by Clendinnen and other historians, he writes, 'Some critics assure us that our novels are irrelevant in discussions of the important issues facing our society. I don't share that view. As well as entertaining us, our novels have always explored the individual's relationship to the great moral questions of the day.' But notice that he says 'explored', not 'answered' or 'resolved', and he goes on immediately to say, 'Not answers, but an awareness of the questions we need to face.' Nowhere is this clearer than in Miller's complex and nuanced treatment, through the lens of fiction, of the issues of reconciliation. On this, as on so many other issues, his subtle and flexible writing eludes reductive accounts and glances away from moral simplifications, always returning us to the complexity that is inherent in our relation to the other, and our failure to see complicity and ambivalence in ourselves. Miller points out, 'it is not a question simply of reconciliation, important as that is, but is the far more difficult question of the acknowledgement of difference' (104). The end point of this ethical relation to the other, Rooney suggests, is often a relinquishment of the desire for knowledge of the other grounded partly in an ambivalent apprehension of its impossibility and undesirability. The novels of Alex Miller offer a wealth of examples of such ethical circumspection and withheld certainty: Lang Tzu's enigmatic disappearance from the final pages of *The Ancestor Game*; the *absence* of Jessica Keal from the artist's portrait of her in *The Sitters*; the *absence* of a film in Annabelle's camera when she takes a photograph of Bo at the Mount Coolon cinema, or her decision not to accompany him on the last stage of their planned journey to the stone country; and John Patterner's decision, in *Lovesong*, to accept Sabiha's pregnancy.

Brenda Walker helps us to see that there are many reasons why we might now begin to speak of the 'greatness' of the novels of Alex Miller. One is the scope of their collective subject matter and the profundity with which they reflect upon it. As Walker and Webby both observe, there is a certain 'imaginative plasticity' in his work that allows him convincingly to portray people, places and events at a great cultural distance from each other and from ourselves. At another level, he has the courage and high seriousness to engage with major events that might be thought of as world historical because they recur throughout human history. In correspondence with Shirley Walker, cited here, Miller describes these as the 'vast impersonal forces of culture and history' (156). No one is unaffected by such events, no one ethically immune, as August Spiess comes to see when he is made responsible for the executions of those who have attacked him. Similarly, *Landscape of Farewell* brings together the Holocaust and the settler invasion of Australia in ways that challenge us to think about the persistence or, as Hannah Arendt would have it, the *banality* of evil throughout human history; and yet, as Raimond Gaita points out, without simply equating them or attempting to 'weigh the gravity of one against the other'. To achieve that, as he rightly says, requires 'great moral tact' (229). Miller's novels are also stylistically varied, from the multiple narrative viewpoints and settings of his most postmodern work, *The Ancestor Game*, to the convincing ekphrasis of *The Sitters* and *Prochownik's Dream*, with their rich insights into artistic practice, to the more contemporary, more 'nationally oriented' narratives of the Central Queensland novels. The novels of Alex Miller are concerned with enduring questions about art and literature, about aesthetics and ethics. In this regard they are also concerned with the dialogue between Australian and European literature, whose great masterworks are often referred to and threaded through them—the work of Heine, Rilke, Goethe, Nabokov and Proust. Commenting on the two-way relationship between national and world literatures, David Damrosch points out that 'even the most influential works of world literature usually achieve their first life in a national tradition'. At the same time, 'national literature specialists should also allow that most of their favourite authors were deeply influenced by a wide range of foreign works ... often read in translation' ('All the World', 8).

It is one measure of a great writer that his novels demand attentive readers who cannot or will not reduce them and the complex issues they reflect upon to singularities. It is another that they can support richly varied readings that go against their grain, such as David Brooks's meditation on the species barrier in *Landscape of Farewell*. As Brenda Walker argues, quoting Philip Roth, Miller's thinking is always concerned with nuance, and politics cannot afford nuance (42). The idea that literature helps us to see things from another's point of view, for example, is questioned by Miller, since empathy and insight into the other can be exploited strategically, as it can in the hunt, in the warrior Gnapun's quest to kill the missionaries who invaded his land, or in Sabiha's search for a father for her child regardless of the consequences for her husband or her lover. And books, as Walker observes, including the great masterpieces of the European tradition, appear mockingly in the library of Ward Rankin and in the library at Ranna in *Journey to the Stone Country*. For all their indebtedness to the history of the European novel and as a means of expression, Miller's novels speak from the dislocated postcolonial perspective of contemporary Australia, which Elizabeth McMahon describes as the 'fractured' perspective of late modernity (128).

A belief that the European dreaming is a broken legacy has long been a theme in Miller's essays. Writing in 1992 on 'Modern, European and Novel', he set himself apart from Milan Kundera's identification with European modernism, speaking instead of his own sense of 'displacement from it'. This sense of displacement is a consequence not only of migrancy, but is inherent in Australia's condition as a settler society in which the European dreaming finds itself inadequate in the face of the very Indigenous dreaming with which it struggles to reconcile itself. This sense of inhabiting a 'disestablished world' (42)—or a series of contingent disestablished worlds—is one key to Miller's empathy with Indigenous Australia, which also finds itself inhabiting the ruins of its own past as a consequence of the damage done by European settlement—'the landscape of ruins' that the Urannah Valley has become since the arrival of Europeans' ('Sweet Water', 103). Yet in both cases, Miller is able to see this process of ruination as a paradoxical legacy for an imagined future: 'My perception as an Australian ... is that displacement has constituted a positive endowment in the elaboration of our culture—displacement, not tradition, has been our workplace in Australia' (42).

Miller has also written, 'We will not be in a post-colonial age until we are in a post-European age' ('Sweet Water', 104). We glimpse what this might mean in the core event in *Landscape of Farewell*, Max Otto writing down the story of Dougald's great-grandfather, Gnapun. Bill Ashcroft speculates that in the context of contemporary Australia, this act of a white historian writing down an Indigenous man's story could be seen as 'an act of effrontery, an appropriation of cultural story' (25). Indeed it might. But it is also a profound act of sharing which allows Indigenous cultural memory to survive by undergoing the translation into writing, and which allows the two men to share what Ashcroft calls, after Ernst Bloch, a moment of 'anticipatory illumination', a sense of future possibility focused on the country of the old people, the '*Heimat*'. Ashcroft describes this moment of writing as 'a powerful gesture of reconciliation because not only does it effect a transformation in Dougald by saving his story ... it transforms Max by allowing him to enter a different understanding of ... place'. It is a reconciliation 'administered by the utopian function of literature' (26), which anticipates the apology given on 13 February 2008.

Elizabeth Webby reminds us that Miller began publishing in 1988 at the height of an intense period of debate about the politics of representation that was informed by feminism, multiculturalism and postcolonialism. We remember it well: 'who speaks for whom?' Miller's novels belong to a type of fiction that has flourished *since* that time, including the work of Amitav Ghosh and JM Coetzee, that Shameem Black calls 'border-crossing fictions' (*Fiction Across Borders*, 3). After a time of heightened awareness about the pitfalls of writing across lines of social difference, such novels call attention to the *process* of imagining the lives of others, inviting their readers to question assumptions about identity and imaginative projection, and exploring the ethics of representation. To understand them fully, Black argues, we need to move beyond the relentless negativity of identity politics and postcolonial critique (5). In what I think is one of the most telling observations in this book, Raimond Gaita describes Miller as the 'least didactic' of writers (218). His novels ask hard questions but they do not offer in return clear-cut answers or comfortable resolutions. Mindful that the Central Queensland novels emerged in the context of Australia's History Wars of the 1990s, and speaking as a moral philosopher rather than a literary critic, Gaita reminds those of us who *are* literary critics—and also, perhaps especially, those readers who are historians—that the novel as a form of imaginative and re-creative writing is not answerable to discursive academic disciplines like anthropology or history or political philosophy. Miller's novels do not express and cannot be reduced to opinions; rather, they ask questions and hold things up for meditation and reflection. I am reminded of those music critics who would explain Elgar's symphonies as an epiphenomenon of Edwardian imperialism; in reality, each contains its dark inner core, the elusive and disturbing cadences of their closing bars disappearing into the ether like vast unanswered questions.

WORKS CITED

Anderson, Amanda. *The Powers of Distance: Cosmopolitanism and the Cultivation of Detachment.* Princeton: Princeton University Press, 2000.

Ashcroft, Bill. 'Australian Transnation'. *Southerly* 71.1 (2011): 18–40.

Black, Shameem. *Fiction Across Borders: Imagining the Lives of Others in Late Twentieth-Century Novels.* New York: Columbia University Press, 2010.

Caterson, Simon. 'Playing the Ancestor Game: Alex Miller interviewed by Simon Caterson', *Journal of Commonwealth Literature* 29.2 (1994): 5–11.

Damrosch, David. 'All the World and the Time'. In David Damrosch, ed. *Teaching World Literature.* New York: MLA, 2009.

McIntyre, Stuart and Anna Clarke. *The History Wars.* Carlton, Vic: Melbourne University Press, 2003.

Miller, Alex. *Lovesong.* Sydney: Allen & Unwin, 2009.

——. 'Waxing Wiser Than Oneself'. *Australian* (Australian Literary Review), 7 October 2009: 24–5.

——. *Landscape of Farewell.* Sydney: Allen & Unwin, 2007.

——. Email to Robert Dixon, 6 December 2006.

——. 'Written in Our Hearts'. *Australian* (review), 16–17 December 2006: 8–9.

——. *Prochownik's Dream.* Sydney: Allen & Unwin, 2005.

——. 'Sweet Water'. *Bulletin.* 16 December 2003–13 January 2004: 100–4.

——. *Journey to the Stone Country.* Sydney: Allen & Unwin, 2002.

——. *Conditions of Faith.* Sydney: Allen & Unwin, 2000.

——. *The Sitters.* Ringwood, Vic.: Viking, 1995.

———. 'This is How It's Going to Be Then'. *Australian Book Review* 127 (December/January, 1990–91): 30.
———. 'Choosing My Tale'. *Kunapipi* 15.3 (1993): 1–6.
———. *The Ancestor Game*. Ringwood, Vic.: Penguin, 1992.
———. 'Modern, European and Novel'. *Overland* 128 (Spring 1992): 38–43.
———. *The Tivington Nott*. London: Robert Hale, 1989.
———. *Watching the Climbers on the Mountain*. Sydney: Pan, 1988.
———. 'Comrade Pawel'. *Meanjin* 34.1 (Autumn 1975): 74–85.
Pierce, Peter. 'The Solitariness of Alex Miller.' *Australian Literary Studies* 21.3 (May 2004): 299–311.
Van Teeseling, Ingeborg. Interview with Alex Miller. 5–6 June 2008. Unpublished.
White, Patrick. *Flaws in the Glass: A Self-Portrait*. London: Jonathan Cape, 1981.

- 1 -

The MASK of FICTION: A Memoir

ALEX MILLER

I'VE BEEN ASKED FOR a memoir for this occasion yet I am uncomfortable writing directly about myself. I prefer the mask of fiction. In this preference it is self-deception I fear most, for who but the self-deceived would claim to be able to write with moral detachment about themselves? I am also cautious of the fate of WB Yeats, the poet, of whom Richard Ellmann wrote, 'The autobiographical muse enticed him only to betray him, abandoning him to ultimate perplexity as to the meaning of his experiences' (*Yeats*, 2). Memoir does not offer us a sure means for contacting the deeper dualities of the self. For this journey to the heart of darkness, fiction is a more certain, if more oblique, way.

Voltaire is said to have remarked of Michel de Montaigne that he does indeed confess his faults, but only his endearing ones. We are human, after all, and we love ourselves. When writing about ourselves the inclination for a self-portrait in an endearing light is not to be resisted. Oscar Wilde famously said of it, 'Man is least himself when he talks in his own person. Give him a mask and he will tell you the truth.' It is the mask that enables detachment from self. All fiction, after all, is self-portraiture and truth is ever an elusive tiger. It is best to take an indirect approach. The obvious is never the true goal. One needs to don a mask in order to become the other, to get behind the mirror-image of self, and see what is truly there. It is no wonder it was flaws that concentrated Patrick White's attention when he abandoned fiction for a moment in order to gaze directly into the glass of self-portraiture. In White's determination to confess himself, his fear was that the devil of vanity would mislead him. If the unconscious is to be our guide it can't be self-consciously so. First we must see ourselves as the other. It is by this path that fiction seeks its truth. For me it is a sacred path. For better or worse I have devoted my life to it.

I'll try to say something here about the place of my novels in my life, and to speak of their interconnectedness with each other. My writing life began in Melbourne when I was twenty-six after I graduated in English and history from the University of Melbourne, having entered the university as a mature-age student. Writing became my way of locating connections in a life which up until then had been characterised by a series of disconnections. The earliest of these disconnections occurred when I was two and a half years of age and was sent to a children's home for a week while my mother went into hospital to give birth to my younger sister. The child did not know his exile was to be for a week. For the child the terrifying abandonment was forever. The experience left a mark on me that has never completely faded and it is disconnection and detachment that have been my minor gods. And wasn't it Virgil who said, 'We make our destinies by our choice of gods'?

From occasional verse and entries in day books, soon after university my writing began to develop into an attempt to make sense of my worlds through reflections on my various selves and on the cultures I had lived within, and they were plural, selves, worlds and cultures. As a result of this self-absorption, this lack of external subject matter, my writing was far too introspective to appeal to either publishers or readers. With my writing I was trying to mend something in myself and I looked inward for the broken ends that I might fit them together. In this preoccupation with self I was mistaken, and it was not until I ceased writing directly about myself and began to write imaginatively of the people and the places most dear to me that my writing began to appeal to publishers and subsequently to gain me a readership. It was also with this change that writing ceased to be a kind self-inflicted torture to me and I began to experience the joy of it. The person most directly responsible for this change of direction in my writing was my friend and mentor, Max Blatt. My novel *The Ancestor Game* (1992) is dedicated to Max and his wife Ruth, and *Prochownik's Dream* (2005) is dedicated to my wife Stephanie and to the memory of Max Blatt. My friendship with Max was the single most important influence on the development of my writing. To this day I write with the question before my mind: Would Max find this interesting? I ask that question of myself at this very moment. It is the challenge, the accompaniment, and the inspiration of my work. Max was a richly cultivated and highly intelligent central European and his standards in literature were the most exacting I have met with.

I came out of the bush when I was twenty-one and went to the University of Melbourne when I was twenty-three. I did not return to Queensland until after I had begun teaching at Holmesglen TAFE, around 1987. For more than twenty years I thought my Queensland days would never be part of my life again. My life as a stockman was foreign to my friends and teachers at university, and to my colleagues and acquaintances in Melbourne, who all looked towards England or Ireland or Europe for their literary antecedents and the sources of their inspiration.

I wasn't aware of any Australian literature being taught at Melbourne in the early sixties. There seemed to be no connection between my world of ringing in Queensland (even the term had a different meaning in Victoria) and the life of writing in Melbourne. They were mutually unvisited landscapes and were unknown to each other. There was no common language of cultural memory or association for me to deal in and I carried the precious memory of my days in Queensland with me secretly for more than twenty years. *Watching the Climbers on the Mountain* (1988) was my second attempt, after *The Tivington Nott* (1989), to reclaim an important period of my past and to make something meaningful of it in the social context of my present.

The Tivington Nott, my first novel, was conceived initially in two parts: the first part was to be set on Exmoor, where I had worked as a farmer's boy for two years, and where I had become close friends with the labourer Morris Aplin; the second part was to be set in the Gulf of Carpentaria, where I had worked as a stockman, and was to be called *Jimmy Diamond*, in tribute to a tribal Aboriginal friend of those days. Jimmy and I had worked side by side as friends just as Morris and I had worked side by side on Exmoor. This book was going to bridge the two lives, the two worlds, and their apparently unconnected realities. My hope was to connect these experiences and to arrive at some sort of sense of wholeness about myself.

I had loved my Exmoor days and my Gulf Country days and possessed a vivid memory of them. I not only wished to celebrate them by re-enacting the country and the people I had loved, but was enticed by the ironies between my position on the bottom of the social scale as a labourer on Exmoor and my elevated status on the cattle station in the Gulf of Carpentaria, where I, the newcomer, was paid ten times as much as the expert Aboriginal stockmen. I understood that this social reversal expressed something of the essential reality of the deeply troubled white Australian culture in which I lived; something of the injustice and unease with which white Australians live, or which we push aside and try to forget about, migrants and invaders all, valuing the title of native born and counting our precious generations, longing for the confidence of an authenticity that can never be ours until it is bestowed on us by the first people of this land. I wanted to explore all this, to review it, to revisit it, and to examine the quality of its humanity and its inhumanity, and to see, hopefully, how it had affected me and my own humanity.

The Tivington Nott was, in its original conception, an unwieldy and far too ambitious project. When I got to the end of the Exmoor part of the book I saw at once that the story was complete and would bear no further additions. Much of *Jimmy Diamond* had been written by then but I knew it would never be published. The original plan had been flawed and my ambition for the book had to give way before the integrity of the story. I learned that it is the story that is master of the author, not the author who is master of the story. I learned something of the subordinate role in the making of story that is the conscious performance of the storyteller. The secret of the story is that it serves a purpose unknown to the writer, and responds to its own mysterious tides. In every story ever told it is the unconscious that has spoken. A story's power to beguile the reader or the listener lies in what has been left unsaid. The manifest content of the story is an artful carapace for its silent meaning; that place into which the reader's imagination is enticed.

My third novel, *The Ancestor Game*, explores the ambiguous liberties bestowed on artists and writers by cultural displacement. The book began as a celebration of the life of a Chinese-Australian friend who was defeated by Melbourne's racism and cultural elitism in the 1980s and who despaired and shot himself. *The Ancestor Game* was my attempt to make sense of my friend's life and death, to see his alienation from his community and culture as something of exceptional value, and to bring him back into my own life and into the lives of his other friends—those who missed him and had believed in him as fiercely as I had.

The success of *The Ancestor Game* came as a surprise and the subsequent international travel was a diversion from the steady daily task of writing. It was three years before I published my next book, *The Sitters* (1995). I wrote *The Sitters* while I was trying to write the novel that eventually became *Conditions of Faith* (2000). The impulse for *Conditions of Faith* came to me when my brother sent me my mother's early diaries after her death. As I read my mother's tiny girlish handwritten notes in a small pocket book I seemed to peer into the shadows of her past and to glimpse her life when she was a young woman and was not yet my mother or the wife of my father, but was gazing into her own future as a place of possibility. I saw in my mother's youthful longings the same longings to escape that had preoccupied my own youth, and which had fired my decision to get away from the grey landscape of a council estate in post-war London and go to the charmed rural landscape of Exmoor.

When I left home at the age of fifteen I did not understand the depth of my mother's suffering at the loss of her oldest son. It was not until my brother told me after her death that she had always spoken of the day when I would return, and when she was dying had said to him, 'Everything will be all right when Alex gets home.' In writing *Conditions of Faith* I imagined myself to be rescuing my mother's memory and giving her the independent life she had dreamed of as a young woman, whereas in fact I may have been dealing indirectly with her loss of her favoured child and how she might have justified that loss to herself and have come to terms with it. I knew she would not have agreed with my sense that she had been oppressed by marriage and family. My motives were complex and poorly understood by me. Consequently the book resisted me for a long time.

It was at last in the landscape of Tunisia, in the filthy cell beneath the ruined amphitheatre of Carthage, once occupied by the grieving mother, Vibia Perpetua, that I found the key to the conundrum and the story began to unfold for me. What I had found in that cell was in fact my own story disguised by my love for my mother. I began to understand this only after I had finished the book. While I wrote it I did so with my love of my mother foremost in my mind, masking the deeper impulse to tell my own story, indeed to conflate her story and my own, as if we two were one person. *Conditions of Faith* contains my own private truth of my youthful struggle to find a way to become a serious novelist from a beginning where such an ambition was laughable and unheard of. In fiction, as in the telling of our dreams, we reveal more than we imagine.

The Sitters persistently distracted me while I was writing *Conditions of Faith*. It was partly my preoccupation with *The Sitters* that inhibited my progress with *Conditions of Faith*—our impulses are rarely the result of one simple cause, but are fibrous and collective in their force, and consequently nearly impossible to resist. I thought, with *The Sitters*, that I was writing about a working-class Australian woman who had gone from Australia to England and had become a professor, and had now returned to visit her aged mother in the country (country where I'd had a farm for several years while writing my pre-novels, country that had been my own escape from the demoralising false urbanities of a public service job in Canberra). *The Sitters* was to offer a kind of reverse version of my own history—a mirror-image of my own portrait, perhaps. I now acknowledge *The Sitters* to have been a meditation on my relationship with my father and my lost sister. A book about the way my family, through my father's emotional and physical wounding during the war, became a distant silence for me: a painful absence that was forever present to me. That family wound remained as a permanent shadow on my life.

I have a self-portrait in pastels that I did fifty years ago in which I am struggling to free myself from the shadow. It was my writing that eventually freed me, not my art. *The Sitters* is a haunted book. A book haunted by my father's wounding and by my inarticulate despair at losing him. Towards the end of the war, when my father returned wounded in mind and body, we did not know him. He was changed. *The Sitters* was my faltering approach to the loss of my beloved father, the man who had taught me to paint and to fish and to enjoy the beauties of nature and music. He had been the childhood storyteller in my life. My dad. He disappeared into the horror of war for four years and another, crueller man, wearing his tortured mask, returned in his place. It was an event that was not to be forgotten.

It wasn't until ten years after I wrote *The Tivington Nott* that I recovered the impulse to write about my experiences in the outback. *Journey to the Stone Country* (2002), though not set in the Gulf of Carpentaria, nevertheless embodies the spirit of that first book, but transformed and elaborated in ways I could not have foreseen or imagined. *Journey to the Stone Country* also came to me through friendships; and, once again, it was a book about people and places that are dear to me. It is a reflection of my own realities and the realities of those friends heightened, simplified and transmuted into the organic whole of story. My own displacement from one side of the world to the other, my loss of culture and home, is dealt with silently in my empathy with the displacement and dispossession experienced by the book's principal characters, black and white. It is a book about friends, people who, in their lives and experiences, connect aspects of my own past experience that had remained until then mysterious and intractable for me. It is also a book about my love of country, the Australian outback of my youth.

My friends Liz Hatte and Col McLennan gave me the bones of the story and blessed the project with their enthusiasm to see it come to completion. Without them that book would not have been written, and those connections would have remained unmade for me. It was when I was writing *Watching the Climbers on the Mountain*, my first published book, and my first book set in Queensland, that I met Liz Hatte and began, through my friendship with her, to reconnect my Melbourne life to my Queensland past. Liz, it turned out, was born on a cattle station in the Central Highlands of Queensland and was intimately familiar with the culture of the people and the country on which I had based my novel. Meeting Liz felt like meeting a long-lost sister. As with all great friendships we each had an effect on the other's life. When Liz told me she loathed teaching and wanted to be an archaeologist, I said she must risk everything for her dream, and have the courage to get out of teaching and go and become an archaeologist—I knew by then that the first step in realising one's dream is to make oneself vulnerable to failure. Liz returned to Townsville not long after this and set up her business. Col and the Jangga became her most important clients (and Col her life partner).

When I visited them in Townsville, Col and I shared stories of our days as Queensland ringers. We understood each other and became friends. With Col it was the first time I had spoken with a ringer from the old days and there was for me in my meeting with him a poignant sense of homecoming; a return to the familiar place of my first boyhood dream. A vital connection was made for me through Col and his story between the two worlds of my early years in North Queensland and my subsequent university and writing life in Melbourne.

To encourage me, Col showed me the country of his people, the Jangga. He gave me the history of black and white betrayal that lies at the heart of this book. He also placed in my trust the spirit of Grandma Rennie, a spirit that lifts the story above the level of race conflict and endows it with the human dimensions of a love story; love for country, that is, black and white. I saw *Stone Country* as the original impulse of *Jimmy Diamond* finding its time.

It was Col who told me I would write *Stone Country* and it was Stephanie, my wife, who told me I should write *The Ancestor Game*. We do nothing alone. I hadn't seen either book coming, but once they were suggested to me I fell in love with both projects and began to understand how important they were to be for me. In writing these books I was aware that they were expressions of communal realities and longings that we share with each other, and were not simply explorations of self. They made my fragile sense of connectedness stronger and more real to me.

When Col first took me on the journey to see his country he introduced me to his friend and old droving and mustering partner, Frank Budby, elder of the Barada people. In Frank it soon became obvious to me that I had met a heroic and selfless man. A quiet, unassuming and deeply intelligent man, Frank rescued his people from the depredations of white culture—from alcohol, prison, drugs, despair and the dole, the terrible loss of self-esteem, the loss of aim and the will to live well—and reclaimed for them, and with them, by the force of his character and his inspired leadership, an ordered and purposeful life. It was Frank's remarkable example, and meeting the writer Anita Heiss in Hamburg, that led me to write *Landscape of Farewell* (2007). Near

Springsure (the location of *Watching the Climbers on the Mountain*) there is the site of the largest massacre of white people by Aborigines in Australia's history, the Cullin-la-Ringo massacre. I was haunted by local accounts of the Cullin-la-Ringo massacre, which I'd first heard when I was a stockman on a cattle station near Springsure, my first job in Australia. I had also carried since my childhood an unexamined sense of guilt-by-association with the events of the Holocaust. *Landscape of Farewell* brings these two unconnected events together. As a primary school kid I had sat among the assembled school in the hall while we watched in frozen silence the horrifying black and white films of the Allies entering the death camps of Belsen and Buchenwald. The overwhelming impression left on us young children by these nightmare images was that we (human beings) do this to each other. A sense of guilt-by-association was inescapable. I had never dealt with it.

In Hamburg, meeting Anita Heiss and witnessing her fiercely honest defence of her people's rights, made the connection for me. I found young Germans as eager to speak with me about the unspeakable as their elders were reluctant. The elements came together for me in Hamburg, my own unvisited guilt-by-association for both our treatment of the Aborigines and the images of Belsen and Buchenwald, the Germans' own intractable sense of guilt-by-association, the silence in Australian history about the massacre at Cullin-la-Ringo, and the inspiration of Frank's heroic reclaiming of the dignity of his people. In my hotel room in Hamburg I began with great excitement to sketch these lines of intersection and to see how they fitted together into a whole, not an Australian or a European whole, but a human whole.

As a child of nine in the assembly hall at school, watching in rigid silence while the unspeakable horrors unfolded on the screen, I saw how we humans were all touched by these evils in ways that ought to prevent us from speaking of *them* and *us*. Surely it was all *us*. All humanity. The great European civilisation and its astonishing self-assurance of superiority in the face of Indigenous cultures had been the author of the greatest evil of all time. And here were Frank Budby and his people not only recovering from that predatory civilisation but reaching out to it and teaching it something of profound significance, offering a gift from the Indigenous sensibility. It is the Aboriginal leader in *Landscape of Farewell* who gives to the European professor of history the hope of redemption from what has been the professor's crushing and intractable sense of guilt for the evils of his father's generation. The contemporary human, the private moral dimensions, of this situation clamoured to be explored. I was eager to contextualise historically the actions of the Aboriginal leader of the Cullin-la-Ringo massacre, Gnapun the warrior, whose strategic intelligence and leadership had resulted in the annihilation of the strongest and most well-armed party of colonists ever to settle in the Central Highlands of Queensland. Gnapun's was a raid that resulted in no black casualties that day. His leadership and organisation were exemplary. He had never been credited. White retribution followed the massacre and continues to this day to echo in our silence, in our failure to celebrate Gnapun's heroic, indeed his Homeric, leadership of his people. The real celebration, of course, is of Frank Budby's contemporary success.

My ninth novel, *Lovesong* (2009), has its seed not only in my visit to Tunisia in search of *Conditions of Faith* in 1998, but also, and more deeply, in my wife's powerful desire for a second child, a child she always knew with uncanny certainty was to be a girl. In Stephanie's need, in her certainty, I saw a new level of the mystery of the impulse to motherhood and I set out to explore it. At least I *think* that is what I did. It may well be that I am still too close to this book to know yet what it was really about.

Autumn Laing (2011), my tenth novel, has its origins in the same period of my life as my first, *The Tivington Nott*. My association with Sidney Nolan's life and work began when I was a boy working on Exmoor. An Australian came to live near the farm and he and I became friends—he is memorialised as the stranger who owns the black entire, Kabara, in *The Tivington Nott*. We talked of what we hoped for from life. I told him I dreamed of going to the frontiers of civilisation. He gave me a book illustrated with richly suggestive black and white photographs of the Australian outback. The photographs enthralled me and I longed to go and find the Australian outback for myself. Many years later, in 1961, the year before I went to the University of Melbourne, I bought the first monograph to be published on Nolan and sent it to my father as a Christmas present. In the first few pages of *The Ancestor Game* I refer to the gift of this book and how I came to get it back without it having ever been opened. My father was a lover of the faded watercolour landscapes of Cotman and Crome, and viewed my gift of Nolan's bleak modernism as a provocation.

After the English edition of *The Tivington Nott* was imported into Australia (I had failed to find an Australian publisher for the book) I received a letter from an old friend of Sidney Nolan's, the poet Barrett Reid. Barrett was then living at Heide, the house which had stood at the centre of Australia's modernist art movement, and where Nolan had found his muse and his sustenance for the practice of his art in the person of Sunday Reed, a woman deeply loved and respected by Barrett. Barrett's letter praised *The Tivington Nott* and asked me who I was and why no one in Melbourne had heard of me. When he and Paul Carter awarded *The Tivington Nott* the Braille Book of the Year Award in 1990 (five years after I had written it), the three of us met and became friends. Sid Nolan, his art and life, and the life of Heide when John and Sunday Reed made it the centre of our new art, were often the subject of conversation with Barrett. He pointed out to me that it was most likely that the book given to me by the Australian on Exmoor had been illustrated by Nolan's photographs of the outback. For me, as you can imagine, this was a magical connection. *Autumn Laing* fulfils a lifelong preoccupation with Sidney Nolan and his life and work. Nolan's anti-establishment energy and anger were well-known to me and I strongly identified my own youthful situation with his.

The idea for *Autumn Laing* came to me in London. The link with the England of my childhood, Exmoor and the outback of my early days in Australia were all brought together in this book. At the end of September 2010, the day before I was due to fly home to Australia from a month-long tour of the UK with my previous novel, *Lovesong*, I was sitting in the sun on a bench in Holland Park watching a squirrel and daydreaming of being a boy in London's parks, when an old woman's voice interrupted my reverie with the words, 'They are all dead.' It was a realisation. Autumn Laing (the woman) sprang into my head fully formed that day. She sprang, however, not from nowhere, but from the springboard of my previous work on this book and from my decades-long preoccupation with certain tides in the life of Sidney Nolan, tides towards which I had always felt a deep sympathy and curiosity. I recognised in Autumn's voice that day a prompt of my imagination. It was a precious gift from my unconscious, the writer's source. And it was in her voice, the voice of Nolan's muse transmuted, that I wrote the book. It felt right for me to do so, for in a way, of course, in following Nolan's struggle to become an artist I was following my own struggle to become a writer.

In writing my novels I have learned that the writer is not master of the story but that the story is master of the writer. I have learned that it is the writer who serves the story, not the other way around. As early as my failed original plan for *The Tivington Nott*, I learned that fiction won't be squeezed and warped into self-conscious symmetries of organisation without losing something of the vitality of its spirit. Fiction, I believe, obeys deeper and more hidden laws than plotted narratives. Despite the contemporary desire to exchange the word narrative for story, mere narrative is not story. Story obeys mysterious laws embedded in the human unconscious and is made available to us only through the prompts of our imagination. To trust these prompts is not as straightforward as it might seem. The novel as a form of storytelling may die, but we will always find ways of telling our stories. No one speaks of the death of story.

As I said, I don't like writing directly about myself. Truth evades us by means not perceived by us. Truth is not a given but requires a continuous effort to be won. We are fools if we think we are masters of the truth (as I once foolishly assumed I was master of the story). We stumble towards our truths and our stories with uncertainty. Finding truth is like understanding ourselves; it is a view through the window of a moving train. Next time we look the landscape has changed. Truth and understanding are not static. They are a project that is never finished. Never done with. Never completed. Death finishes it for us. Truth, like understanding, changes with our days. The impulse towards it, however, I believe remains constant in us. Our desire for it. Our desire to *be* true. The urge we have to claim it for ourselves. Our own truth. To know in our hearts that we have not fooled ourselves, but have truly understood.

It is I, not my readers, of course, who must be beguiled by the mask for it to be an effective means of achieving detachment from the mirror-image of self. The mask, as both metaphor and reality, was known by the classical dramatists to reveal more than it conceals. The goal of all storytelling is finally to account for one's own story and it is through the poetics of my fiction that I have sought my personal truths. Writing is a joy to me. When I'm not writing I feel unplugged. Powerless. Disconnected from myself. When I am writing I enjoy a mysterious illusion of invincibility and connectedness.

NOTE

Since writing this I have found out that I have four generations of Millers on my father's side of the family recorded as living in Castlemaine and Melbourne, and so find myself even more literally 'at home' than I had imagined.

WORKS CITED

Bakewell, Sarah. *How to Live: A Life of Montaigne*. London: Chatto & Windus, 2011.

Ellmann, Richard. *Yeats: The Man and the Masks*. London: Macmillan, 1949.

White, Patrick. *Flaws in the Glass: A Self-Portrait*. London: Jonathan Cape, 1981.

- 2 -

ALEX MILLER and LEO TOLSTOY:
Australian Storytelling in a European Tradition

BRENDA WALKER

ALEX MILLER MAY BE Australia's greatest living writer. I certainly believe this to be the case. I base my view on the depth and range of his narrative preoccupations. He writes about love but his lovers often come from very different cultural backgrounds, and this illuminates what is foundational in love while respecting diversity in the most intimate of human connections. He writes with scrupulousness about the human complications of invasion, massacre and armed conflict. The American novelist Philip Roth writes that art is concerned with nuance, and politics cannot afford nuance (*I Married a Communist*, 223). Nuance is the most welcome and apparent characteristic of Miller's understanding of the politics of territorial dispossession. He writes, also, about art and literature as cultural forces and as imperatives within the lives of individuals. In all his fiction, he is both a great writer and a great thinker. This chapter offers a much more brief appreciation of his work and thought than I would wish, more brief than it deserves. In it, I plan to consider Alex Miller and Tolstoy: both great writers, both great thinkers, especially on matters of love and war.

In *Lovesong* (2009), a pair of young lovers, the Tunisian girl Sabiha and the shabby and bookish Australian traveller John Patterner, are resting beneath a willow tree in Chartres. This is the only time they have been alone together. It's the third time they've met. The first occurred when John, on his way to Chartres, was so engrossed in his reading that he missed his train stop and found himself in an unfamiliar area. He sheltered from a summer storm in a café belonging to Sabiha's aunt Houria. The first time Sabiha sees him he is reading in the empty café. The clientele of the café is almost exclusively workmen from North Africa and it is not located in a tourist precinct—this is not the Paris of postcards, nor is it the Paris of popular romance. Romance is a complicated and deeply moral matter in this book. Astonishingly but convincingly, on the basis of two meetings, John and Sabiha are drawn to one another. They barely have a common language. They communicate in French, and John's French is imperfect. Sabiha's Arabic is incomprehensible to John and in any case her deepest understandings—the threads of truth that come to her in her grandmother's Arabic songs—hold a meaning that is personal, a matriarchal inheritance only available to her. He offers to learn Arabic and she warns him that there is no point. It is too difficult. There are so many differences between them. Almost indecently, in Tunisian terms, he has no moustache. He unsettles Sabiha, she rejects and longs for him during his absence from the café, and this irritates her.

Yet in Chartres they are at the very lip of their lives together, at that over-earnest and also childishly joyful moment when each has the unspoken understanding that the other is for them. As Sabiha feeds bread to ducks under the willow tree, John states his situation bluntly: 'I love you,' he tells Sabiha (68). This is before he has so much as embraced her. Then, a little later, 'I'll always love only you' (69). Sabiha objects to this. It violates the light-heartedness of tender early courtship. His declaration is exciting, but it's also too sudden and too serious. She is probably eighteen or nineteen. 'There will never be anyone else, Sabiha', he continues (70). She counters with something more playful and casual, observant and less intense. She tells him that 'Your eyes are the colour of Tolstoy's eyes' (70). Tolstoy, she explains, is the name of a grey-eyed wolfhound, a Russian borzoi owned by Houria's neighbour, the stationer André. So John offers Sabiha his love; she tells him he's like a familiar dog. She does turn this into a compliment: the wolfhound Tolstoy is descended from hunters; like John, it has visions of distance. It, too, is a kind of traveller. It is an animal to respect. They are lying under the willow tree in one another's arms. Then, for the first time, they kiss. The uncertainty that unsettled Sabiha before this stranger from Australia made his feelings so very clear has been resolved. But the difficulties are just beginning.

Sabiha has, in her levity, said something far more grave than she might be expected to realise, for the name Tolstoy signals the great complications of love and misunderstanding, of loss, sundering and calculated personal and military destructiveness that play out in Tolstoy's novels *War and Peace* and *Anna Karenina*. To tell any man, but especially a bookish man, that his eyes resemble Tolstoy's is to anticipate that he may at some point be looking at human complication and historical catastrophe. To commence to love under the name of Tolstoy is to invite exactly the kind of difficulties Sabiha encounters in the course of *Lovesong*: difficulties of betrayal and passionate intransigence and misunderstanding. This will not go away: as one borzoi dies André replaces it with another. There is always a great grey-eyed creature called Tolstoy in the vicinity. Moreover the wolfhound is not only a domestic animal, it is, ancestrally, deeply foreign. It is from an ancient ritual world of strategy, of swift chance and equally sudden death for both human and animal: the world of the hunt—a world Miller has written about in his second published novel, *The Tivington Nott* (1989). In *Lovesong* the wolfhound Tolstoy consciously inhabits this predatory world. Even as it is physically confined to the rue des Ensclaves at the side of its owner, André, it is also somewhere else: '[while walking] its grey eyes [are] fixed on the bloody deeds of ancestors who had ripped wolves apart on the wintry steppes of Siberia' (184). When Tolstoy wakes and howls at dawn, the cry is a response to a sudden vision of foreign solitude: 'the beast waking from his dreams to find himself alone on the snow-covered steppes of his ancestors' (325). The wolfhound is both in a laneway behind a café in Paris, and in Russia, either watching the climax of the hunt or isolated from both its quarry (the wolf) and its pack. Tolstoy's dawn cry slips into the dream of John Patterner, who is by then married to Sabiha and living in rooms above the café. In John's dream the sound is transformed into the whistle of a train, speeding towards him, as if he has dreamed he is the writer Tolstoy's desperate character, Anna Karenina, moments before the impact of the train that takes her life. Earlier in the novel, John tells Sabiha, apologetically, that 'I read too much' (118). I'm not sure that this is possible, myself. What is certain is that John is open to literature; it has made him porous. A literary and Russian grief, originating in the throat of a strange and visionary animal, takes form in his dream. He dreams himself into the position of Anna Karenina because the problem that has befallen his marriage to Sabiha is aligned with the situation in Tolstoy's novel: a passionate necessity—in Sabiha's case, the need to bear a child after years of fruitless marriage—has created a great disturbance in that marriage. The adult Sabiha has become a huntress, reprising an old song she heard from her grandmother about a woman who goes, alone, to kill a lion that menaces the children of her village and eludes the men who try to destroy it. Sabiha does not take her husband with her on her hunt for a father for her child.

This is a visible deployment of Tolstoy's work on Miller's part, but I hope to do more than consider his direct references to prior writers—European literature is often mentioned in Miller's novels. I hope to use the correspondence I see between Miller's fiction and Tolstoy's to consider the way that each novelist writes about invasion and conflict, paying particular attention to the insights of each into the function of identification and empathy during deadly conflict. This has much to teach us, I believe, about the workings of empathy itself, and has implications not only for our attempts to understand conflict and destruction, but also for our consideration of the effects of literature, given that there is currently considerable emphasis on empathetic engagement as a function of reading and a way of ameliorating hostility and estrangement. It is possible to see common ground between Miller and Tolstoy in relation to this issue. It is also possible to situate these writers together in view of the relationship between Australian and European art that is established in Miller's own writing.

In *The Ancestor Game* (1992), Miller's character Steven Muir is in the sad position of selecting a book, a keepsake, from his dead father's library in England. He chooses a book on Sidney Nolan which he had sent, as a gift, to his father some time previously, unaware that this would antagonise a man devoted to the traditions of English watercolour painting. Steven sees Nolan's work as 'located deep within the embrasures of a European tradition' (8), that is, lying within the openings—embrasures—of European art. The

Australian and the European may be, according to this view, almost structurally interrelated. The relationship between the Australian and the European is apparent in a deeply significant way in Miller's writing, which threads phrases from Flaubert, Goethe, Nabokov and others into its most strongly freighted exchanges of meaning, and which, in *Journey to the Stone Country* (2002), folds European and Australian history together in the Queensland bush, where 'a wooden board was nailed to a dead tree, an arrow crudely carved in the grey and weathered timber of the board pointing down the spur, the word BLENHEIM in letters of faded carmine, as if the Duke of Marlborough's decisive battleground really lay that way, the lost resting place of ten thousand defeated Frenchmen' (126). 'Blenheim' is more than a colonial place-name here. It is a reminder of European military death and destruction in a novel that is deeply concerned with massacre. The seamless encompassing of European—and, indeed, Chinese and North African—history and artistic traditions in fiction which requires us to consider the urgent issues of Australian post-invasion culture is one of the things that makes Miller's fiction great. It is a refusal of limitation, in terms of culture and cultural responsibility for the predatory and the destructive elements of our history. I use the term 'great' quite deliberately. One of Miller's characters cautions against the attribution of greatness. In *Prochownik's Dream* (2006), Theo, contradicting an effusive viewer of his drawings, remarks that 'Great is not a word you should splash around' (134). This is so. But for me as for many of his readers one of the great things about Miller's fiction is his unflinching imaginative examination of the terrible enterprise of human destructiveness, an enterprise that is, in his work, profoundly implicated in literary traditions as old as Homer. He frees us from the view of massacre, for example, as simply the deed of culpable individuals in ignorant and vicious times. Without diminishing this culpability, he places the enterprise of destructiveness within European traditions so that we understand its terrible and historic force. At the same time, due to the great plasticity of his imagination, he looks across the divisions of cultural and imperial aggression and convincingly imagines the circumstances and consciousness of people very different from himself. In both these respects, an obvious European predecessor is Tolstoy.

In a piece in *The New Yorker*, Louis Menand observes that 'There is history the way Tolstoy imagined it, as a great, slow-moving weather system in which even tsars and generals are just leaves before the storm. And there is history the way Hollywood imagines it, as a single story line in which the right move by the tsar or the wrong move by the general changes everything' ('Wild Thing', 69). He goes on to write: 'Most of us, deep down, are probably Hollywood people' (69). We might be, in our popular entertainment, but I like to think we ask more of those novelists who engage with history. In *War and Peace*, Tolstoy uses the hunt—both as an exhilarating experience where Nikolai Rostov, 'whistling up his own leash of borzois' (541), sets out to kill a wolf, and as an emblem of the self-destruction of Napoleon's forces in retreat from Moscow. The Rostov wolf-hunt is vast and disciplined—with 'about a hundred and thirty dogs' and 'twenty horsemen' (542). There are 'forty' borzois (542). Nikolai is stationed near a thicket, imagining how he might deal with a wolf, should one emerge. Like so many of Tolstoy's characters, he's wildly emotional. At first, he thinks of strategies. Then he loses hope and prays, asking God to flush out a wolf. This gives way to an angry outburst against God [I am quoting from the translation by Anthony Briggs]: '"No, I won't get that kind of luck," thought Rostov. "And it would cost Him so little! No chance! I'm always unlucky—at cards, fighting in the war, everything"' (547). Nikolai Rostov has a lot of growing up to do. We witness this, in the course of the novel. But in the wolf-hunt his prayers are immediately answered—just after he reproaches God a she-wolf crosses his path. Exactly as he had hoped, the wolf is seized by Nikolai's dog. It is, Tolstoy writes, 'the happiest moment of his whole life' (549). It is a happy moment for the reader, too, as Nikolai is amusingly rewarded at the very point that he seems to shake his fist at the sky. The wolf-hunt surges into an evening of Russian celebration with dancing to a balalaika and sledding through wood smoke over snow.

Late in *War and Peace*, Tolstoy considers the final devastation of the French invaders, defeated, after sacking Moscow:

> The plight of the army was like the plight of a wounded beast that realises the end is near, but doesn't know what it's doing. Studying the subtle manoeuvres and general aims of Napoleon and his army from

the time they entered Moscow to the moment of their destruction is rather like looking for meaning in the jumping and twitching of a mortally wounded animal. Very often the wounded creature will hear a slight movement and rush towards the shooting huntsmen, lurching forward, then back again, hastening its own end. This is what Napoleon was now doing, under pressure from the entire army (1120).

The great battles of *War and Peace* are disillusioning in their chaos, their false pomp, their sheer human cost. Napoleon's defeat resembles the meaningless and involuntary movements of an animal that has almost ceased to be a quarry. Tolstoy and Miller share a thoughtful narrative interest in hunting and invasion that provides insight into the complexities of each.

Miller's novel *The Tivington Nott* is about hunting deer, and it is centrally concerned with the situation of the outsider. A young Londoner works on a farm on Exmoor. The life of a farm labourer is comfortless. The narrator lives in the home of one of his co-workers and although he has an immense wooden bed with a down-filled mattress, his room is invaded by rats that make their way through the rotting timber beneath a chest of drawers. The rats come one by one, then in a presumably breeding pair. They are passive, 'big, slow and easy to kill' (49). He says, 'I'd never killed anything before, not a decent-sized animal anyway, and hadn't realized quite how committed and violent it was necessary to be' (48). The rats are like 'puddings' and killing them is 'repetitive' slaughter (49). They are, specifically, not quarry in the sense that a hunted animal—a fox, for example—is quarry. Instead they are designated as colonists: 'They're congenital colonists' (53)—and disgusting ones—against which he must wage 'war' (53). In *The Tivington Nott* war is waged against the invasion of comfortable personal territory. It is horrible and simple. In contrast, the hunt is a complicated enterprise. In its own way, it is about insiders and outsiders, but the Londoner making an incursion into the inhospitable world of rural Exmoor is no colonist.

The nott of the novel's title is a kind of stag: solitary and unusually cunning and dangerous, familiar to the narrator because he has uncovered one of the nott's hidden mud-wallows and actually seen the determined and elusive animal—the great prize of local hunters whose hostility to the nott stems from the belief that it may alter, and in their terms damage, the bloodline of the deer herds. The very name 'nott' indicates refusal. This is an animal that will not fit into the local scheme of things. The narrator joins the local hunt because Tiger Westall, his boss, is stabling Kabara, the temperamental and beautiful stallion owned by a local Australian who is no longer able to ride. The Australian is an obtuse outsider. Westall sends the narrator into the hunt because he is thinking of buying Kabara. The youth from London and the horse have their performance tested, but it is clear from the outset that Westall himself falls far short of the mark, and the process of the hunt establishes this. It is the narrator, not the boss, who is present in the final moments of the hunt, the narrator who witnesses the stag at bay, and the narrator who organises the sale of the horse Kabara to a more appropriate owner than Westall. Through his own position as an outsider and because he has access to the secret places of the nott, he has an intimate understanding of the hunt as a ritual of triumph or annihilation, where the survival of the outsider is at stake. The novel is a meditation on issues of territory and intrusion in human and animal form. This intrusion is nuanced. There is a difference between the transient worker and the colonist, and territoriality can be unpleasantly parochial—this is established through the Exmoor locals—rather than legitimately defensive.

Tolstoy and Alex Miller both imagine young men who are deeply taken with the hunt. Nikolai Rostov is at the heart of an aristocratic family enacting one of its privileged traditions and he is a naive and excitable character. Miller's solitary Londoner is wiser and more watchful; it is hard to imagine that the day of the hunt is the happiest day of his life, although it may be among the most significant.

The point of similarity between Miller and Tolstoy lies in the fact that both writers cast invaders in the role of self-destructive animals. In Miller's case, the colonising rats, too, are beyond strategy; they simply arrive and wait to be killed, and although the narrator speaks to them and attempts to concede limited ground to them by tolerating a single rat for a time, a larger invasion is intolerable. The position of animals—the wolf, the deer—in ritualised killing is a very important field of inquiry but it is not an issue I will consider here. My point is that, as Menand reminds us, Tolstoy's sense of history is the opposite of Hollywood plotlines that confer massive agency on a single authoritative figure, and Miller, too, has a usefully complex sense of war and invasion.

Miller and Tolstoy each imagines the experience of warfare as a complex process of identification between adversaries. In popular art—action movies, for example—the division between adversaries is usually very clear. But both novelists suggest an intense relationship between the two, and this simultaneous identification and enmity is part of the wisdom each has to offer on the subject of war.

In *Landscape of Farewell* (2007), a recently bereaved widower, Professor Max Otto, gives a conference paper on 'The Persistence of the Phenomenon of Massacre in Human Society from the Earliest Times to the Present' (11). He is well aware of the inadequacy of his work, and although the subject has fascinated him in the past, he has evaded it because he is conscious of his own limitations. He plans to kill himself after the conference: this is to be his last public utterance. However, the genteel aftermath of his delivery is shattered by an outburst from the crowd. Professor Vita McLelland, from the University of Sydney, is infuriated: "'How can this man presume to speak of massacre . . . and not speak of my people?'" (15). She is speaking of Indigenous Australians. The confrontation mellows into a night of conversation. He confesses his plans for suicide. She responds with: 'The time to kill ourselves is after we've paid our debts, not before' (51). Instead of committing an act of violence against himself—a possibility that implicates him directly in the destruction of a human being—he is encouraged to travel to Australia and befriend Vita's Uncle Dougald, also a grieving widower, who lives in Central Queensland. Otto, who had assumed that his life was ebbing, there finds a great purpose: Dougald asks him to write the story of his great-grandfather, the Aboriginal warrior Gnapun. Max Otto becomes a scribe in the service of a tale of massacre, not an analyst of the phenomenon, or a participant, through suicide, in the death of a human being. With uneasy determination and the understanding that this is his 'version' (170) of the events that Dougald told him, Max composes a tale of massacre. Gnapun, a traditional Aboriginal man, is living at the time of European incursion into neighbouring country. He is prescient, and prior to conflict he enters the being of the man he will destroy: a missionary who has inadvertently desecrated the sacred stones of local Indigenous people. He experiences the missionary's hopes, his view of the land, his tender regard for his wife and his sons. Gnapun experiences the death of this man, not as an outsider, but from within. Gnapun knows intimately what it means for this man to die, right down to the missionary's physical agony, his last view of clouds and his final breath. No identification, no instance of empathy, could be more complete. Yet when the time comes, Gnapun kills him. This is entirely convincing. When land and faith are at stake, empathy and identification may not prevent bloodshed—indeed they may be part of the process of bloodshed.

After the 9/11 bombings in New York, Ian McEwan wrote a piece in the *Guardian* in which he argues that 'If the hijackers had been able to imagine themselves into the thoughts and feelings of the passengers, they would have been unable to proceed' ('Only Love'). I'm not so sure about this. *Landscape of Farewell* gives a less optimistic or, rather, more nuanced view of empathy. It is reinforced by a short passage from *Conditions of Faith*, in which the Tunisian nationalist Hakim describes an entirely misplaced sense of kinship with a French soldier: 'As you observe him you begin to think of him as a man just like yourself. When his bayonet is fixed, however, then he fixes his gaze on you. And you see in the pale eyes of this French boy from the pastures of the Val-de-Loire, with its camellias and roses, that he will kill you in the same lazy, easy going way that he fixed his bayonet to his rifle' (201). Projecting fellow-feeling on to a military adversary is delusive, and it may be dangerous.

Tolstoy, like Miller, has a sense of the complexities of identification and enmity, and this is apparent in his stories about Russian military action in the Caucasus, especially in the story 'Hadji Murat'. Tolstoy served in Chechnya in the 1850s, at a time when the local ruler, Imam Shamil, had a dispute with his subordinate, Hadji Murat. Murat joined the Russians, hoping to take control, but was killed by them. According to Rosamund Bartlett, in her recent biography *Tolstoy: A Russian Life* (2010), Tolstoy is highly regarded in Chechnya because of his ability to write convincingly about that culture and about an important historical combatant in their resistance against Russian invasion (7). This is an instance of the great imaginative plasticity that I attributed to both Miller and Tolstoy: the capacity to portray characters convincingly at a great cultural distance from themselves. 'Hadji Murat' is a late piece of writing, published after Tolstoy's death, and it is one of his most skilled works. Hadji Murat surrenders, for his own strategic purposes, to Prince Vorontsov, a wily military politician who has no illusions about the loyalty of his new ally. It's clear that Tolstoy admires Hadji Murat far more than the Russians, who are self-indulgent, undisciplined and conventional. Tolstoy remarks of one Russian officer: 'Unconsciously, to preserve his poetic notion of war, he ... never even looked at the killed and wounded' (449). This same officer is entranced with Hadji Murat and his men: 'He acquired a beshmet, a cherkeska, leggings, and it seemed to him that he was himself a mountaineer and was living the same life as these people' (461). This is the most simple and delusive form of impersonation. It really comes down to costuming. The local people do not dress up like the Russian invaders: 'The feeling that was experienced by all the Chechens, big and small, was stronger than hatred. It was not hatred, but a refusal to recognise these Russian dogs as human beings, and such loathing, disgust, and bewilderment before the absurd cruelty of these beings, that the wish to exterminate them, like the wish to exterminate rats, venomous spiders, and wolves, was as natural as the sense of self-preservation' (450). The invaders have the luxury of identifying, however crassly, with locals who wish at all costs to be free of them.

My larger point is that Alex Miller and Tolstoy, two highly nuanced writers, have a sense of the complexity of identification and empathy, and this is especially important because of recent discussions about empathy and literature in general. A capacity for imaginative identification is said to be the basis for the value of the humanities in Martha Nussbaum's *Not for Profit: Why Democracy Needs the Humanities* (2010). She writes about the democratic value of 'what we can call the narrative imagination. This means the ability to think what it might be like to be in the shoes of a person different from oneself, to be an intelligent reader of that person's story, and to understand the emotions and wishes and desires that someone so placed may have ... the humanities and the arts ... activates and refines the capacity to see the world through another person's eyes' (96). She qualifies this reasonably carefully: not all works of art promote a constructive view of other people (109). Nevertheless she is hopeful about the positive possibilities of a liberal and literary education, an education that encourages an expansive, empathetic view of others.

Some see empathy as the central function of the novel. Suzanne Keen argues that 'emotional contagion comes into play in our reactions to narrative, for we are . . . story-sharing creatures. The same drive to affiliate with others for comfort and safety that expresses itself in empathy and sympathy may also play a role in our species' enthusiasm for narrative' (*Empathy and The Novel*, 5). We may indeed be 'story-sharing creatures', or many of us may be, under the right circumstances. We may have mobile and capacious imaginations and this may lead to altruism. However there are problems. First, 'emotional contagion' seems character-based. Narrative is not entirely about character and action. It's also about literary style. The critic James Wood writes in *The Irresponsible Self*, 'if the philosophical question is, How do we know ourselves? the literary question is always both the philosophical question of how we know ourselves and the literary-technical question of how we *represent* knowing ourselves' (33). Second, we may be hopeful about the benefits of imaginative empathy, but we can never be sure that it will be socially valuable. Sophie Ratcliffe, in *On Sympathy*, opposes what she calls the 'fuzzy' (5) claims for the value of literary empathy and points out that there are problems with 'merging the idea of imagination with that of goodness, and, to a certain extent, between the upholders of the imagination—our poets and novelists—and the achievements of political peace and unity' (227). I hope that Nussbaum is right, and that literature and the imagination have a generous and connective function. The 'narrative imagination' (96) that she venerates, however, deserves to be considered with the subtlety that Alex Miller and Tolstoy bring to the subject. Empathy and identification can mean so many things in so many contexts, and not all of them are generous and constructive. In at least two novels, *Watching the Climbers on the Mountain* (1988) and *Journey to the Stone Country*, Miller emphasises the part that literature has to play in territorial conquest by placing stale or deliquescent books in the libraries of European landowners. These books have not opened the minds of their readers to the plight of Indigenous people.

In conclusion, I want to return to the observation of James Wood: 'if the philosophical question is, How do we know ourselves? the literary question is always both the philosophical question of how we know ourselves and the literary-technical question of how we *represent* knowing ourselves'. 'How do we know ourselves?' It's a good, and difficult, question. But we might begin by facing our history, as Alex Miller does. How do we represent knowing ourselves? Again, we can point to Miller's work and suggest that in his case representation is conducted with nuance, with scrupulousness, and with the materials of Australian and European narrative traditions.

WORKS CITED

Bartlett, Rosamund. *Tolstoy: A Russian Life*. London: Profile Books, 2010.

Keen, Suzanne. *Empathy and the Novel*. Oxford: Oxford University Press, 2007.

McEwan, Ian. 'Only Love and Then Oblivion'. *Guardian*, 15 October 2001.

Menand, Louis. 'Wild Thing: Did the O.S.S. Help Win the War Against Hitler?' *New Yorker*, 14 March 2011: 69–72.

Miller, Alex. *Lovesong*. Sydney: Allen & Unwin, 2009.

——. *Landscape of Farewell*. Sydney: Allen & Unwin, 2007.

——. *Prochownik's Dream*. Sydney: Allen & Unwin, 2005.

——. *Journey to the Stone Country*. Sydney: Allen & Unwin, 2002.

——. *Conditions of Faith*. Sydney: Allen & Unwin, 2000.

——. *The Ancestor Game*. Ringwood, Vic.: Penguin, 1992.

——. *The Tivington Nott*. London: Robert Hale, 1989.

Nussbaum, Martha C. *Not for Profit: Why Democracy Needs the Humanities*. Princeton: Princeton University Press, 2010.

Ratcliffe, Sophie. *On Sympathy*. Oxford: Clarendon Press, 2008.

Roth, Philip. *I Married a Communist*. London: Vintage, 1999.

Tolstoy, Leo. 'Hadji Murat', in *The Death of Ivan Ilyich and Other Stories*. Trans. Richard Pevear and Larissa Volokhonsky. London: Vintage, 2009.

——. *War and Peace*. Trans. Anthony Briggs. London: Penguin, 2005.

Wood, James. *The Irresponsible Self: On Laughter and the Novel*. New York: Picador, 2005.

- 3 -

'MY MEMORY HAS a MIND of ITS OWN':
Watching the Climbers on the Mountain and *The Tivington Nott*

PETER PIERCE

NOT LONG AGO, ALEX Miller remarked at a literary event (my witness is a bookseller from Launceston) that 'My memory has a mind of its own'. What might this mean? Perhaps a memory that is truant, given to reinvention, but also set free. Another implication might concern the double insecurity of memory: the tenuousness of our hold on what we can recollect from the past, and the uncertain hold that memory gives us on our present. In any event, that remark by Miller began and then informs this discussion of the first two novels that he wrote, works that draw closely on some salient events of his youth. They are *Watching the Climbers on the Mountain* (1988) and *The Tivington Nott* (1989). Because they were written in reverse order of their dates of publication, and in autobiographical sequence, I will talk first about *The Tivington Nott*, which is set on a west Somerset farm and on Exmoor in the early 1950s, and whose principal character is an unusual youth: secretive, stubborn and down from London to work. His older counterpart in *Watching the Climbers on the Mountain*, Robert Crofts, has 'a closed solitariness about him that was not natural in a young man' (10). He, too, is from London and has come to Australia where he works on a station in the Central Highlands of Queensland. The two books were conceived to begin with as one, with the first part set on Exmoor, the second in the Gulf of Carpentaria. The book would be a bridge between two crucial periods in the author's life. Soon enough, *The Tivington Nott* seemed to Miller to be a work complete in itself and as such it was published first—in London, rather than in Australia.

In the case of the two books that came to be written, there are close correspondences with the writer's experiences more than three decades in the past. Both novels involve intense retrievals of distant but indelible experiences. The new 2005 edition of *The Tivington Nott* comes with an Author's Note and photographs that insist on the veracity of the story. Here Miller is pictured, at sixteen, in the same pose as Morris (who bears that name in the book), but who is described as 'the genuine West Country farmer'. The author declares that 'the events of this book took place in 1952' and then he equivocates: 'As a novelist, I have been not so much a liar as a re-arranger of the facts. That is the kind of writer I am' (vii). Soon after the events narrated here, Miller migrated to Australia, inspired—as he has often recollected—by a black and white reproduction of a Sidney Nolan photograph of an outback scene. So the story goes, he hitchhiked from Sydney in search of that enchantment the painting had afforded, and came to the upland Queensland town of Springsure. As he said in an interview with the *Australian* on 16 February 2008: 'the dramatic escarpments of the Central Queensland ranges and the fast-flowing streams and open ironbark forests were not Nolan's outback, but I fell in love with the country'. Here he found the setting of what would eventually be his first novel, *Watching the Climbers on the Mountain*, published when Miller was in his early fifties.

In that note to *The Tivington Nott*, Miller also wrote that 'Although this story may not be autobiography in the conventional sense, it is nevertheless deeply revealing of the author' (viii). But which author? Or, more exactly, at what time of his life: is it the author as his young self that is revealed, or the writer in middle age, seemingly compelled then to revisit powerful early memories? We may never know the trigger that led to Miller's first two novels of the late 1980s, although a belated return to Queensland in the middle of the decade was probably a factor. By then, he had had a long career in the arts. 'He began writing in 1972' (533), *The Oxford Companion to Australian Literature* (1996) baldly informs us. He wrote both poetry and plays, taught creative writing in Melbourne at La Trobe University and helped to found both the Anthill Theatre and the Melbourne Writers' Theatre. So there had been a long apprenticeship before that memory with a mind of its own sent Miller towards fiction.

In *The Tivington Nott*, this took him back to his teenage years in England and to a rural world that was more barbaric than idyllic. The title of the novel refers to a stag without antlers, a rare animal that is feared and loathed by those who hunt deer because of the harm that it might do if allowed to breed others of its kind. On the nott, it is always open season. Miller's narrator comes by accident upon a lonely spot on the moor that is 'the soiling pit of the Tivington nott', the place 'where the great stag without horns rolls and soils' (20). This gift is a secret that he will keep from a community in which he is naturally enough treated as an outsider. His affinity is with the stag: 'Solitary. Always on guard. Never at ease with the herd' (22). He is granted a terrifying audience, in which Miller's descriptive powers are first unleashed. The nott has 'the wide-set, slanting eyes of the satyr. Wild and aggressive. Staring directly into mine. Neither of us moving. His thick neck-hair shaggy and standing out, knotted and sopping; with black mud cascading from his flanks. Something wild and savage rising from the wallow to confront me' (24).

The youth lives with the aforesaid Morris, rural labourer and nephew of Bill (Tiger) Westall, the canny tenant farmer who employs them, but whose potential undoing is his passion for the hunt. Morris is not from this district, but his wife is: 'her parents eke out an abandoned existence in a decaying stone cottage up behind Monksilver in a sunless cleft of the moor' (1). Here, in two lines, is another novel that might have been. In the one that is, there are three main animal characters, as it seems right to call them: the Tivington nott, the two-and-a-half-ton bull, Vern Diplomat VII, 'eaten up with a soured energy' (4), that Morris has to lead to a cow in season, and 'Kabara the black hunter' (3). This black stallion, 'this entire with the strange Australian name'—stranger still when its name probably means 'Place of Rest'—is indeed owned by an Australian, Major Fred Alsop, who prances round with the Exmoor hunt in fancy dress and who is another outsider, quietly despised by the locals. But it is the youth who comes to tend, groom and ultimately ride Kabara to the hunt. Formally, *The Tivington Nott* is a novella (as defined by the American poet and critic Howard Nemerov), in particular as it deals with the relationship of intimate dependency between two characters—in this case, the youth and the stallion.

In the land across which they will hunt, the wild red deer has outlived the bear, the boar and his natural predator, the wolf. Coming upon the nott, the youth confronts something primeval. Besides what he has seen, this is what he hears: 'The whole darkening combe around me filling and echoing with his deep bellowing, low, archaic and malicious towards men and hounds and horses, tailing off into a bolking rattling in his throat' (26). It is prose of remarkable suppleness, impelled forward by the eight present participles, slowed by the succession of long vowels. The last three-fifths of this short novel are occupied by the hunt, whether for the nott here discovered, or for the so-called Haddon stag. Early one morning, the youth grooms Kabara and then, with Tiger Westall, rides into 'the last ancient homeland of the wild red deer of England'. Thus, 'we're intruders, outsiders' (75).

As—in English class terms—they are. Assembled for the hunt are Mrs Grant, Lord Harbringdon and Harry Cheyne, the latter Chairman of the Hunt Damages Committee. He 'owns a freehold estate of over 1200 acres and his four sons and their families work it for him' (82). There, too, in her old black motor car is Mrs Allen, over whose land they will hunt. For all their wealth, the gentry are dependent on underlings—Jack Perry, the huntsman, and Mathew Tolland, the outrider, who are in charge of the hounds, and John Grabbe, the harbourer, whose task it is to find and select the stag to be hunted. His main employment is as a rat-catcher and he appears to be 'A troll, [come] out of the earth and bracken and forest' (92). After confusion and delay, the chase begins. Kabara stops to drink and—in the prose register that we have heard before—this is Miller's description: 'his head going down and his lips flapping at the crinkling current, lightly brushing the smooth round stones, playing with it for a delicious moment and sucking the cold water in deep long gulps' (108). This is prose of a tactile precision and we can hear the echo of Hemingway within it.

Discordantly, at other times the prose of the novel is exclamatory—literally so. Scores of exclamation marks stud the narrative, signs perhaps of the youth's unbridled excitement in an escapade where he was meant to play a subordinate part. So he thinks, 'we're a mad tribe of wild savages galloping headlong down the narrow spur into the peaceful valley below!' (133). Yet the base note of the novel is deeper and more protracted. Here it sounds again, as the terrain slows the pursuers: 'As we penetrate deeper into this quaking country we find ourselves sprinting over rotten honeycombed areas, criss-crossed with blind gutters brimming from last night's downpour. A welling-up of water on all sides. Like a monstrous rotten bag full of holes and breached seams, this great sodden spongy mountain is sucking and gurgling, noisily draining itself of all around us' (150). It was not only, after all, what Miller would choose to remember, but the language—here at once stately and wild—in which he would fashion that remembrance.

The hunters have literally set foot on the surface of the underworld, trespassed across it, emerged both febrile and spent. Some early reviewers guessed at the quality of this work. As the blurb to the paperback edition attests, 'This man knows his hunting country' was the sage opinion of the *Somerset County Gazette*, while the reviewer in the now-defunct Melbourne *Herald* ventured that 'this meditation on the condition of wildness, on being an outsider, is one of the most original pieces of writing of the year'. On the last page of *The Tivington Nott*, the narrator confides that 'For Kabara's sake I regret nothing, but I wonder what it is that I am making my way towards' (167). For Miller, at least, that way would be towards Australia and to the events, when recollected, that form much of the action of *Watching the Climbers on the Mountain*.

The move from sodden moorland to arid upland finds its counterpart in prose that, in the second book, which is narrated in the third rather than in the first person, is notably spare by comparison with the baroque flourishes of its predecessor. This is the mild commencement: 'A small Queensland cattle station during the height of summer is a place where events that are quite out of the ordinary may sometimes occur.' The cast list follows: 'the people involved in this tragedy were a young stockman, the owner/manager of the station and his wife, together with their two children, a boy aged eleven and a girl aged thirteen' (9). That is to say, eighteen-year-old Robert Crofts from England, Ward Rankin and his wife Ida, who is from an old pioneering family of the district, and Alistair and Janet. At fifty-six, Rankin is twenty years older than his wife. A hemisphere away, but we are again with a closed rural community, as in *The Tivington Nott*, one that is also about to be disrupted by an outsider, who is the subject of suspicion and unease.

Embedded within the novel is another novella. Of Crofts we learn that 'his beauty and his aloofness disturbed the equilibrium of the Rankin family' (10). This comes to involve the resentment of both children towards him, and his eventual affair with Ida Rankin. Most important, though, is the inexplicable, sudden and deep animosity of the station owner towards his stockman, long before any adultery occurs or is suspected. Rankin 'conjured for himself a fantasy in which he humiliated Crofts. In this daydream the stockman was no longer muscularly beautiful but bore instead the worried hungry look of the local poor' (19). He has, perhaps, 'a daily beauty in his life that makes mine ugly'. The novella, then, concerns the dependent, desperate and ultimately fatal relationship between the two men. In one of its classic forms, this was Melville's story of Claggart and Billy Budd (1886–91, 1924), which told of an envy that is intense and destructive beyond warrant. William Hazlitt said that 'Those who are most distrustful of themselves, are most envious of others', while Joseph Epstein, after quoting this aphorism in his book *Envy* (2003), made this vital distinction: 'one is jealous of what one has, envious of what other people have' (4).

One consequence of Rankin's obsession is the decay in the regard of his family for him. Janet begins 'to see her father as an ordinary failure, instead of the guardedly sympathetic and mysteriously complex man she had previously considered him to be' (52). As the annual boxing matches at Springton [Springsure] near, Ida was 'intrigued by the prospect of seeing the stockman in a situation where he would be forced to abandon his solitariness and reveal himself' (63). That is not quite what happens, although the visceral description of Crofts's fight is as stirring as the hunt in *The Tivington Nott*, albeit involving the tensions of a constricted space rather than the freedom and different dangers of the horseback chase. After their affair begins, instead of revelation, Crofts offers his lover fabrication. When asked by Ida to recollect his past in England, to offer her a dream of elsewhere, 'An image of the grey cliff-face of the Council flats obediently waited to be described' (146). Instead he substitutes a false memory, inventing as home 'the façade of one of the comfortable semi-detached houses that he used to pass on his way to school'. Thus 'he began to re-invent himself. The fiction was not a lie—he was not trying to deceive her—but was a metaphor for the richness which he believed was in himself, but for which he could see scarcely any external evidence' (146).

The remarks are suggestively confused. His inner 'richness' is expressed and justified by the 'external evidence' of a home where he never was. The seduction of the substitute memory is plain, if perilous. And in the implications of the comment for the act of authorship, we recall Miller's note to *The Tivington Nott*: 'I have been not so much a liar as a re-arranger of the facts'. In the event, Crofts finds himself the passive main character in the stories that others are trying to weave around him. Janet harbours a bitter adolescent sexual desire for him. For Ida, this affair might be the escape from her marriage, while in the cases of Alistair and his father, if for different motives, theirs are intended to be stories of revenge. All of them at various times have each other under surveillance, indeed even in the sights of a rifle. This is one of the theatrical elements in a novel about being an active spectator. In its climax, this involves the act of 'watching' the climbers on the mountain. The novel ends with a deceptive quiet, with an observation of landscape: 'the grey forest of brigalow, out of which the oddly misplaced sandstone monolith of Ida's mountain rose into the empty sky' (224)—and with much business not yet concluded.

Although it is mentioned only once, there is a key remembrance early in this book (and one that will be re-remembered in two subsequent novels by Miller). This occurs when we are told that a previous generation of the Sturgisses, Ida's family, had settled 'on the Nogoa River in 1862, less than a year after the local Aborigines had been exterminated in retribution for the massacre of the Wills family at Cullin-la-Ringo' (20). This refers to the largest massacre of Europeans (nineteen of them) by Aborigines in recorded history. Horatio Wills had overlanded with his party from Brisbane to take up land that he had brought from the squatter, PF McDonald. The massacre was in revenge for depredations against the Kairi Kairi people of the region by settlers and the Native Mounted Police. In turn, revenge for the killings at Cullin-la-Ringo led to the slaughter of some two hundred Aborigines. (Horatio Wills's son Thomas was away at the time of the massacre. He went on to take an Aboriginal cricket team to England, found Australian Rules football, become an alcoholic and commit suicide.)

In the fourth volume of his *A History of Australia*, subtitled 'The Earth Abideth Forever' (1978), Manning Clark wrote that 'Reports came down from central and northern Queensland of all the abominations committed by the savages against white settlers. In the Leichhardt district on the Dawson River nineteen white men were murdered in 1857' (215–16). It is Clark's memory of his research notes that is at fault here. He has conflated the killing of eleven Europeans at Hornet Bank on 27 October 1857 with the massacre at Cullin-la-Ringo of women and children as well as men. The Hornet Bank episode, by the way, formed part of the childhood memory of novelist Rosa Praed, who grew up nearby in the Burnett District. Shocking reprisals followed each of these massacres. Praed remembered and fictionalised the Hornet Bank killings in *Fugitive Anne* (1903), among other novels.

Transplanted to different Queensland locations, the Cullin-la-Ringo massacre is retold graphically in Miller's novel, *Landscape of Farewell* (2007). When once I mentioned to him that he had already used this story in *Watching the Climbers on the Mountain*, his response was that he didn't remember having done so. His memory has a mind of its own. But consider the layering of memories that the Cullin-la-Ringo story has in Miller's fiction, almost as its primal scene. First the massacre, and the killings that preceded and came after it, was embedded in the memories of the victims and avengers on each side. Long afterwards, these events were recollected, if not strictly remembered, by those with whom Miller worked at Springsure and who told him a version of the story, most likely showed him some of its sites. In turn, the memory of what he had been told became part of the memories of characters in his fictions. It is an archetypal memory of bloody racial conflict on the frontier, treated obliquely in *Watching the Climbers on the Mountain*, crucially in *Journey to the Stone Country* (2002) and in *Landscape of Farewell*.

A scene of massacre is the operatically staged and frightening climax of *Journey to the Stone Country*. The Aboriginal stockman Bo Rennie and his lover, the Melbourne academic Annabelle Beck, come back to the ancestral country of each of their families. Their intention is to visit the stone country, 'the playground of the old people' (341), but first they must confront Rennie's great-aunt Panya. It is 'as if he had been called before the ancient dark of this old Jangga woman's judgement to answer for all the wrongdoing of his life' (336). It is Panya's personal memory of the events she survived that authenticates her arraignment: 'that grandfather of hers hunted us in the moonlight'. This was her place of safety and vantage: 'Me and your Grandma was all curled up inside that carcass looking out through the old bull's skullholes watching them murderin our people in the moonlight' (339). Fifty years after he had first heard the story of Cullen-la-Ringo, Miller would summon that memory to create this confrontation between the old Aboriginal woman and those whom she believes bear guilt down the generations.

In *Landscape of Farewell*, Miller brings back the Aboriginal man Dougald Gnapun from *Journey to the Stone Country*. With him comes an ancestral memory of the Cullin-la-Ringo story. This he confides to the ageing German historian, Max Otto. On Miller's part, a meeting with the Aboriginal academic Anita Heiss was the spark for his return to his memories of what he had been told so long ago. In the *Australian* interview, he remarked that 'I first began to see the configuration of an outline to how the whole Cullin-la-Ringo massacre story might be told'. Accordingly, he invented Dougald's forebear, the warrior Gnapun, whose patient planning and infiltration of their settlement enables the swift killing of the nineteen Europeans. As he tells his followers, 'If any of them live they will continue their leader's enterprise of the Book and will make of this their own story, and we shall not figure well in it but will be portrayed as the evildoers' (201). Gnapun's implacable calm during the killing that he initiates is the chilling ground note of the narrative. The story that young Miller heard in Springsure has travelled on a long and increasingly complicated journey, in the course of which it has been found that no unequivocal judgements can be made of any of the characters who met on the contested frontier, but that memories of what did occur are morally bound to be preserved.

Now to return to Miller's first two novels, those ventures, ambitious and unusual in themselves, that surely gave him the confidence to continue, to strike out on new paths, to some of which he would return. Thus Chartres and Tunisia are among the settings of both *Conditions of Faith* (2000) and of *Lovesong* (2009), as the story of Cullin-la-Ringo is a point of reference in three of his novels, the inspiration of much of his unobliged thinking about the history and memory of race relations in this country. At first, though, his fictional project was on a smaller scale. Here was a sixteen-year-old nestled in 'a great labourer's dream bed' (45), reading *The Master of Game*, which was published in 1406 and written by Edward III's grandson, who died leading the vanguard at Agincourt. The youth comments: 'I have read in an old book on venery that men are better when riding, more just and more understanding, and more alert and more at ease' (13). Here—two years later as it were—is Robert Crofts in his hut, sewing, a copy of Jonathan Swift's fantasy, *Gulliver's Travels*, loaned to him by Ward Rankin, spurned, lying on the floor. These outsiders, these disruptors, know—instinctively rather than rationally—the cares and the consolations of solitariness, separation from home, the venture into a future and to other places dreamed of, but more precarious than they had supposed. So it is that Alex Miller's first two novels, initially conceived as one work, *The Tivington Nott* and *Watching the Climbers on the Mountain*, seem like the two parts of a whole, or indeed the four differently paced movements of a single symphony, instinct with memory fictionalised, memory claiming a mind of its own, transformed, mellowed and deepened by the distance of decades, and tempered by craft hard-won.

WORKS CITED

Andrews, Barry, William H. Wilde and Joy Hootton, eds. *The Oxford Companion to Australian Literature*. Second ed. Melbourne: Oxford University Press, 1994.

Clark, Manning. *A History of Australia IV: The Earth Abideth Forever*. Melbourne: Melbourne University Press, 1978.

Epstein, Joseph. *Envy*. New York: Oxford University Press, 2003.

Miller, Alex. *Lovesong*. Sydney: Allen & Unwin, 2009.

———. *Landscape of Farewell*. Sydney: Allen & Unwin, 2007.

———. *Journey to the Stone Country*. Sydney: Allen & Unwin, 2002.

———. *Conditions of Faith*. Sydney: Allen & Unwin, 2000.

———. *The Tivington Nott*. London: Robert Hale, 1989; new edition Sydney: Allen & Unwin, 2005.

———. *Watching the Climbers on the Mountain*. Sydney: Pan, 1988.
Nemerov, Howard. *Figures of Thought*. Boston: Godine, 1978.
Perkin, Corrie. 'Journey into the Heart of a Massacre'. An interview with Alex Miller. *Australian*, 16–17 February 2008, pp. 14–15.
Pierce, Peter. 'The Solitariness of Alex Miller'. *Australian Literary Studies* 21.3 (2004): 299–311.

- 4 -

ALEX MILLER: Migrant Writer

INGEBORG VAN TEESELING

ALEX MILLER, A TWO-TIME winner of the Miles Franklin Literary Award, has written ten novels, all of them featuring protagonists who are outsiders, often in more ways than one. In most, if not all of them, Miller's narrators grapple with personal and societal questions of alienation. Miller's books offer sophisticated literary investigations into issues relating to the 'ownership' of place and landscape, the impossibility of an uncomplicated identity after migration, the role of history, and the nature of belonging and home. Critical reviews of his work have, over time, acknowledged this presence of migrant themes, but the connection between the migrancy of the writer and the content of his work has hardly ever been noted clearly. In fact, the *Oxford Literary History of Australia* categorises Miller, a little mystifyingly, as a 'non-migrant Australian writer' (Lever, 325). My argument here is that this is not just factually false, but that reading Miller's work as unproblematically Australian takes the sting out of what he is trying to say, and not just about the migrant experience but about Australia as well.

Alex Miller was born in London in 1936, the son of a Scottish father and an Irish mother, and raised in a poor neighbourhood. In an interview I conducted with him in 2008, Miller said that his first realisation of non-belonging came to him when he was a child. Because his parents were working class and not English, it was 'made very clear' that they were not 'part of the ruling culture', and this made it difficult for him to find a 'meaning and a purpose' to life. Miller's father, who resurfaces in various guises in many of his books, was traumatised by his years as an infantryman during the Second World War, which left him wounded and unable to work. Miller's novel *Landscape of Farewell* (2007) can be read as a study into both the psychology of this complicated man and the difficult relationship he had with his son. It not only addresses the issue of guilt and the silence that was its product, but also recalls an incident that was, as Miller only recognised after the writing, 'straight autobiography, from the point of view of the emotion and the dynamics of the situation'. It concerns a severe beating the boy took from his father, because he realised that the older man needed an outlet for his 'reasonable' anger and the boy felt he 'owed it' to him: 'I have his name, I am his son, an extension of him. That makes me responsible.' (Van Teeseling, Interview)

Living with a parent who 'had lost faith in the human project', coupled with a desire for adventure, eventually instilled in Miller an overwhelming need to get away, preferably to a place that was 'unconnected to family, past and history'. (Van Teeseling, Interview). In *The Ancestor Game* (1992), Miller describes this yearning in an almost mythical way: 'Look for something you can't name ... and call it Australia. A thing will come into being ... A land imagined and dreamed, not an actual place ...' (259); 'From my European perspective, Australia looked like this fantastic blank page, free of the "too much" of European history. I freed myself, in a way' (Van Teeseling, Interview). The idea of Australia had been born when, after leaving school at fifteen, Miller worked as a farm labourer on Exmoor, an experience he wrote about in *The Tivington Nott* (1989). One day an Australian migrant showed him a Sidney Nolan photograph depicting a group of stockmen staring into the distance, a great empty landscape in front of them. A year later he convinced his parents to let him go, and in 1952, at age sixteen, Miller arrived in Australia by ship. He recalls the first time he saw the land he had been dreaming about:

> The sun was rising and then I saw this thin line. I clearly remember the excitement, the 'Christ, this is finally it!' A magical moment. The place that is ready for me, the place I am going to inhabit, the place that will be mine. A clear, clean tabula rasa. Not theirs, not full of stuff, but mine. Ready for me to write on. (Van Teeseling, Interview)

In my reading of his novels, all of Miller's work deals with what are usually considered migrant themes, such as fragmentation and displacement, difference, nostalgia and history, landscape and belonging, home and story. I also propose that for Miller these issues are not abstract concepts, as they are for many Australian-born writers, who are fascinated by the role they, and migrancy, play in 'the story of the nation'. His novels are crucially informed by his own experience, and the vision that permeates them is one of eternal homelessness. Reviews of his work often do not acknowledge this and to find out why requires, I think, some understanding of how multicultural Australia has been shaped.

The word 'multiculturalism' was first used in Australia in 1973 by the then Minister for Immigration, Al Grassby, to denote a fairly broad idea of 'the family of the nation' (Preface, 5). In the roughly forty years since then, it seems to have evolved from this inclusive notion to a designation 'related more directly to the social position and interests of ethnic minority groups (Ang and Stratton, 'Multicultural Imagined Communities', 137). Writers like Ien Ang, Jon Stratton and Stephen Castles, as well as literary critic Sneja Gunew, point to the consequence of this way of thinking for the division of Australian society into core and non-core communities. The core consists of white, Anglo, English-speaking, culturally similar 'non-ethnics', while the non-core contains everybody else. 'Multiculturalism', in this way, has been transformed from a term used to describe the values and practices of the whole of Australian society (denoting the fact that it is a multicultural country) into something that is associated with '(non-English-speaking) migrants' (Ang and Stratton, 'Multiculturalism in Crisis', 100). 'Multiculturalism' functions, then, as a measure of difference, defining who belongs to the nation and who does not. This binary opposition leaves no apparent room for individuals or groups who do not fit easily into either category. Stratton, James Hammerton and Alistair Thomson make this case through an investigation into the position of Irish and British migrants respectively, while David Mosler and Bob Catley have looked into the location of their American counterparts. They conclude that the Australian multicultural binary has made these particular migrants 'invisible' because they are not only English-speaking, but also mostly white. Whiteness, therefore, emerges as yet another important field of investigation here. Theorists of whiteness such as Ruth Frankenberg define it as a dangerously 'unmarked and unnamed' category (*White Women, Race Matters*, 2). Whiteness refers also to 'terms of acceptable moral difference' (Stratton, 'Multiculturalism and the Whitening Machine', 165), to an undiscussed and undefined 'white' morality that is the norm and into which writers like Miller have been uncritically assimilated.

The concept of migrancy in Australia therefore has a sliding scale. Older immigrant groups like Western Europeans, who came here after the Second World War, were classified then as migrants and 'ethnics', but with the influx of newer migrants their status has changed. People arriving now from Somalia or Lebanon fit into this category, while the Dutch and Germans have become part of the core. Also, there are people who are called second- or third-generation migrants, a contradiction in terms. As a consequence, the simple dictionary definition of a migrant as someone who migrates seems to have been erased, making way for a rather confusing version of the nation as one in which everyone is a migrant and yet only newly arrived, non-white, non-English-speaking migrants are considered really to be so. This obscures both certain migrant stories and discussion about the consequences of migration in general. If migration is 'the quintessential experience of our time', as John Berger contends (*And Our Faces*, 55), the analysis of this important global occurrence should be based in clearly defined understandings of the central concepts. Miller's friend, the historian, writer and artist Paul Carter, who is himself an English migrant to Australia, is right in insisting that 'it becomes more than ever urgent to develop a framework of thinking that makes the migrant central, not ancillary, to historical processes' (*Living in a New Country*, 7–8). Doing that requires adopting definitions of both the migrant and the nation (and the relationship between them) that are less based in tacitly selective models.

Taking all of this into consideration makes it easier to understand the ideas surrounding migrant literature within Australian literature. From the early 1980s onwards, Sneja Gunew has taken the lead in positioning migrant literature as signifying 'difference' ('Migrant Women Writers', 18), denoting writers with a non-English-speaking background who can be considered 'ethnic' (*Beyond the Echo*, xiii) or 'marginal' ('Postmodern Tensions', 22), and who come from 'cultural traditions which do not derive from either England or Ireland' (*Bibliography*, viii). Later, Graham Huggan introduced the notion of the 'exotic' (*The Post-Colonial Exotic*, vii) and attached it to migrant or multicultural literature. Huggan argues that difference is not necessarily produced by migrant writers themselves, but by the way the observers—here the white Anglo-Celtic core—view and 'designate' them (134). In looking at the work of white, English-speaking, culturally similar migrant writers, the seemingly inflexible binaries and their consequences pose a problem. This particular group of writers, whether they migrated from Britain, America, New Zealand, South Africa or elsewhere, challenge easy dichotomies of the Anglo–ethnic binary. The work of some of these white, English-speaking writers sometimes suffers from a limited or biased reading because of a lack of appreciation of how they occupy this ambiguous position of both mainstream and migrant.

Let me now come back to Miller, and discuss three of his novels in order to show where migrant issues are, to my mind, central. *Watching the Climbers on the Mountain* (1988) is the first book that Miller published in Australia. It introduces one of his recurrent protagonists: an Englishman in Australia, here a young stockman (Miller's first job in his new country) called Robert Crofts. On the surface, the book looks like a simple love story between Crofts and Ida Rankin, the frustrated wife of Crofts's employer, Ward Rankin. In fact, *Watching the Climbers on the Mountain* is a continuation of a theme Miller had already touched upon in *The Tivington Nott* (1989), the novel he actually wrote first: the individual (outsider) versus the group (of insiders). Crofts and Ida Rankin are both strangers. Crofts is an Englishman who does not talk about his family (or when he does, he fabricates a story about them) and who irritates Ida's husband by how seriously he takes his work. Ida does not feel connected to either her husband or her children, and feels that the only time she was really herself was when she was climbing the highest mountain in the district as a girl. This feat has made her an oddity in the area, where women are not supposed to do things like that. Miller writes about everybody else as belonging to a tribe, and about those tribal members as interchangeable smiling assassins, out to force the outsiders to make a choice: conform and 'belong', or keep your individuality and run the risk of being driven out of town.

In *Watching the Climbers on the Mountain*, Miller uses the landscape as an actor in the decision about who belongs and who does not. The protagonists' positions in the community are reflected in their relationship to the landscape. Rankin, the station owner, has long ago lost interest in his surroundings. He sees the land as hostile, something to escape from whenever he can, something that he has given up on after too many years of trying to domesticate it. His descriptions of his property are mostly negative, with a focus on the heat, the flies and the bush taking over. Crofts (who can be read as a portrait of the writer as a young man) is the quintessential new colonist, working himself into a sweat to organise, categorise and order the bush. He clears, builds and uses his physicality to do the opposite of Rankin: he wants to forget about his past in his old country by almost literally hacking himself a way to a future in the new one. Then there is Ida, the only one who is connected to the actual landscape and not simply to some idea of it. The mountain she once climbed feels to her very much like her soul, the place where her true identity lies, and Miller portrays her as inhabiting every piece of scrub around her. She is genuinely of the place, which her husband labels as an 'eccentricity, a lingering symptom' (149). I would argue that such an interest in landscape and estrangement is thematically rooted in the migrant experience. It is reminiscent of Elizabeth Jolley, for example, who wrote that for migrant writers especially there is a difference between 'stored landscape' and the one you live in and with. 'Stored landscape', according to Jolley, can be used to 'heighten contrasts', or, specifically in the case of the writer, 'to create parallels which reveal aspects of human behaviour'. Only by realising the difference between then and now, between there and here, and acknowledging the role of memory in this process, did Jolley feel it possible to write about the Australian landscape (quoted in Lurie, *Central Mischief*, 99). Miller likewise seems to feel his way into his new country by concentrating on landscape and how old and new inhabitants deal with it, and it with them.

Miller's next book brought him national literary celebrity, ironically with a story that questioned the very existence of 'Australia'. *The Ancestor Game* (1992) is a big book, a masterpiece in the original sense of the word: something you make to prove you are not an apprentice anymore and that you belong to the professional ranks of your particular guild. Miller once said that his books are 'part of a buried city of great complexity', and that they have 'a confessional nature' ('This Is How', 30). In this buried city, *The Ancestor Game* is the cathedral, complete with hundreds of little sculptures, carvings and stained-glass windows that tell the sub-stories which make up the overarching one. Again, this novel came out of a personal experience, in this case the death of a Chinese-Australian friend who had always felt 'he only partly belonged' in Australia because of his status as a Chinese migrant. Miller 'wanted to validate him', then realised, in the course of the four years it took to write the book, that 'he could have been me'. The book turned from an ode to a friend into 'this enormous project . . . challenging the whole sense of homeland, identity, nationality—what this means to us' (Miller quoted in Ryle, 'An Author Arrives', 1–3).

The Ancestor Game begins with English-Australian writer Steven Muir going 'home' to be present for the British release of his first novel. He hopes that the book, 'which was set in England, might prove the basis for a reconciliation with the country of [his] birth', and desperately wishes that 'something might have healed between us by now' (4). Instead, something entirely different happens. His father has just died and his mother is in no mood to placate her son. She blames him for never writing letters home and just sending his parents a book about Sidney Nolan—something he did as a way of explaining his fascination with Australia, but which was instead seen as 'a taunt' (6). Steven realises quickly that he has written himself out of his mother's story of her life and that 'she couldn't wait to have done with me': 'her verdict, it seemed, was that if I'd wished to belong in England then I ought to have stayed' (5). Steven's mother, who, like Miller's, has a 'Scottish husband and an Australian son' (8), has, like his birth country, become alien to Steven, who wonders whether he is 'returning to Australia in the morning to continue [his] exile, or was [he] going home?' (8).

Two of Steven's colleagues also struggle with the consequences of their migrancy and its family complications. Gertrude Spiess has a problematic relationship with her father and Lang Tzu (in Mandarin: 'the son who goes away') has a troubled relationship with his past. Mourning his father, Steven realises that Lang and Gertrude have started to 'occupy the vacated homelands of [his] interior, which were in danger of being colonised by the chanting spectre of my father' (17): the old home is being taken over by his new friends, who are also trying to come to terms with issues of belonging and alienation. All of them look for a unification of their identity, and their temporary solution is what they call 'extraterritoriality, as signifying both an enviable liberation and as a fate more terrifying than any [they] had imagined' (94). They realise that going back is not an option, that it is nothing more than an 'old illusion', a myth 'dragged out and given a shake every time there had been a crisis in [his] life' (147). Having left comes at a price and that price is the loss of the old identity. When Lang goes back to the town he was born in, the town that harbours his past and traditions, he is suddenly unable even to remember his own name. Lang is the quintessential Flying Dutchman: 'He knew the journey had begun, his travelling, his campaign, his going from one place to another, and he knew that it would only be halted again by death' (192). Living with fragmentation as a given is the only thing any of Miller's protagonists can do.

In *The Ancestor Game*, Miller concentrates on the intellectual and emotional result of that realisation. His protagonists desperately try to find some purpose, justification and a place of their own, and finally locate it where postcolonial theorist Homi K Bhabha said it would be. As Miller writes: 'Boundaries . . . exist to be transgressed, they are there to facilitate crossings, not to frustrate them. It is not . . . in those places whose exact frontiers have already been defined for us, but in the regions of uncertainty where definitions have yet to be located, that we must find our place' (194). That place, more an idea than a delineated reality, is Australia. Australia, the land where the national story is that almost everybody is from somewhere else, is for Miller's protagonists the only place to be: 'There's nowhere better. You'll be able to imagine it into being for yourself. You'll be able to make it visible. Think of that! You couldn't do that with Paris or Berlin or London, could you?' (261). The colony is the opposite of any mother country, free of the tired and tiresome burden of history and family of Europe (or even Lang Tzu's China). It has the excitement Miller himself felt when he first saw the country: 'A clear, clean tabula rasa. Not theirs, not full of stuff, but mine. Ready for me to write on.' Australia, the book concludes, is 'a divided landscape waiting to be inhabited' by people for whom 'exile is the only tolerable condition' (302). The effort made by Miller's characters appears to consist of finding similarities with others who do not belong, and also of delineating Australia as the country where non-belongers can imagine belonging (as long as they are prepared to pay the price). The country and its new inhabitants have much in common: invisibility, strangeness, something as yet undetermined. Furthermore, it is 'imagined and dreamed, not an actual place' (259), and this is the main problem; it is an Australia of and in the mind, not a comfortable habitual home.

In Miller's novel *Lovesong* (2009) people are also struggling with home and belonging. John Patterner is an Australian who falls in love with Sabiha, a Tunisian woman running a café in Paris that caters mostly for North African migrants working in France. Sabiha desperately wants a child, and promises John that she will migrate to Australia as soon as the child is born and she has been able to show it to her father in Tunisia. Over the years it seems that their wish to become parents may never materialise. This starts to taint their relationship and locks them into a stalemate: both their love and their lives are put on hold waiting for this child to set them free. Eventually Sabiha decides to force a pregnancy into being, risking the relationship, but giving both herself and her husband the opportunity to leave. Like *Watching the Climbers on the Mountain* (and many other Miller novels), *Lovesong* is a novel about migrancy disguised as a love story. There are 'strangers' everywhere; even within the marriage of John and Sabiha, closeness is overshadowed by strangeness. When Sabiha meets John for the first time, Miller's narrator introduces him as 'the stranger', somebody who 'disrupts everything', somebody as well who brings an 'absence' where once there was a whole contentment (55–9). John loves his wife and their home 'in a quite painful way', even labels it 'sacred', but recognises that 'even if he lived in this place for the rest of his life it would never be real . . . It stood away from him, and he was not admitted to it . . . He could feel the deepening of his isolation, his absence, his drifting' (84–5). Thinking about the future and fatherhood, there is only one thing clear to John: 'If his children grew up in France they would be strangers to him and to his country, and he couldn't bear the thought of that' (87). For Miller, the point of *Lovesong* seems to be that belonging and home are mirages, fantasies that do not even command consideration anymore:

strangeness and displacement are the only certainties. For John Patterner, everything and everybody has become a stranger: white, native French in the little Tunisian enclave, Tunisians both in Paris and their homeland, the Australian even within his marriage. I suggest Miller's main investigation here is whether it is possible to find belonging anywhere, even in relation to people, if an actual home is too difficult to find. Especially from the relationship between John and Sabiha, the impression the novel leaves is that the answer to that question is negative. Although they love each other, when John thinks about 'his beautiful wife', he concludes: 'What strangers they really were to each other. Strangers to each other's language. To each other's childhood. Strangers to each other's tribe' (192–3). It makes his love 'helpless', and creates a distance both of them find it difficult to bridge. Sabiha too uses the word 'stranger', both to describe 'her stranger, her husband' (231) and 'the stranger in the mirror, the enigma of herself' (245). When Sabiha and Nejib, one of the patrons of the café and a fellow Tunisian, make music together, John realises that '*this* was the place in her heart to which [he] would never be admitted ... It was not something that could ever be learned. One had to be born with it. To know it in one's heart as a child, the way he knew the bush and the sounds and smells of his own childhood home. Nothing would ever replace it. And it could never be shared. Except with another born to it' (310–11). The memory of home, shared with somebody on a basic emotional level through music, gives (temporary) access to home and belonging. But when the music stops, John Patterner is still in a strange country, uncertain of both identity and place.

Throughout Miller's writing career he has tried to explain to his readers what strangeness and non-belonging feel like from the inside. His novels have also been a call to core Australia: we live among you, see our confusion and our struggle. Within this call there is a question about multiculturalism: are we really Grassby's family of the nation, or is it more complicated than that? To Miller it is obvious that 'this writing is about migrancy, there is no getting around that. Even if you don't want to see it, it is still there' (Van Teeseling, Interview). Reading Miller as a quintessentially Australian writer, then, is to miss out on the essence of his work, grounded as it is in the condition of migrancy. Miller is a communicator of difference, not difference in terms of 'them' and 'us', but difference that speaks of fragmentation and dislocation from a deep well of lived experience and understanding. From that migrant place, 'the story of the intimate and private lives of us' (Miller, 'Truth in Fiction', 6–7) is a story that shows its readers a very particular kind of Australia. To be able to hear it properly, it is imperative to know who its writer is.

WORKS CITED

Ang, Ien and Jon Stratton. 'Multiculturalism in Crisis: The New Politics of Race and National Identity in Australia', in Ien Ang, *On Not Speaking Chinese: Living Between Asia and the West.* London and New York: Routledge, 2001.

———. 'Multicultural Imagined Communities: Cultural Difference and National Identity in Australia and the USA', in David Bennett, ed. *Multicultural States: Rethinking Difference and Identity.* London and New York: Routledge, 1998.

Berger, John. *And Our Faces, My Heart, Brief as Photos.* London and New York: Pantheon, 1984.

Carter, Paul. *Living in a New Country: History, Travelling and Language.* London: Faber, 1992.

Frankenberg, Ruth. *White Women, Race Matters: The Social Construction of Whiteness.* Minneapolis: University of Minnesota Press, 1993.

Grassby, Al. Preface, in A Dezsery, ed. *The First Multicultural Anthology in English and Other than English.* Adelaide: Dezsery Ethnic Publications, 1973.

Gunew, Sneja. 'Postmodern Tensions: Reading for (Multi)Cultural Difference', *Meanjin* 49.1 (1990): 21–33.

———. 'Migrant Women Writers: Who's on Whose Margins?' *Meanjin*, 42.1 (1983): 16–26.

Gunew, Sneja, Lolo Houbein, Alexandra Karakostas-Seda and Jan Mahyuddin, eds. *A Bibliography of Australian Multicultural Writers.* Geelong: Centre for Studies in Literary Education, Deakin University, 1992.

Gunew, Sneja and Jan Mahyuddin, eds. *Beyond the Echo: Multicultural Women's Writing.* St Lucia: University of Queensland Press, 1988.

Hammerton, James and Alistair Thomson. *Ten Pound Poms: Australia's Invisible Migrants*. Manchester and New York: Manchester University Press, 2005.

Huggan, Graham. *The Post-Colonial Exotic: Marketing the Margins*. London and New York: Routledge, 2001.

Lever, Susan. 'Fiction: Innovation and Ideology', in Bruce Bennett, Jennifer Strauss and Chris Wallace-Crabbe, Eds. *The Oxford Literary History of Australia*. Melbourne: Oxford University Press, 1998.

Lurie, Caroline. *Central Mischief: Elizabeth Jolley on Writing, Her Past and Herself*. Ringwood, Vic.: Viking, 1992.

Miller, Alex. *Lovesong*. Sydney: Allen & Unwin, 2009.

——. 'Alex Miller: Truth in Fiction and History'. *The Book Show*. ABC Radio National, transcript 30 November, 2006.

——. *The Ancestor Game*. Ringwood, Vic.: Penguin, 1992.

——. 'This is How It's Going to Be Then'. *Australian Book Review* 127 (December/January, 1990–1): 30.

——. *The Tivington Nott*. London: Robert Hale, 1989.

——. *Watching the Climbers on the Mountain*. Sydney: Pan, 1988.

Mosler, David and Bob Catley. *America and Americans in Australia*. Westport and London: Praeger, 1998.

Ryle, Gerard. 'An Author Arrives, With A Work of Love'. *Age*, 26 May 1993: 1–2.

Stratton, Jon. 'Multiculturalism and the Whitening Machine, or How Australians Become White', in Ghassan Hage and Rowanne Couch, eds. *The Future of Australian Multiculturalism: Reflections on the Twentieth Anniversary of Jean Martin's* The Migrant Presence. Sydney: Research Institute for Humanities and Social Sciences, University of Sydney, 1999.

——.'Not Just Another Multicultural Story'. *Journal of Australian Studies* 66 (2000): 23–47.

Van Teeseling, Ingeborg. Interview with Alex Miller. 5–6 June 2008. Unpublished.

- 5 -

The PRESENCE of ABSENCE in *THE SITTERS*

RONALD A SHARP

IN THE SECOND PARAGRAPH of Alex Miller's *The Sitters* (1995) the narrator informs us that his memory of Jessica Keal allows him 'to approach the last enigma of my life—my family and my childhood. That cold legacy of silence and absence' (2). Bernadette Brennan's fine essay on *The Sitters*, in the context of Maurice Blanchot's meditations on death, notes that the narrator never explains 'why his experience with Jessica has given him the energy to begin painting...his childhood' (104). That it does so is indisputable, and Peter Pierce points us in the right direction, in his article on 'The Solitariness of Alex Miller', when he observes that Jessica functions as 'a Wordsworthian trigger to recover past "spots of time"' (305). The connection between the story of Jessica and the story of his childhood family constitutes the central frame of the entire narrative—and I use the word 'frame' not only to indicate a narrative frame but also in the sense of a picture frame, since this is a novel that foregrounds the connections between literary and visual art, between a novelist creating a character and a painter creating a portrait.

Throughout the novel Miller continually calls attention to such parallels by employing explicitly painterly imagery and framing devices. Even the narrator's back pain is rendered in the language of painting. He describes it as 'gradually losing its urgency, spreading out and thinning down to a sensation that was almost pleasant, a background wash' (111). Jessica is frequently portrayed in images of light—for example: 'The light falling across her lower arm makes it look like an arm cast in some resilient metal, yellow bronze' (66). In another image that calls attention to the analogy between creating a literary character and a visual portrait, Jessica 'stands straight, making a picture of herself, then she stretches, embracing her childhood playground. Her bare arms in the sunlight' (75).

Miller extends this parallel between creating a character and painting a portrait to include the construction of a memory and the creation of an identity, which also entail making a whole out of parts or fragments and thereby confronting the complex dialectics of truth and fiction, revelation and deception, presence and absence. Thus we should probably amend Brennan's point by clarifying that it is not the 'experience' with Jessica that has allowed the narrator to paint his childhood but, as he specifies, the 'memory' of Jessica. As the rest of the novel demonstrates in great detail, the actual experience is only available to us through the tricky mediation of memory—a point the narrator emphasises in the second sentence of the book: 'Under the influence of this memory, revisiting me in its new disguise, I was able to paint again' (1).

From the outset, Miller makes it clear that, far from being a quibble, this distinction constitutes the aesthetic, metaphysical and epistemological framework of the entire novel. The gift the narrator receives from Jessica is an 'altered memory, a memory entangled with certain family likenesses and forgotten moments of my childhood' (1). Memories can never be unmediated. They are always, to use Miller's word, 'altered' because they are already partly the creation of the mind that remembers. We simply have no access to them in some pure, unmediated form—a point that was made most memorably by Wordsworth two centuries ago in *The Prelude* when, in a long epic simile, he compared the process of remembering his childhood to that of a person looking over the side of a boat into the river as the boat moves through the river, and trying to disentangle what he actually sees in the water—fish, roots, stones—from what is reflected in the water from the sun or trees above it, or from the reflection of his own face as he gazes into the water from the moving boat.[1] The 'entire episode' with Jessica 'is contained for me in a single image,' the narrator of *The Sitters* says, which is 'my portrait of Jessica'—'an image in which I'm content, for once, to recognise myself' (1–2). The 'portrait of Jessica' in which he recognises himself refers to both the actual painting the

79

narrator makes of Jessica and the character of Jessica that Miller creates in his novel through the narrator painting a portrait.

The Sitters is both a brilliant meditation on, and an elaborate demonstration of, the complex relations between fiction and reality, image and truth. Miller is willing to place at considerable risk the narrative line of the novel and the plotting of events in time and space in order to emphasise the slipperiness of cognition and interpretation and the ubiquity of masks, deceptions and fictions as components of even our simplest attempts to construct or establish a storyline in the actual events of our lives. He is deeply attuned to the abundant variety of such enticements and seductions, in much the way Nabokov is—a writer whom Miller quotes in *The Sitters* (85) and who in recent years has, not surprisingly, become of central importance to him. It is a 'mistake', the narrator says, for the artist to 'look for the perfect image. That's Greek philosophy. It's the antique error. The error of monotheism. It gets you nowhere. The longing for a fixed truth resident behind the reality we've brought into being ourselves ... The fallacy of the Western intellectual tradition, the idea of perfection' (39). While Miller is profoundly interested in the interaction of fiction and reality, he is never led to the paralysing conclusions that some other postmodern thinkers and writers have accepted. The difficulty of interpretation and the constant interplay of fiction and reality, presence and absence, do not lead him to a deconstructionist labyrinth in which there is an endless deferral of truth, meaning and value. Instead, Miller discovers within this very dialectic the seeds of value and meaning.

It is in the relationship between presence and absence that Miller finds his deepest source of affirmation. Throughout *The Sitters* he plays literally dozens of variations on this aspect of the dialectic, which culminates in the portraits of the narrator's father and sister as belated but resonant and moving portraits of love, guilt and forgiveness. The first reference to the powerful presence of absence is the intense persistence of the narrator's lack of contact with his family, which, as we have already seen, is presented in just these terms in the second paragraph of the novel. As he is coming to know Jessica, 'an enormous feeling of regret came over me' (5) when he barely acknowledges her in the hallway at the university—a feeling he has again when he feels strongly 'her detachment ... The withholding of herself that was the foreground of something of great substance' (6), and then again: 'The remembrance of seeing her in the common room and then leaving without speaking to her' (7). Miller considers the aesthetic implications of this dialectic of absence and presence when he has the narrator tell us that 'It's not in what we say but in what we leave unsaid that we reveal the shape of our deepest motives. In the places between the words. In the tacit and the implicit. In the silence beyond the words' (15–16). As a child, the narrator's father would 'tell me his dreams, for me and for himself and for our life after the war. And that's what I'd begun to live for, these strange, beautiful and romantic fancies, this future that was never going to be part of our real lives' (11). That his father tells him these dreams while they are painting together is significant for the emerging aesthetics of both the narrator and Miller. And the bleak underside of that aesthetics is thrown into relief by the horrifying image of his war-torn father sitting at the kitchen table 'drinking watered whisky from a tumbler like the one he'd kept his teeth in on the bathroom shelf when I was a kid' and 'dabbing oil or glue or something on the spine' of one of the endless broken books he was always repairing, 'pretending', as the narrator says, that 'he was a craftsman' (29–30).

After his father returned to the war following a brief leave at home, the narrator as a child 'hid under the table and pressed my nose against the precious painting box and breathed its rich sad smell and I cried for a long time' (10). Far from being an exclusively aesthetic phenomenon, this unrelenting presence of absence can have the most lacerating effects on a person's actual life. Think, for example, about the ironic brutality the narrator's father visits on his children when at Christmas he generously invites derelicts into their home for the holiday and then pathetically uses them as a shield, hiding behind their presence to stage his aggressive absence from his own children on this special day. His father, who is radically transformed in the war, barely acknowledges the narrator when he returns from Australia to pay him a visit in London. And here the parallel with Miller himself, who like the narrator was born in England but made his life in Australia, bathes this passage in even more intense emotion. The father's bitterness, we are told, has grown into 'a tumour of hatred . . . He wants me to know that all the time I've been living in Australia, ever since I emigrated on my own as a boy . . . that I've been killing him. He blames me ... for the failure of those old dreams' (30–1). And then, in perhaps the most searing image in the novel of the power of the presence of absence, the narrator tells us that by 'looking into' his father's 'secret' and seeing that 'it's empty', he leaves his father utterly exposed: 'he doesn't know how to defend its emptiness from the destruction of my gaze' (31).

While the persistence of absence—its fierce and relentless presence—can be toxic and destructive, it can also be creative, as it is, for example, when the narrator paints the portrait of his friend Henry not after having Henry sit for him while alive but rather after visiting his house and doing various sketches after Henry has died. Likewise, it is by discovering Jessica's absence in her own portrait that the narrator feels he is making progress on his project. 'I hadn't known I was going to leave her out of the picture till I'd finished it,' he says (111). 'Then in the end I began to like the fact of her absence in the picture ... Then I realised that's what I was painting. Her absence' (112). It is exactly this dialectic that for Miller most characterises the creative act, as he indicates in what may be the single most striking statement of his *ars poetica* in all of his work:

> The silence we work in. At the centre. Working with the absence. Our anxiety. Trying to bring something into being there. Hoping to coax it out. Holding our breath. Waiting for that first little sign of presence. That offer. The first shuffling movement in the dark ... What are we looking at? And then the happy accident, the distraction of our thoughts, the way the paint begins to go on while we're thinking of something else, and suddenly it's happening. It's not our intention. But here it comes. We're alone. We're in the great isolation. Alone with the great absence. It's always the same ... Then it's greeting us. And we've never seen it before. It's the same old thing and we've never seen it before. It's new. It's completely new and unexpected and we know it and we've always known it. (114)

Immediately after this passage, which is preceded by the narrator's realisation that it is indeed the presence of Jessica's absence that he has been painting, he climbs up the hill where Jessica is sitting under the walnut tree. 'I was going to explain to her,' he says, 'why she was absent in my picture. I walked up the hill with the explanation ready in my mind. My explanation was going to link us up . . . But when I got to the tree I didn't say anything about it' (115). A few pages later, after Jessica returns to England, the narrator talks with her on the telephone and says, 'I'd like to tell her certain things. Even now I'd like to explain that absence thing. To explain it fully. Even though she'd laugh and tell me not to be silly' (121). Like the first conversation, that one never occurs, but if it did I would imagine the narrator beginning his explanation of 'that absence thing' by recounting to Jessica the moment described on page 118 when he is looking at an old photograph of her as a schoolgirl standing with her grandmother waiting for the school bus. 'Vulnerability,' he says, 'that's what it is, to time. The quick leap of time' (118). This is a phrase that Miller also uses in *The Ancestor Game* (1992)—'vulnerable to time' (51)— and which he picks up again just a few pages later in *The Sitters*, when the narrator is remembering the birth of his son: 'The way his little blue body turned pink and he started to live for himself . . . It was the moment I became vulnerable' (125).² The connection between absence and vulnerability is that it is because of absence—of loss, of heartbreak, of separation or disconnection—that we are vulnerable in the first place. But, paradoxically, it is that very vulnerability that makes possible meaning and value. Painful as it may be, death, as Wallace Stevens said, 'is the mother of beauty' ('Sunday Morning' [63]), and it is because of the harsh fact of absence that presence must be created and embraced—in personal relationships and in art. That is what artists do: they make something out of nothing. Out of absence they make presence.

It is precisely this process that emerges in the portraits that, the narrator tells us at the end of the novel, he is 'nowadays' (127) painting of his sister and father. In crucial ways it is the narrator's sister and father who turn out to be the real 'sitters' of the title. Speaking as a portrait painter but still again implying a parallel with the work of the novelist, the narrator acknowledges that 'titles have always been important to me. They've always been half the story' (76–7). In one sense, of course, the plurality of the title refers to Jessica and the narrator since, as he says explicitly, ' It takes two to make a portrait.

And one of them's always yourself' (40). Later, he repeats the point: 'a portrait's always a portrait of the artist' (71). This is Miller's variation on Oscar Wilde's claim in *The Picture of Dorian Gray* that 'every portrait that is painted with feeling is a portrait of the artist, not of the sitter' (8). But as the narrator of *The Sitters* explains immediately after making this statement, 'Except that nothing's ever as simple as aphorisms' (71). For there is another sense in which the two most vivid portraits that emerge from this novel are those of the narrator's sister and father, and it is of particular note that both are the very embodiment of absence. To the extent that a portrait is always at one level a portrait of the artist, it is no accident that in revealing his own self-portrait in this novel, the narrator creates two vivid and moving portraits of his sister and father—and both by indirection rather than intention. 'That's it,' the narrator says. 'I can't ask them to sit for me. That's all there ever is. Fragments' (127).

What emerges in these portraits is both the vulnerability of his sister and father and the paradoxical revelation that their beauty is inseparable from their vulnerability in much the same way that, as I have been trying to demonstrate, presence and absence are profoundly intertwined throughout this novel. 'I'm painting the absence and the silence of my childhood,' the narrator says about what he calls his 'family portraits' (127). Miller clearly deploys this dialectic to explore the aesthetic and epistemological complexities of the relations between truth and fiction, revelation and deception, disclosure and distortion. But I want to emphasise that he gives equal weight in *The Sitters* to the *ethical* dimension of the dialectic of presence and absence. *The Sitters* is just as sharply focused on the implications of this dialectic for questions of meaning and value as it is for cognition and art, or for metaphysics and epistemology. The very first time the narrator mentions his family and childhood in the novel—in a passage that I quoted earlier—he refers to 'that cold legacy of silence and absence' (2).

Far from being merely an epistemological or aesthetic concern for the narrator, the presence of absence in his life—and specifically the absence of his family—is a scorching reality, a painful presence that shapes his entire vision and way of being in the world, which is to say both his personal experience and his artistic vision. Even as he is leaving England for Australia, which is long before he returns for a visit, the narrator is haunted by the pain of absence. He recalls his father waving goodbye to him at Paddington Station. 'I still see him waving now,' the narrator says many years later. 'I can still feel his despair. His defeated hope' (99). When he does return home from Australia, his father's rejection of him is unbearably painful, and its toxicity erupts again when his own son comes to visit him near the end of the novel. One feels in equal measure contempt for the father who could so cruelly turn on his son and empathy for a war-battered old man whose dreams have been so painfully shattered, as in the image of the father's endless attempts to repair books with broken bindings, which the narrator tells us, in still another haunting image of the presence of absence, 'stood for something he'd never had. They stood for education . . . Refinement . . . A better life. A . . . productive life that he'd long ago despaired of' (14).

That same vulnerability to time and its ravages characterises his sister, who is originally introduced to us as a helpless child being hurled against a wall by her father, and then beating her brother, which 'hurts her more than it hurts me', which makes her 'weep helplessly' (103) in her vulnerability and retreat to her bedroom, where as a child the narrator listens at the keyhole of her door. 'That's what I do,' he says. 'I gaze into space and witness her crying in her room, sitting on her bed staring out of her window' (103). This image of his sister lying in bed in her childhood bedroom is reminiscent of Jessica staring out of the window of her own childhood bedroom, as she does more than once in the narrator's account of their time together but not, significantly, in the actual painting of her in her bedroom. The image also recalls another woman in her childhood bedroom: namely, the young lover whom the narrator leaves in England. Just before he leaves her, he is overwhelmed with this same heartbreaking imminence of absence as 'she lies on the bed with her back to me, curled away from me, curled into herself and into her despair' (35). When the narrator returns to visit his family, his father complains that the girl had come to visit them while he was away. 'I remember only her nakedness,' the narrator says, 'cool and pale and glowing on the bed . . . She's still with me. There's the guilt, the secret joyful guilt, and there's this faint arousal, like an old song carried to me then lost' (36–7).

The narrator is also racked by guilt about his sister: 'I didn't write to her, ever. Not one letter in all those years' (104), and then a couple of years later he receives a letter from one of her children informing him of her death from breast cancer. He is haunted by the news, especially because just a few years earlier his sister had sent him a letter in which she told him she had taken a few days off work to travel from Leeds to see a show of his in London. 'She'd seen me talking to people and she'd hung about but had thought it best not to interrupt me' (104). This may be the most powerful image in the novel of the excruciating presence of absence, and it bleeds directly into the narrator's account of never replying to his sister's letter and then, after receiving the news of her death, putting 'the letter from my sister's son to one side on my painting trolley' (105) and proceeding with 'applying paint to the canvas. It was as if my sister had crept up quietly while I was working and had closed a door, trying not to disturb me, trying not to interrupt my work with her bit of news, trying not to draw attention to herself, to her death, not wanting to waste my time' (105–06).

The portrait that emerges on this canvas is a portrait of his sister. 'By lunchtime,' the narrator says,

> I realised I hadn't been thinking about the *Tan Family* but had been laying the paint on all morning as if someone else was doing it for me. I'd been talking to my sister and watching someone else do the painting... I hadn't been aware of painting it. I'd been acknowledging my sister in the gallery in Mayfair. We were laughing and embracing and saying what a great thing it was and who would have thought when we were kids in the flats that we'd be doing this one day. (106)

This is clearly a fantasy of reconciliation that never occurred, but notice that even as the narrator allows himself this fantasy, he refuses to exculpate himself: 'And there was her husband and her two boys,' he continues in his fantasy, '—whom I'd never had the grace or the generosity to meet in real life—and I was taking them all to dinner at the Savoy' (106). But again, even as he dreams of hosting a conciliatory dinner, the narrator tells us that he 'could still feel her little body hitting that wall. Trembling afterwards. Taking the blame for something I'd done, I'll bet' (106).

Clearly his sister's absence has been a central presence in the life of the narrator, and hence of the portrait painter, all along. 'We paint landscapes,' he says,

> from our sense of loss and alienation from the real landscape. We paint portraits from our alienation from people. It's nostalgia for company we don't have and can't have. Absence and loss. People we've lost. We're haunted by our memories of them, of ourselves with them. We're always dealing with these things. How to deal with them, that's always the problem. How to visualise them in their absence. (110)

The presence of absence in *The Sitters* leads simultaneously to the torment of guilt, the fantasy of reconciliation, the refusal to seek a facile exculpation simply by admitting the guilt and, most importantly, a heartbreakingly beautiful portrait of the consequences of loss, separation and missed opportunities for human connection—between the narrator and both his sister and his father, and his son as well. Human connection, compassion and love are not, for Miller, mere artifacts that have no more meaning or value than their opposites. I would argue that Miller affirms, in this novel as in the rest of his brilliant work, that death is indeed the mother of beauty, and of value and meaning as well.

NOTES

1   See, in the 1805 version, Book 4: 247–67.
2   In *Landscape of Farewell* (2007) the image, if not the exact wording, is also central. Because the sacred stones have been moved by the white settlers, 'Time has been brought to the stones and they are lost to the eternal present of reality . . . They have lost their position in the sacred Dreaming' (189). As a result, 'No man will ever again live within the moment but all people will be the victims of Time, this terrible thing that has been set free among them like a pestilence and will devour their souls' (205–6).

WORKS CITED

Brennan, Bernadette. 'Literature and the Intimate Space of Death.' *Antipodes* 22.2 (2008): 103–9.

Miller, Alex. *Landscape of Farewell*. Sydney: Allen & Unwin, 2007.

——. *The Sitters*. Ringwood, Vic. Viking, 1995.

——. *The Ancestor Game*. Ringwood, Vic. Penguin, 1992.

Pierce, Peter. 'The Solitariness of Alex Miller'. *Australian Literary Studies* 21.3 (May 2004): 299–311.

Stevens, Wallace. *Collected Poetry and Prose*. Ed. Frank Kermode and Joan Richardson. New York: Library of America, 1997.

Wilde, Oscar. *The Picture of Dorian Gray*. Ed. Joseph Bristow. Oxford: Oxford University Press, 2006.

Wordsworth, William. *The Prelude: 1799, 1805, 1850*. Ed. Jonathan Wordsworth, MH Abrams, and Stephen Gill. New York: Norton, 1979.

- 6 -

LIKE/UNLIKE:
Portraiture, Similitude and the Craft of Words in *The Sitters*

BRIGITTA OLUBAS

IN A SHORT ESSAY about novel writing published in 1993, Alex Miller writes:

> The novel retells again and again the story of the person who is marooned on some kind of island of metaphor and who comes upon the tracks of another self. Which might be the story of two people who fall in love or it might be the story of two warriors who fight each other, or two kingdoms or peoples who challenge each other for occupation of the ground. But it is always the story of the isolated self seeking to transcend its isolation by becoming the other, the other self, through the communication of the subjective reality of the self. ('Chasing', 6)

This comment, which provides the conclusion of the essay, speaks in a very precise way to the preoccupations of Miller's subsequent novel, *The Sitters* (1995), through its focus on an agonistic narrative of self-creation and self-reflection. In addition to this, it draws attention to that novel's concern with layers of otherness constituted primarily for the protagonist through the work of memory and friendship. Miller's comment also folds metaphor into the schematic of fiction, suggesting that the novel's capacity for iteration—its brief, as he puts it, to 'retell again and again'—lies in some fundamental way in the metaphoricity of the 'island', a move that works to displace setting within the narrative, to shift it sideways. A little earlier in the same essay, Miller makes explicit the connections between a fictional and alienated selfhood that is 'seeking to transcend its isolation by becoming the other', as he puts it, and the larger processes of meaning-making that are the proper work of the novel, when he writes 'Fiction is not invention but is in the process of making subjective the alien fact and of communicating its subjectivity within the artful carapace of story. Fiction is engaging meaning in the subjective life, so that one is not overwhelmed by futility' (6).

Meaning and significance in human life, then, constitute the real work of fiction, not so much in constructing a new world—the task, Miller tells us, is rather what to leave out: 'The problem is never what to invent. It is not necessary to invent anything. There is already too much' (5)—but in expressing what it is that we apprehend in our engagement with the world: 'the process of making things of our imagination tangible' (5). In this chapter, I want to make use of this thoughtful account of the work of fiction as a way to approach *The Sitters*, an enigmatic, arresting novel about the slippages between painter and subject, between visual art and writing, and between actual and imagined or remembered worlds. I want to propose that the larger question of metaphor informs and orchestrates these oppositions—and the others that trail around them in the novel: oppositions of gender and time and geographical space—and that Miller's repeated returns across his writing to the question of how the artist lives in the world might be informed by the aesthetic questions being raised here.

Central to Miller's engagement with the work of the artist, with the representation of human selfhood through the mechanism of the portrait, is the question of metaphor, defined as 'the recognition of likeness in unlike things' (O'Rourke, 'Aristotle', 158). I want to signal here two important features of metaphor, drawing from Fran O'Rourke's extensive commentary on Aristotle's account of metaphor. O'Rourke draws attention in the first instance to 'metaphor as a token for the analogous unity pervading the diversity of the world, and as an index of man's psychosomatic unity. The key to Aristotle's approach is his understanding of metaphor as analogy . . . Analogy is of the essence of metaphor. It relies on the diversity and unity both of human knowledge and human nature, and on the diversity and interconnection of beings within the cosmos' (156).

Following on from this, metaphor provides for the complexity of human selfhood:

> Metaphor is the 'imposition' upon the object of a name belonging to another ... Is there a tautology here? Is Aristotle's definition circular? Perhaps, but not viciously so. It reveals rather a hermeneutic circle in which we find ourselves firmly centred and which allows us to extend the horizon of our world. We are on sure ground, since we spontaneously affirm the existence of diverse beings, recognise simultaneously their similarities, and deny their identity. (157)

O'Rourke's second point is that the 'similarity' between two unlike things, enacted through the copula '*x* is like *y*' or '*x* is *y*', is 'glimpsed only through the creative imagination'. Aristotle, according to O'Rourke, 'repeatedly notes that one of the primary virtues of analogous metaphor is to "place things before the eyes..." i.e. to bring them to life. Things are set before the eyes, [Aristotle] says, by words which "represent them in a state of activity..." A metaphor may be nominally complete, but will lack vitality unless it conveys the notion of activity' (168).

Further, 'the expression to "place things before the eyes" is itself metaphorical for the sensible character of metaphor' (168), and 'the power of metaphoric expression comes from its sensible, imagic character. "The faculty of imagination, [which Aristotle] states, "is identical with that of sensation"' (169).

My proposal here is that Miller's novel grounds its interest in the complex unity of the human self, and in the capacity of language and art to animate the world, to bring it to life through the work of the imagination in its focus on metaphor, on the recognition of likeness in unlikeness, which is in turn at the heart of its interest in portraiture. Before moving on to consider the question of portraiture in greater detail, I want to examine the question of visuality in the novel, in particular as it concerns the subject of the portrait. The novel's account of Jessica Keal is determinedly visual: she is always a figure defined by the space around her, in relation to other forms and figures, and in terms of the planes of her body, the surfaces of her skin and clothing, the play of light and shadow. This visuality comes almost immediately to stand in for her, for her known or imagined selfhood. She is described in terms of her enactment of a certain detachment. The first time the artist sees her, the impression of detachment is understood as 'something that belongs to her', we are told: 'She's like that.' She is, moreover, at this moment, bound into the artist's own history as artist, in that her image resembles another: 'Observing her you might imagine there's something Mediterranean in her ancestry, perhaps even Spanish. This, and her air of detachment, remind me of the woman who in my youth convinced me that the artist's occupation could be a noble thing, for *she* had been like that, handsome and aloof and troubled' (3).

The artist's account of Jessica in this early section of the novel—speculative and scrutinising—and her response—'her gaze was filled with enquiry and challenge, and even with a certain enmity' (3–4)—reads like an encounter with a figure in a painting, awash with the very precise mix of unfamiliarity and intimacy that comes to structure and determine relations between viewing subject and object. Some time after that first encounter he meets her again, briefly, and later that day, he tells us, 'I elaborated what might have been the possibilities of our meeting'. The domain is insistently visual, but also fictional, speculative, and desiring: 'And I saw her turn away again. The withholding of herself that was the foreground of something of great substance, some unshakeable purpose, a private and unspoken intention that she had dwelt on with care and singleness of mind over the decades of her life' (6).

It is here that he is most explicitly the artist: 'I played with this idea and drew it out and pursued it' (6). Veronica Brady has written eloquently of this moment in the novel, proposing that:

> It points us to the real subject, a ceremonious introspection, at once profoundly intimate and yet paradoxically impersonal, as the artist pursues her in himself and himself in her through the labyrinthine ways of memory as well as of the unfolding of ambiguous relationships. But this is not as merely subjective as it sounds. There is a kind

of unshieldedness about the gaze brought to bear here upon the movements of perception and intuition, and a melancholy of retrospection which is yet also somehow peaceful, even joyous, creating a sense of life as at once monumental and fugitive. ('A Portrait', 43)

The novel imagines the space of the portrait as comprised of multiple images and planes, as a point of meeting, observation and entanglement. Although the relations of looking are clearly gendered, Jessica is never simply a passive object. The novel sets out to imagine the nature of the relation more minutely, more comprehensively, to configure the point of intersection of artist and subject. What is more, it becomes clear that Jessica is not the only figure becoming entwined with the artist; as I've already noted, hers is not the only portrait painted in the course of the novel. And these other portrait subjects are in turn bound up with their antecedents and offspring. Likewise, the portrait is the place where the painter's journey from England to Australia comes to meet Jessica's reverse migration from Australia to England and her brief return: the narrator observes on hearing her story that 'it's a kind of reverse of my own story, though I haven't remarked on this because her telling is complicated by other things, and because to have mentioned myself would have been to deflect her from her own story, which I was eager to hear' (43). The stories are brought together in the work of the portrait, a form that yokes together divergences of time, space and human experience, compressing vastness into the depiction, or the absence, of a single figure as a point of intensity, of overreaching expressiveness.

In addition to the portrait of Jessica Keal, produced over an expanse of novelistic time and space, and which is revealed ultimately to be a portrait of her absence, there are the portraits of two of the artist's other friends: the scandalous painting of the corpse of the dead Henry, and the portrait of his agent, Michael Vay, 'with his back to the viewer in his gallery, he's looking at a portrait of me facing the viewer' (96). Finally, there are also the promised, putative, posthumous portraits of the artist's sister and parents. In other words, portraits are not singular; they reproduce, diversify and proliferate. In the careful discursus it provides on the nature and practice of portraiture, *The Sitters* takes us decisively back into the question of metaphor.

Portraiture, moreover, comes to this novel with its own story: within literary history, the portrait enacts a highly conventionalised relation of opposition, even antagonism, between word and image, drawing in turn upon the traditions and practices of ekphrasis, which is itself, of course, central to Miller's novel, and to its account of the agonistic play between male artist and female subject. James AW Heffernan's influential account of the central role of ekphrasis in Western aesthetics foregrounds this dimension, 'Because it verbally represents visual art, ekphrasis stages a contest between rival modes of representation: between the driving force of the narrating word and the stubborn resistance of the fixed image. [Moreover] this struggle for mastery between word and image is repeatedly gendered' (*Museum of Words*, 6).

Elizabeth Hollander argues that in Victorian fiction at least (her particular focus is *Middlemarch*, a novel as centrally concerned with portraiture as Miller's), the portrait 'necessarily punctuates the action of a story, simultaneously effecting both change in, and commentary on, its procedure', constituting a 'device for shifting and enhancing narrative perspectives' ('Ariadne', 171). In narrative terms then, a portrait enacts change, preempting fixity and singularity, which is, I think, what Miller meant when he said in an interview about *The Sitters* that 'Portraiture is always a portrait of yourself' (5). He is suggesting here that subjectivity shifts between—at least—the poles of self and other in a portrait, or to put it the other way around, that a portrait tells us or reminds us that this decentring of the self, 'becoming the other, the other self', is what happens in our engagements with the world, and that portraiture is an enactment of this process.

The narrator takes up the question of portraiture quite explicitly once he decides to paint a portrait of Jessica; that is to say, to move from the 'likeness' he has been commissioned to do, to the more substantial and compromising work of the portrait. But the novel has already announced its interest in the conflicted narrative of portraiture right at the start, in its dramatic opening paragraphs, which see the artist imagining, in a way, his own posterity as a past event, as a future product of memory. He begins: 'When I was old and could no longer hope for new friendships', his words presenting both an imaginative leap into the future of old age and a picture of retrospective continuity and reflection through his entanglement with the subject of his painting. Portraiture is thus inseparable from memory, and no more beholden than memory to the literal truth. A few lines later on the first page we read, 'And that is what she gave to me, Jessica Keal, the subject of this altered memory, a memory entangled with certain family likenesses and forgotten moments of my childhood; her roots and mine mysteriously grown together' (1).

In other words, the portrait is the point where two stories, or the stories of two lives, grow together—the organic metaphor of growth suggesting something of Aristotle's sense of the animating capacity of metaphor—in what Miller's narrator calls 'a single image'. Portraiture is about connected or overlapping likeness, about memory brought together with forgetting, about grief and joy aligned, working together to produce an image of another self 'in which', the narrator tells us, 'I'm content, for once, to recognise myself' (2).

Portraiture becomes a more explicit concern of the narrative again a little later, when Jessica looks at the 'likeness' the artist has produced of her in the form of 'a proof of the etching', and struggles to see herself, 'Twice removed. She didn't know how to approach it. Screwing up her face in an effort to see into the likeness, a feeling of herself in there. The two-dimensional image calling her in and warding her off at the same time' (38).

Here the two-dimensionality, the flatness of the pictorial medium, opens up duality; it bifurcates a self that has been imagined previously as whole. So the etching, the literal 'likeness', is differentiated from the portrait, which is, explicitly, an 'unlikeness'. However this distinction cannot be sustained, as this rich 'likeness' opens up the possibility of portraiture's uncanny sense of the self. When she looks at the etching, Jessica does not see something that can be claimed or possessed by her, but rather she is confronted by an encounter with her own duplicity: 'She didn't know what to think. It disturbed her to see this image that was her and not her. Seeing herself as strange, flat and familiar for the first time. Disquieted by the gulf of detachment opened for her by the print. The printed drawing. The intimate sign of my hand moving across the page. A touch she'd scarcely felt' (37).

The image of the likeness is emphatically the space of attenuation, of divergence, as well as intimacy, a space where the self is complicated by its capacity to be represented as an image, as a likeness. This duality is mirrored by the associated bifurcation of the artist figure in the lens of memory, intimacy and disputed truth, in addition to his being split across the roles of artist and narrator.

At first the distinction is clear: the physical process of making etchings signals likeness unmistakably, the impress of displaced and repetitive similitude. The likeness begins, moreover, as a proper and public expression of status, in the commission to produce etchings of 'ten eminent Australian women' (16). As a commission, it is also linked to the substitutive field of commerce: 'It didn't appeal to me. I didn't need the money' (17). With the differentiation, however, comes the confusion of repetition—of the word 'like' in its different forms—and it becomes more and more difficult to separate the two, once again through the operation of the copula, or the enactment of 'x is y': 'Portraiture is the art of misrepresentation. It's the art of unlikeness' (38).

So the idea of unlikeness challenges and complicates the idea of singular identity, of a one-to-one fit, of replication and of representation. And this impossibility is played out through repetition of the word, sliding into its contrary, and into different grammatical forms. This complexity is present within the word itself: according to the *Oxford English Dictionary*, the etymological roots of 'like' lie in the first instance in the Old English verb 'lician', 'to like', meaning 'to please' (in other words the reverse of the modern form) and the adjectives 'like' and 'alike' from the Old English 'delic'. Etymonline has a further derivation for the adjectival form, signalling 'appearance' or 'form' from a Middle English shortening of Old English 'gelic', meaning 'like, similar', 'having the same form', or literally 'with a corresponding body', a compound of 'ga-' meaning 'with, together' and 'likan', meaning 'body', a form also found in the Old English 'lic' meaning 'body', itself from the Germanic 'Leiche' for 'corpse'. Mortality, the slide from life to death, as a fundamental precondition for representation, seems to be intimately bound up with our grasp of similitude in English, and likewise embedded in the historical form of the word is the converse flow from active to passive, the somewhat slippery agency, the 'shifting narrative perspective' carried in the fictional invocation of portraiture.

The first viewing of her likeness by Jessica Keal anticipates the later portrait of her absence. After taking her likeness with multiple quick sketches, the artist refuses to let her look at what he has drawn, replying to her incredulity: 'There's nothing to see yet', and adding for the benefit of the reader, 'I don't really know anything about her. I've finished getting my information for the likeness. That's all it's going to be, a likeness' (21). The dispute between artist and subject is a dispute over ownership of the likeness: 'That's why she's been patient, so she can claim her likeness from me at the end of the session ... The likenesses are hers, that's what she thinks' (22). This dispute and the way it brings *his* sense of *her* 'vanity' to the fore, thus instantiating the gendered roles of portraiture, inaugurates the dialogue that will itself *become* the portrait, signalled for the reader not by a literal conversation so much as through the lexical transfer from repetition of the word 'likeness' to the word 'portrait', which dominates the next couple of pages. Here again the literal and repetitive impress of printmaking provides an alternative and insistent movement to interrupt the flow of narrative.

In its likeness to likeness, portraiture provides the subject of a narrative excursus. Defined in negative terms as mis-representation and un-likeness, that is to say with its difference located in the prefix, it preempts, at the level of the lexis, the possibility of identity, of sameness. But the spatiality of likeness is not fixed—metaphorically, we are told, it is located somewhere to the side: 'you've got to slip past the likeness ... reach into the dark and touch something else' (39). And, again metaphorically, it is the 'Beast' hidden behind the 'mask' of 'beauty' (39). The work of metaphor here is to animate the spatiality of likeness, to amplify the space between the prefix and the word, to sidestep as it were the conflation of the two, which is a confusion, 'That's the mistake we make, to look for the perfect image. That's Greek philosophy. It's the antique error. The error of monotheism. It gets you nowhere. The longing for a fixed truth resident behind the reality we've brought into being ourselves' (39).

The work of portraiture, then, is to argue against the conflation of appearance and reality, to avoid the 'misunderstanding' of the likeness, to get the wrong 'impression'. Portraiture reinserts the duality: 'It takes two to make a portrait. And one of them's always yourself' (40).

With the suggestion that similitude is presented as a space, we are able to take up the insistent similes in the novel's account of landscape, marked through the repetition of the lexical figure of 'as if'. The insistent repetition works further to spatialise the quality of similitude, to render it material, aesthetic and dimensional, so that like an etching, it functions to impress, to mark itself on the surface of the image. The narrator tells us, as he is preparing to visit with Jessica her mother's home in the Araluen Valley, the site for the new work is grounded in repetitive proximity and utter familiarity:

> I'd heard of the Araluen Valley but had never been there. It's two hours drive. People in Canberra often spoke to me of the Araluen Valley. They always said how beautiful it was, *as if* they owned it, or *as if* it owed its beauty to their appreciation of it, *as if* knowing about it made them superior to me for not knowing about it . . . *As if* they were responsible for the beauty they were acknowledging. So it had never occurred to me to go to the Araluen Valley. (40) [italics added]

The narrator distances himself from this space, noting the 'mistake' made by others in conflating their appreciation of its beauty with that beauty itself, collapsing the space between themselves and it, mistaking the space of similitude. I have suggested that the sense of 'unlikeness' at the heart of portraiture challenges the idea of singular identity, of a one-to-one fit, of replication and of representation. This impossibility is, I want to argue, further played out at the level of stylistics, in the flattened prose and the piling up of apparently simple statements, observations and accounts of events. At the same time, the insistent focus on similitude, the repetition of the words 'like', 'unlike', 'portrait' and 'likeness', and now of the phrase 'as if', brings to mind and to life—it animates—the problem of writing itself. Within literary poetics, a list of similes typically works to amplify the work of analogy, of poesis, but at the same time speaks to a diminished capacity to represent or express. Erik Gray argues that this is Shelley's preoccupation in 'A Defence of Poetry': 'while Shelley recognises that to compile a list of similitudes is self-perplexing, he nonetheless considers such effort to be necessary. The vain and perpetual search for an ideal is the common endeavour of love and poetry. Hence it is nothing short of fundamental' ('Faithful Likenesses', 301).

The arrival of the two protagonists in the Araluen Valley is a moment indelibly marked by similitude: 'Jessica switches off the motor and we sit in the car. It's *as if* she's made a decision. *As if* she's arrived at a decision to stay in the car' [italics added] (42). Similitude is followed by uncertainty, insisting on a point of distance, of non-arrival, as much as of contingency: 'It's possible we won't be getting out of the car. It's possible she'll give me a look at the old place from where we are then drive back out to the road again, *like* strangers who've taken a minute to decide they've driven to wrong place' (42) [italics added].

'In 'On the "Likeness" of Similes and Metaphors', Teresa Bridgeman argues that 'When the reader cannot justify similes and metaphors on a semantic basis, when s/he considers their pragmatic force to be an invitation to reverie, their effect can be seen as shifting to the realm of the imagination, the "as if" of an alternative view of the world, which, for Kant, is the domain of aesthetic experience' (69).

In even its most prosaic and inconclusive moments, like the uncertain, unmoving vehicle that carries artist and subject in this scene, *The Sitters* provides its readers with just such an 'invitation to reverie', tracking repeatedly and compellingly the 'domain of aesthetic experience' at the heart of fiction reading and writing.

WORKS CITED

Brady, Veronica. 'A Portrait of Absence and Silence'. *Australian Book Review* 170 (May 1995): 43–4.

Bridgeman, Teresa. 'On the "Likeness" of Similes and Metaphors'. *Modern Language Review* 91.1 (January 1992): 65–77.

Daniel, Helen. 'An Interview with Alex Miller'. *Australian Book Review* 170 (May 1995): 44–6.

Etymonline. http://www.etymonline.com/index.php?term=like. Accessed 15 June 2011.

Gray, Erik. 'Faithful Likenesses: Lists of Similes in Milton, Shelley, and Rosetti'. *Texas Studies in Literature and Language* 84.4 (Winter 2006): 291–311.

Heffernan, James AW. *Museum of Words: The Poetics of Ekphrasis From Homer to Ashbery*. Chicago: University of Chicago Press, 2004.

Hollander, Elizabeth. 'Ariadne and the Rippled Nose: Portrait Likenesses in *Middlemarch*'. *Victorian Literature and Culture* 34 (2006): 167–87.

Miller, Alex. *The Sitters*. Ringwood, Vic. Viking, 1995.
——. 'Chasing My Tale'. *Kunapipi* 15.3 (1993): 1–6.
O'Rourke, Fran. 'Aristotle and the Metaphysics of Metaphor'. In *Proceedings of the Boston Area Colloquium in Ancient Philosophy*. Vol. 21. Ed. John J Cleary and Gary M. Gurtler. Leiden: Brill, 2006: 155–77.

- 7 -

An ARTIST in the FAMILY:
Reconfigurations of Romantic Paradigms in *Prochownik's Dream*

ADRIAN CAESAR

I SHOULD BEGIN BY making clear that there is little I can say about *Prochownik's Dream* (2005) that the novel doesn't say better itself. One of the reasons I left academe some years ago was that I began to feel all literary criticism was reductive. The point of art, I think, is to embody something of the complexity, mystery, beauty and pain of life. Criticism turns it all back into argument. And the more theoretical the criticism the more distorting and reductive it becomes. It seems to me that literary 'theory' has become a kind of substitute belief system. There is a fundamental paradox, I think, in 'believing' in theory. As I heard one scientist remark recently: 'Most theories are wrong!'

Though my chapter leans to some small extent on the bundle of theories we have come to know as 'Romanticism', it does so only as a way of trying to illuminate the manner in which Alex Miller's novel eludes theoretical categorisation to give us a story which has the ultimately inexplicable richness of life.

Romantic paradigms insist on the necessary loneliness and suffering of the artist. DH Lawrence writes of the artist's 'crucifixion into isolate individuality' (*Letters*, 694). Rilke, perhaps a more pertinent example with respect to Miller's work, advises a young poet to 'love . . . solitude and sing out with the pain it causes', and furthermore to perceive the world from the 'vastness' of his own solitude, 'which is itself work and status and vocation' (*Letters*, 41, 55). There are moments in *Prochownik's Dream* when one might detect the influence of Rilke, and in its emphasis on the irrational, intuitive and mysterious in the creation of art, we may perceive Miller's affinities with the Romantic tradition. But the novel's distinction, I believe, resides in its portrait of the artist as embedded and enmeshed in family. Not only are Toni Powlett and his work seen in relation to his father, wife and daughter, but also in relation to his friends, who constitute another 'family'.

This chapter seeks to tease out the creative connections and tensions between families and art as they are represented in the novel, and attempts to demonstrate the way Miller's novel subverts the Romantic idea of creative genius to insist on the often unacknowledged collaborations necessary to the making of art. 'We're all collaborators,' the artist Marina Golding says to Toni in the novel. 'All of us. None of us does this completely on our own' (156).

In a recent essay, Miller recalls the occasion when his friend Max Blatt asked the question, 'Why don't you write about something you *love*?' ('John Masefield's Attic', 269) The advice implicit in the question becomes explicit in *Prochownik's Dream*, which is dedicated to Max Blatt, when Moniek Prochownik advises Toni, his son, to 'Paint what you love' (65). Though this injunction has an elegant simplicity, we all know that love is complex; the novel dramatises this in the profoundest ways as Miller shows that great art, alluded to in the novel as 'the real thing' (121), can only be created by mining the unconscious, which in turn necessarily involves one's most intimate relationships. The risks and hazards entailed by this pursuit are forcefully explored in the novel, as I hope now briefly to demonstrate.

Everywhere one looks in the novel there is collaboration. And in every case, love, familial and/or erotic, is implicated and expressed. Further complicating matters are the conflicts and correspondences between literal families, the Schwhartzes and the Powletts, and what is called in the novel the 'other family', the metaphoric 'larger family of the life of art' (103). These tensions go beyond the ample demonstration of the psychological commonplace that our relationship with our parents provides a basis for all future significant relationships. They also allow Miller to articulate various propositions about the relationship between life and art, and draw into the ambit of 'family' other characters, like Andy, the art dealer who sells and shows Toni's work, and the curator Oriel Liesker.

The central conflict of the novel concerns a literal and metaphoric collision of collaborations, with Toni Powlett/Prochownik at their centre. Much of the dramatic tension and narrative impetus of the book derives from Toni's artistic collaboration with Marina Golding and the suspicion and jealousy this arouses in his wife, Teresa, thereby placing enormous stress on the Powletts' domestic life and marriage. But before I look at this conflict more closely, I'd like to notice some other collaborations in the novel within and between the Schwartz/Golding and Powlett/Prochownik families.

Robert Schwartz and Marina Golding are a married couple who are also married to art. Marina is described early in the book as 'a faithful collaborator' (15), existing in Robert's shadow; later they are described as 'the collaborative team of Schwartz and Golding' (29). Unlike Toni and Teresa, Robert and Marina have made a conscious decision not to have children. In Marina's words, '*We decided it is enough we are artists... We realised we couldn't have everything, and we chose art*' (196). At the opening of the novel the couple have just returned from Sydney to Melbourne. Robert no longer paints, but provides the ideas that Marina executes on canvas. He also works as an academic. As the novel proceeds, we realise that Marina is in the process of struggling with Robert's domination. Her collaboration with Toni is a further part of that process.

Toni's relationship with Robert Schwartz prior to the opening of the novel has been one of student to teacher, developing into friendship. Toni was once one of Robert's 'most gifted students' (16), and was drawn into the Schwartz/Golding circle in that role. Later, he became a tutor under Robert and we are told that he often stayed at the Schwartz/Golding home, so much so that one of the rooms became 'Toni's room' (24). At the beginning of the novel, when Robert and Marina invite Toni to collaborate with them on a show, they are described watching Toni's reaction 'like parents who have given a favourite child a present' (29). It is tempting, then, to see here the suggestion of a transferred Oedipal triangle between Robert, Marina and Toni, though this may impose too programmatic an interpretation on fluid friendships. However this may be, it is clear that, despite protestations of affection and regard, there are elements of rivalry and aggression between Toni and his erstwhile mentor. Early in the novel, following some mild intellectual sparring between the men, we hear of 'the old attraction, the competing visions of master and pupil' (33).

If competition had a place in the 'old attraction', it is not to be thought that this has diminished in the new ambivalence. Though Robert is described through Toni's eyes as 'reliable and perceptive' (34), and Toni finds in Marina's painting of Robert's ideas an example of the former's 'generous, calm and reliable good sense' (22), we are made to feel that Robert is a passionless man dominated by his intellect, and that Toni is intent upon asserting the superiority of his vision, which depends upon mystery, the exploration of the unknown, the dialogue with the unconscious.

It is clear throughout that Marina and Toni's 'friendship' is full of libidinous energy. When they begin their collaboration and start to modify the painting that Toni has begun alone, we have the following: 'They worked in silence, conscious of the nearness of each other. It was Robert's vision they were obliterating: the knowing comment of the artist on his image, the self-conscious inquisition of the subject' (159).

In the same painting, which includes a portrait of Robert, Toni notices that the frames of Robert's spectacles 'resembled the slits of a gun turret', and regrets that 'it was not a more generous portrait of his friend' (165–6). Toni acknowledges that the three of them are 'linked to each other in ways they would never unravel or fully understand' (160). It is the transformation of this human mystery of relationship which makes art, rather than academic theories.

If Robert provides an authority figure that has to be in some way challenged and usurped, other father figures in the novel provide different kinds of positive example for Toni. Theo Schwartz, Robert's dying father, has worked in Europe as a commercial graphic artist and for thirty years has made drawings in a series of sketchbooks. Now, in his last days, he makes exquisitely detailed pen and ink pictures which feature his daughter-in-law and himself in a number of erotic poses and situations. Bondage is a motif and sado-masochism suggested. That these images are described as 'innocent' by both Theo (121) and Toni (193) challenges the reader. We are alerted to the possibility that Toni's point of view may not be invariably incontrovertible as we ask ourselves if anything and everything in art is innocent. Theo gifts the sketchbook to Toni, thereby enabling Toni to solve a problem in his own work.

Like Robert and Marina, Theo becomes a subject for Toni's art as well as a collaborator in its creation. Robert, Marina and Theo, Toni says, 'become his fictions' (114). Toni speaks of 'mining the intimacies' (132) of their lives for his art and, further, 'that it was like a surprising gift that had been brought to him, a trust that had been laid upon him, for which he was grateful and of which he was a little afraid' (133). The relationship between Toni and Theo is reciprocal. Theo sees in Toni the young man he wishes he could have been, the dedicated artist, while Toni recognises the quality and value of Theo's drawing and the passionate imagination that underlies it. He draws upon Theo's 'illicit intimacies' (221) in his own work. Theo also helps Marina see what she has to do in creating the background for her collaborative painting with Toni. Theo is acknowledged by them both as their 'secret collaborator' (244).

While he is thus a successful father figure in the family of art, Theo is less so in life. (One of the great strengths of the novel is that within the fictional artifice Miller successfully creates the simulacrum of a distinction between art and life, thus enabling a comment like this.) Theo has been a largely absent father figure to Robert. Theo abandoned his seven-year-old son to follow an affair of the heart which led to a life lived in Europe for forty years. 'I'm not a great moral example to anyone' (125), he says. Theo confides to Toni that he has come back to Australia not to be reunited with his son but in an attempt to distract himself from the grief of losing his beloved Marguerite. The attempt, he says, has failed: 'You won't tell Robert, will you?' (128).

Just as Theo's drawings constitute 'illicit intimacies', so too do these shared words, which place Toni in a position of privileged knowledge with respect to Robert. There is a sense in which Robert is betrayed here as Toni takes his place in Theo's affections. This is a prelude to the greater betrayal when Toni makes love with Marina, Robert's wife. That Robert seems to accept all this without demur is one of the mysteries of the novel. The reader is left wondering if he embodies an ideal of unselfish, liberal intellectual wisdom, or is an over-cultivated, passionless eunuch. Miller seems partly to paint-out Robert;

he is there and not there, just as he is there and not there in Toni and Marina's painting.

So far, the collaborations I've noticed have existed between Toni and members of the Schwartz/Golding family, who are all very much associated with the wider family of art. Toni's other collaborations are with members of his own family: his father, wife and daughter. Though these relationships also feed and sustain Toni's art, they constitute and take place in a world of domestic and economic practicality which exists in a problematic relationship to the 'magic zone' (198) of art.

At the centre of the novel is the life, work and example of Toni's father. He is the hub around which everything in the novel turns. Though the great drama of the book exists between Toni and the two women, Teresa and Marina, it is arguable that the most affecting and influential character portrait offered in the novel is that of Moniek Prochownik. He is a survivor of the Polish labour camps of the Second World War. His boyhood dreams of becoming an artist have been destroyed by that experience, and his subsequent life as a refugee and an immigrant have been hard. In the novel's words, he is 'an artist and intellectual by nature' (145) but is obliged to spend his days earning a living on the moulding line at the Dunlop factory in Port Melbourne. By night he is a painter. Art is his consolation. He paints still lives composed of the familiar objects that constitute and symbolise the life of his beloved family. Moniek Prochownik, we are told, doesn't paint the figures of the people he loves because they are 'too precious for him to risk [their] likenesses' (42).

The paintings remain private, stored in his battered suitcase: his art, Toni tells us, 'wasn't something for outsiders to admire or strangers to buy ... Dad was building a temple to our lives together. The intimate things of our daily use. To be a family was deeply precious to him. The domestic realities ... He never complained. The Dunlop factory was like his second prison. He was more familiar with prisons than he was with temples' (45).

Moniek Prochownik's past and present remind the reader of the Holocaust, and this implicitly raises questions about the relationship of art and the imagination to those terrible events. The language, imagery and action of the novel won't let the reader forget the place of violence in human affairs. Repeated allusions to freedom and imprisonment are similarly significant.

When Toni strolls away from Marina on Bream Island early in the book, he imagines the place as 'a truant's island. A place for escapees.' It's a place where 'the hunter could hide or approach the enemy's camp unseen'. His imagination takes him to the next step: 'A pulsing of bullets through the leaves and the felled bodies lay twitching on the grass. Step in and finish them off. The *coup de grâce . . .*' (48). Australia's convict history and its history of massacre between Aborigines and settlers are economically suggested here, as is the idea of the island as a place for imaginative freedom.

Later in the novel, dismantling an installation, Toni drags a timber rack 'out of the tangled pile of clothes, as if he were dragging a body out of a bomb site' (58). When Toni takes his daughter out to his studio with him at night they are described as 'alert, like refugees who have tricked the guard into letting them slip across the border, aware of the guard's suspicious gaze following them, tense in case his voice suddenly calls them back' (200). In this case, the metaphoric 'guard' is Teresa, Toni's wife, who on another occasion worries that the way she's 'set things up' for Toni constitutes a 'trap', a suggestion that he passionately refutes (87). Nevertheless, when he isn't working is likened to being imprisoned and painting constitutes being 'let out of prison' (263); painting also means forgetfulness towards his domestic circumstances and duties. In the face of this familial pressure, Teresa is described as 'like a woman in a war zone waiting for the resumption of normality' (227).

These figures of speech operate in an ambiguous way. On the one hand they seem to compare incommensurable realities and thus force the reader into a contemplation of the distance between art, language and reality. In this way they partake of a larger tension in the novel between art and life. Toni recognises the force of Theo's advice not to confuse the two. On the other hand, the imagery also operates to remind the reader of the risks and dangers, the potential for damage, in the pursuit of art. In this way they contribute to the counter argument of the novel, helping to illustrate the difficulty, even the impossibility, of always separating illusion and reality. As Toni recognises, they exist on a 'sliding scale' (191).

In view of these linguistic patterns, the very word 'collaborator' takes on added significance. In the novel, the idea of 'collaboration' is largely positive, though its dangers are apparent. Yet the historical connotations of the word, stemming from the various Nazi occupations of the Second World War, allow the reader to contemplate the idea of destructive as well as creative collaboration.

Though the novel is narrated in the third person, the prevailing point of view is Toni's. Given that it is by his father's side that he learns to draw and paint, there is a psychological realism to the way that past violence haunts the narrative. The fate of Toni's brother, Roy, adds a further dimension to this. In a fight with their father's persecutor, outside the 'rat-flats' where they live, Roy unintentionally killed a man and was imprisoned for his action. This occurred when Toni was only a child. He considers that his brother did the right thing, but for his father he thinks Roy's imprisonment 'must have seemed like a fragment of past horrors come back to lay its claim on him' (145).

It is against this background of his father's suffering that Toni as a child watched and listened and learned at night by his father's side as Moniek Prochownik created his consolatory paintings while sharing with his son powerful epigrams about the nature of art and the artist. These include the idea that '*In art beauty is everything*'; that '*The artist's enterprise is to refuse the world's ugliness*' (38); and, that 'art was something noble ... with the power to lift humanity out of the factory and the prison' (45). As we shall see, the novel implicitly questions these ideas without necessarily destroying their validity.

This sharing of precious time together is the beginning and basis of the collaboration between father and son. 'After a while I took it for granted I was going to be an artist when I grew up. Dad did too. It became our joint project. My future. We worked on it together' (46). In another beautiful piece of dialogue, Toni explains to Roy the reciprocal nature of the collaboration with his father:

> 'Between me and Dad there was never a need for explanations or reasons or why or whatever about what we were doing. We just did what we did. We loved doing it. We both loved doing it. That was it. That was our reason. Love. Dad was my inspiration. And maybe I was his inspiration. It wasn't just me keeping Dad going. We kept each other going. That's why I stopped painting when he died. I just couldn't do it. For a time I hated it'. (184)

The novel shows us the process whereby Toni returns to painting by finding, first in Marina and then in Theo and, indirectly, Robert, the substitute collaborators he needs to rebuild his sense of self and confidence as a painter. It is through his interactions with them that he comes to see the necessity of risking his self in his art and of placing himself within his pictures. We observe how Toni Powlett, erstwhile maker of installations, becomes Toni Prochownik, painter.

The question arises as to why Toni's wife, Teresa, cannot fulfil the role that Marina plays—this is the question Teresa not unreasonably is made to ask herself, since it is she who is supporting Toni's efforts both economically and emotionally. She too is a collaborator in his art. As she says to him, 'When I saw you I realised I wanted you to live your dreams through me. I don't have the passion for my work that you have. But with you I'm a part of it. We're a team. We're a family. When I saw you I knew I'd found the man I wanted to spend the rest of my life with . . . I wanted to support you in your work' (87).

Through the brilliant evocation of Teresa and Nada, Toni's daughter, and the articulation of the palpable love that exists between them, the reader is made to share in the novel's tensions. Teresa's passion is for her family (in this she reminds us of Moniek Prochownik) and her imaginative vision is centred on having another child. All her efforts and energies are focused on supporting Toni and her idea of the family. Ironically and cruelly, it is this immersion in the real, the practical, the economic and quotidian that puts her at a distance from the process of artistic creation and makes her an unsuitable muse figure.

Marina on the other hand is less known to Toni, less formidably present and sure of herself; she is ripe for Toni to invent as he will. She is an artist, ten years his senior, and we feel he identifies with her artistic and erotic struggles. She becomes his ideal imaginary companion with whom he converses as he compulsively paints while neglecting his wife and daughter (227, 235). Marina is a mother/lover/muse figure, her role shifting and unstable, whereas Teresa's presence in Toni's life is more stable, certain, known.

Part of the mystery and fascination of Toni's relationship with Marina is the way it relates to his mother. Toni's first prize-winning painting, completed in the novel's past, was of his mother. Now, after spending several years making installations, it is a female subject who inspires a return to painting. He is not yet ready to paint Teresa, Nada or his father. But he sees in his drawing of Marina an 'authentic mark' which he recognises as the way forward. It is as if he has artistically to connect with the progenitive power of an imagined femininity in order to unlock his latent creativity. (Jungians would perceive here an illustration of Toni's partly conscious, partly unconscious recognition of Marina as an anima figure—the projected embodiment of his own internalised and idealised femininity.)

After he has drawn Marina on the island, Toni takes the drawing pad back to his studio where he seeks out the portrait of his mother. In a complex passage, we are given a description of this painting and Toni's recognition in it of the 'mysterious power of his gift'. It is through a contemplation of his mother's portrait and a musing upon the as-yet-unpainted portrait of his father that Toni comes to recognise what he has achieved in his first drawing of Marina: 'He knew what it was now, this drawing. He understood what he had done' (66).

Part of the importance of Marina to Toni seems to be in the difference of her social circumstances to those of his parents. In stark contrast to the rat-flats, Marina was brought up at 'Plovers', an elegant country mansion. As a student, Toni was 'a little awed by the grand manner of Marina's parents, the ample style of their lives, the imposing gabled front of their enormous old house' (50). Later, Toni watches her and wonders 'if she might elude him'. She is then specifically compared and contrasted to the women of the rat-flats. Marina, he decides, is an 'undamaged woman. Unlike the women in the flats with whom he had grown up'. She seems to Toni 'to have come through unscathed, her dreams intact, even untried, the beliefs of her young womanhood transformed in middle life into a complexity that would escape him' (98). As he worries about capturing her inner life, his father's method, 'to find *himself* in his subject', is compared by implication unfavourably with pinning up a photograph—'Robert and Marina's way' (98).

This is significant, I think, because in painting Marina, Toni is finding the part of himself that is 'undamaged', the part of himself that dares to dream and dares to be a success in the world of art. His previous installation, by his own estimation, had 'represented for him something like his own unofficial history, a kinship history of displacement. A story of losers, not winners, of those who had drifted into the dark without a trace' (33). Later, these 'featureless people' are specifically related to the 'uncelebrated people of the flats', as well as being to do with his 'brother and mother and father' (71). In moving on from his installation and painting Marina, Toni is daring to overcome that past and to join the ranks of the successful, the winners not the losers.

The erotic consummation of Toni's relationship with Marina follows the artistic consummation—the completion of their joint painting. They make love 'like two people who knew something of which they had been forbidden to speak'. Afterwards he holds her, and 'From the top of the plan press the portrait of his mother gazed back at him across the studio' (238). Later, when Toni considers if he has betrayed Teresa, he isn't sure: 'Surely it had been something belonging to another realm, to another dimension altogether... Or had it been merely betrayal after all?' (239). The novel refuses further explication—does the mother's portrait regard Toni reprovingly or is the mother's portrait a marker of some psychological connection or contrast between his mother and Marina that makes the latter a compelling subject for his art?

What is certain is that Teresa's reality, her world and values, exist in opposition to everything Marina and Robert stand for. Interestingly, this is not true of Nada. She is shown becoming part of the Prochownik tradition of artists. She draws with Toni in his studio. She asks to do so at night—just as he used to work with and watch his father. The certainty of her imagination is the power the mature artist seeks to recapture. Even Nada's Snoopy Dog has his integral role in the novel. He is Nada's imaginary friend with whom only she can communicate. We are reminded of this when Toni is having his imaginary conversations with Marina as he paints, when she is described as 'the ideal companion of his hours' (227). Similarly, when Toni thinks of Nada at clown training 'solemnly instructing Snoopy Dog. Keeping the world of her imagination safe from the real world' (297), we are reminded of his wish with respect to Marina: 'He did not want to think about the real world with her... He wanted their friendship to be encompassed by the world of their art. There it would be safe' (243).

The love between Toni and Nada is strongly articulated and yet we are shown how the compulsion of his art sometimes leads to neglect and forgetfulness towards her. This, we are led to understand, is part of the price of the 'real thing'. But for Teresa it is inexplicable and is to go too far. Though Teresa believes in Toni and his art, her other allegiances are with nature and procreation. Her symbol is the water fountain in the courtyard—the fountainhead of life at which the singing blackbird sips and of which the reader is periodically and appositely reminded.

Though tensions between art and life are dramatised throughout the novel, and Toni Powlett's decision that as a painter he will be Toni Prochownik further suggests a schism between Toni Powlett in his role as husband and father and Toni Prochownik as artist, the conclusion to the novel suggests the dangerous collision of the two worlds. Teresa's outburst of jealous rage at the novel's climax results in physical violence. This has been prefigured at least twice when Toni, following moments of dereliction of duty, remarks that Teresa is ready to, or going to, kill him (18, 54). At first the reader takes this as the casual reiteration of a dead metaphor. But then we are told that Teresa is like Roy (and unlike Toni) in that she 'did not know how to back down' and in a fight 'she was prepared to go to the extreme' (207). When she attacks Toni the reader experiences the slide from the metaphoric to the literal within the fictional world. We are reminded of all the previous comparisons of aspects of the creative process to war, violence and imprisonment, which could be read as merely metaphors comparing incommensurable realities. We see the capacity for ordinary, decent human beings to be moved to murderous rage; we see that extremes are part of the human condition; we are exposed to the disturbing paradox that love can find expression through violence.

In the course of the ensuing struggle between Toni and Teresa the nude study of Marina, its paint still wet, is damaged, distorted, transformed. Here, in a brilliantly complex image, art and reality collide, the literal and metaphoric are brought together as Miller delivers a final symbol of collaboration—the result of passion, love and an element of chance. The collaboration with Marina is superseded by the inadvertent and violent collaboration with Teresa. Love—the real thing—finds its uneasy expression. Toni decides not to change the painting. Violence, the ugliness of the world, is taken in and transformed by art.

In the painful aftermath, Toni, who describes himself as 'not a violent man' (279), reiterates to himself, 'no one's dead' (280). There is here, I think, the suggestion that art is the best place for the expression of anger. It is significant that the two non-artists, Roy and Teresa, are the two characters who are prepared to go to extremes in life; who express their love through violence. Through careful juxtapositions within the text, we are left to question the relationship of this insight to ideas of massacre and holocaust. It is as if the theme of Miller's following novel, *Landscape of Farewell*, is foreshadowed in *Prochownik's Dream*.

The climax of the novel also works literally and metaphorically to suggest that the artist is only ever partially in control of his or her material. The 'real stuff' is beyond the ego—it is that which transcends the ego and takes on a life of its own. For it to do so, it must spring from the deepest places—the fountain of life symbolised by Teresa; the maker/muse/mother figure of Marina; the collaborations with the various father figures. Overall there remains an element of surprise or mystery, the inexplicable—the irreducible mark of authenticity. Miller's novel embodies this and in doing so teaches us to recognise it and to aspire to it.

At the close of the novel, Toni recognises that his father 'would have been 'Deeply hurt by the violence and infidelity' and would have seen it 'as a failure . . . to deal with the demands of art in a decent way' (293). Miller is not interested in special pleading for Toni, who is made to face the consequences of his actions and is seen to be culpable, at least in part, for the provocation of Teresa's rage. But we also see love triumphant. Teresa will return to him. He is now ready to paint his father. He will call the painting *Prochownik's Dream*. Aptly the title takes us back to collaboration, for the dream is that of both father and son. Miller makes it our dream as well; for this he is to be thanked and congratulated.

WORKS CITED

Lawrence, DH. *The Letters.* Ed. A. Huxley. London: Heinemann, 1932.

Miller, Alex. 'John Masefield's Attic'. http://www.nla.gov.au/events/flight/John_Masefields_Attic-Alex_Miller.pdf

——. *Prochownik's Dream.* Sydney: Allen & Unwin, 2005.

Rilke, Rainer Maria. *Letters to a Young Poet.* Trans. Stephen Mitchell. New York: Vintage, 1986.

- 8 -

REPRESENTING 'the OTHER' in the FICTION of ALEX MILLER

ELIZABETH WEBBY

ALEX MILLER BEGAN PUBLISHING his novels in 1988 at the end of a period of intense debate in literary circles about the ethics of representation, a debate informed by feminism, multiculturalism and postcolonialism. Put crudely, the debate was about whether white male writers from first-world countries, the dominant literary players up to this point, should continue to feel perfectly free to depict their others—that is, those who were not white or male—now that these others were at last finding their voices and writing back. In Australia, the debate was particularly focused on the question of white writers' representation of Aboriginal people. But in feminist circles male appropriation of female voices was also a major issue. Although a total ban on representations of others would clearly have meant the end of fiction as we know it, these debates did draw attention to the stereotyped representations of 'others' found in much earlier Australian writing.

I first read Miller's *The Ancestor Game* soon after it was published in 1992 and was struck by his empathy for his female characters and their predicaments, as well as his insightful depictions of people from other cultures. These have continued to be hallmarks of his fiction, with representations of 'otherness' also extending to animals, especially in *The Tivington Nott* (1989) and *Landscape of Farewell* (2007). My focus here, however, is on *The Ancestor Game*, *Conditions of Faith* (2000) and, rather more briefly, *Lovesong* (2009).

My attention was drawn to *The Ancestor Game* by an enthusiastic review in the *Sydney Morning Herald* for 15 August 1992 by my then colleague Andrew Riemer. I was shortly to visit China for the first time, and preparing a paper for the 1992 conference of the Australian Studies Association of China, dealing with the representation of China and the Chinese in Australian literature. Obviously *The Ancestor Game* was highly relevant. Reading it, I was intrigued to find that one section, when the first Feng comes to Australia as a ten-year-old boy and ends up working as a shepherd near Ballarat, where he has friendly card games with two other shepherds, an Irishman and an Aborigine, was clearly inspired by a painting that had especially impressed me when seen in the Art Gallery of Ballarat several years earlier. This naïve painting, *Euchre in the Bush* by JCF Johnson, depicts three men sitting around a table in a bush hut, playing cards: one is Chinese, one white and one black. As I learned later from Alex Miller, it had once belonged to a Chinese friend, Alan O'Hoy whose suicide was the inspiration for *The Ancestor Game*. It is reproduced in Alison Broinowski's *The Yellow Lady: Australian Impressions of Asia* (1992), where she notes that: 'The black man in this cross-cultural card game is thought to be not an Aboriginal Australian but an American' (Plate 3).

JCF Johnson, *Euchre in the Bush*, circa 1867, Oil on canvas mounted board, Collection: Art Gallery of Ballarat, Bequest of Clarice May Megaw, 1980

More recently, an extended study by Erika Esau of the cultural context in which the painting was produced has demonstrated that the black man was intended to be an Aborigine. Although *Euchre in the Bush* was Johnson's only known painting—he was primarily a journalist—it exists in several versions, including as a coloured wood engraving published as a special supplement to the *Australian Sketcher*'s Christmas issue for 1876. There was an accompanying text in which Johnson described the scene, referring to 'Jack, the black packer' as Aboriginal (*Images of the Pacific Rim*, 70), as well as indicating the influence of American author Bret Harte's highly popular 1870 poem, 'The Heathen Chinee'. As Esau points out, however, Johnson does not stress the racial antagonism that featured in Harte's poem and was strongly emphasised in illustrated versions of it produced in the United States. For Johnson, *Euchre in the Bush* was to be read as an allegory of the future of Australia: 'The three races have been for some time playing a game for life on this continent. The aboriginal race have very nearly played their last card, and the game is henceforth between the whites and their yellow-skinned competitors . . . there is no reason to doubt that the two races may work on amicably together and aid in the development of an immense territory, where "there's room enough for all"' (71).

In *The Ancestor Game*, Miller clearly shares Johnson's hope for an Australia in which different races can live in harmony, if not his assumption, typical of the period, that the Aboriginal race was doomed to die out. Miller interprets the Aboriginal man's costume—red jacket, tight breeches and high boots—as an English hunting outfit, ironically depicting him as a victim of the European desire to hunt and collect people as well as animals. Dorset, as a three-year-old Aboriginal boy, had been shipped to England 'As a curiosity from the ends of the earth'. There, as Miller explains,

> he lived in opulent splendour with a great and whimsical duke until he was fourteen and the duke died suddenly. The dead duke's son was not whimsical but determined to be a politician, and he shipped Dorset and his chestnut horse back to Australia. So here I am lads! He spoke English with the refined accents of an aristocrat and had been the intimate of many notable personages of London society. (221)

Dorset is one of many displaced figures in a novel that questions concepts such as nationality and homeland, as well as the relationship between nature and nurture, and an individual and his ancestors. While Dorset would seem to have been quite 'at home' in London society and appears equally so when with the other shepherds, he lacks the ability to read the Australian landscape that would have been his if he had not been separated from his Aboriginal family and ancestral country. The white settlers, however, believe in racial stereotypes: Dorset is an Aborigine and therefore must have an innate ability to follow tracks. His failure to find the Aboriginal man believed responsible for killing a settler is read as a deliberate attempt to mislead, and he is accordingly killed in revenge.

The Ancestor Game remains one of the most complex of Alex Miller's novels, ranging widely in both time and space, and introducing an equally wide range of characters. While the present of the novel is set in Melbourne in the 1970s, much of it takes place in Shanghai and Hangzhou in the 1920s and 1930s, while the events outlined above occur near Ballarat in 1850. It is also, I believe, Miller's most postmodern novel, with its multiple narrative perspectives and its emphasis on art as the way to escape the pitfalls of the 'ancestor game'. If the friendly cross-cultural trio of Aboriginal, Irish and Chinese men was an impossible one to sustain in nineteenth-century Australia, Miller offers a more hopeful twentieth-century parallel in the central trio of novelist Steven Muir, born in England to a Scottish father and Irish mother, artist and teacher Lang Tzu, born in Hangzhou in 1927, and artist Gertrude Spiess, daughter of Lang's mentor, the expatriate German doctor August Spiess, and a Chinese woman met in Melbourne in 1937. Lang, who only survives a difficult breech birth thanks to Spiess's skills, is born with 'a disturbing and fixed misalignment to his features' (11). This facial dimorphism is paralleled by his upbringing: his father Feng, a thoroughly Westernised Shanghai capitalist, grandson of the first Feng who came to Australia as a boy and established the family fortune there, agrees that Lang can receive a traditional Chinese education with his mother's father in Hangzhou, but at the age of ten must go to Australia to receive a Western education. Lang's 'ancestor game' is his way of striking out on his own, rejecting the conflicting beliefs of both his parents. He burns his grandfather's sacred book of the ancestors and throws the precious bronze cosmic mirror of the Huangs into the river. Gertrude and Steven, however, play their ancestor games through the creation rather than the destruction of works of art. As Steven realises at the end of the novel, Gertrude's translation of her father's journals, begun immediately after his death, has involved 'the living child ... fittingly taking up and renaming the spaces of the dead parent; making herself at home while making *of* herself an artist' (299). Equally, Steven's narrative of Lang's ancestors, begun after his own father's death, can be seen as an attempt to make himself at home and an artist. There are also clear parallels with Miller's writing of *The Ancestor Game* after the death of his Chinese friend.

The central image of *The Ancestor Game* is the phoenix, which, as Dr Spiess tells Lang, is common to both 'the occidental and the oriental worlds' (259), so representing the common humanity that underlies racial differences. Furthermore, drawing on the traditional Western association of the phoenix with rebirth after death, he claims that 'Art is a phoenix. Art annuls the sterile dichotomy Life/Death and makes for contradiction and fertility. It is both life and death' (260). The ancestral bronze mirror that Lang throws in the river bears an emblem of two phoenixes within 'eight entwining bouquets of vineleaves' (197). The same symbol has appeared earlier in the novel on the front of the house the first Feng built in Melbourne (39), where Lang now lives, as well as on the cover of the novel written there by Feng's daughter, Victoria (40). In *The Winter Visitor: Life in the Northern Hemisphere*, written after her father's death, Victoria recreates his other life in China, where he has had another wife and a son. So, like Gertrude later, Victoria is able to make herself 'at home while making *of* herself an artist.'

Most criticism of *The Ancestor Game* has been written by Chinese scholars and has understandably focused on Miller's representation of China and the Chinese. For me, however, an equally interesting feature is his representation of gender. During that visit to China in 1992, I saw how entrenched gender stereotypes remained there: at the conference dinner in Shanghai, for example, the only woman at the top table was the wife of the Australian ambassador. I was seated at the second table, along with the wives of the male professors and other top-table men. In *The Ancestor Game*, even the thoroughly Westernised third Feng remains sufficiently Chinese to long for a son. After his first two wives have produced only daughters, he marries Lien, daughter of the old literary painter Huang. Finally, after two stillborn sons, he allows Lien to return to her father's house in Hangzhou for the birth of Lang. Lien, Huang's only child, had been brought up by him as though she were a boy. Although her gifts as an artist exceed her father's, she destroys her work when she becomes aware that it conflicts with her traditional role as a Chinese woman, and marries the third Feng in part as revenge on her father. In Melbourne, it has been easier for Victoria Feng to reject her destined role as wife and mother, even though she remains cloistered from the world, and her work leaves no official record. Steven Muir looks in vain for any mention of Victoria's *The Winter Visitor*, supposedly published in 1912, in Nettie Palmer's *Modern Australian Literature 1900–1923* (1924) and 'Ferguson's seven-volume *Bibliography of Australia*' (68). As Sir John Ferguson's great bibliography only extends to 1900, however, Steven really should have been looking in Morris Miller's *Australian Literature, From its Beginnings to 1935* (1940), though of course he would not have found Victoria Feng there either! Finally, in Gertrude Spiess, we have a woman artist who in the 1970s can be publicly acclaimed; fittingly, the novel ends with the opening of her exhibition.

On my second visit to China a year or two later, I was taken around the Forbidden City by a young woman who was writing her PhD thesis on Patrick White. She pointed out to me the lines of phoenixes underneath lines of dragons on many of the buildings, explaining that the phoenix represented the Empress, and the dragon the Emperor. Earlier, however, it seems that the Chinese phoenix, or *Fenghuang*, had both male and female forms, with *feng* being the male and *huang* the female. It is this earlier version that clearly informs *The Ancestor Game*, as seen in the characters' surnames. We are also told that the pair of phoenixes found on the ancient Huang mirror, on Feng's Melbourne house, and on the cover of Victoria's novel, 'appeared to be engaged in a ritual dance preceding either mating or combat' (40). If 'Art is a phoenix . . . that annuls the sterile dichotomy Life/Death' (260), artistic practice can also annul the dichotomy self/other, as we see with Gertrude and Victoria's writing of their father's stories, as well as with Steven's writing of Lang's.

Although Alex Miller's novels, especially his earlier ones, are set in very different times and places, some continuing preoccupations are apparent, such as the focus on solitary figures, as noted by Peter Pierce. In addition, one might add the importance of friendship and the emphasis on the relationships between life and art, and parents and children, especially fathers and daughters. Reading *Conditions of Faith* when it first appeared, I was initially disappointed that it seemed so different to *The Ancestor Game*. Rereading it more recently, however, made me aware of many similarities between the two novels, as well as just how daring *Conditions of Faith* is in its representation of female experience, especially that of pregnancy and birth. While these also feature in *The Ancestor Game* in relation to Lien, she is a fairly minor character, and her experiences come to us through various narrators. Emily, in contrast, is at the centre of *Conditions of Faith*, which has a more conventionally linear structure and a narrative method that gives the reader direct access to her thoughts and feelings. Like Lien, and the three main characters in *The Ancestor Game*, Emily is an only child, whose relationship with her professor father is complicated by his desire for her not only to be beautiful but to excel intellectually. As a young Melbourne woman from a professional family, the 1920s offer Emily more alternatives than China did for Lien, but she still opts for marriage to a man who seems capable of heroic acts, in particular of achieving the engineering feats her father has rejected for fear of failure. Georges Elder also offers Emily an alternative way of escaping from Australia to her father's desire for her to study at Cambridge, but their essential incompatibility is signalled early in the novel when he refuses the challenge of swimming after her to an old shipwreck in the bay (10). Unlike Emily, Georges, another only child, has not rejected his mother's desire for him to achieve success where his engineer father, who died in debt when Georges was ten, had failed (67). So when they return to Paris he is soon immersed in his designs for the proposed new Sydney Harbour Bridge. The neglected Emily finds Georges's Tunisian friend, the homosexual Antoine Carpeaux, a more engaging intellectual companion, someone with whom she can discuss her fears and hopes for the future. Antoine's comment that "'Our passions always require from us a betrayal of our former state'"(55) is proved only too true after Emily makes passionate love with Bertrand, a young priest she meets in the crypt underneath Chartres cathedral while Georges and his mother are at Mass. As well as being a betrayal of Georges, this results in a betrayal of Emily's former state as free woman when she discovers she is pregnant.

Far from being thrilled by this news, and suffering from anaemia, Emily is sent to Tunisia with Antoine to recuperate at his family home. There she discovers the story behind Perpetua's medallion, 'a fragment of an early Christian pyxus' (54) found many years ago, made into a brooch by Antoine's father, and given by him to Emily at their first meeting. She becomes captivated by the story of Perpetua, hailed as an early Christian martyr, but claimed by the radical Arab archaeologist Hakim el-Ouedi to be 'a misunderstood Berber woman [whose] life was a mystery' (164). She also meets the American scholar Olive Kallen who encourages her in her plan to reinterpret Perpetua's story from a secular and female point of view. Returning to Paris, she rejects Georges's gift of a sewing table in favour of library research, determined 'to make Perpetua's voice audible to us at last above the din of Tertullian's bleak and heartless rhetoric' (259). Emily also decides that she must go to Chartres to confront Bertrand before the baby is born, but when she gets to the cathedral her waters break and she falls and hits her head. Bertrand manages to get her to the Elder household, where Georges's mother delivers a baby girl. Miller's account of the birth is one of the most compelling I have read, sparing none of the messy bodily details but graphically conveying the elemental quality of an event that is always both universal and unique: 'The two women were like wrestlers, or lovers, their sweating limbs glistening in the yellow lamplight, knotted to each other by their struggle, unyielding and locked until the tiny shoulders followed the head and the child slithered from Emily's body with a sudden rush into Madame Elder's hands' (289).

The death of Madame Elder shortly afterwards, together with the news that Georges's bridge design has been disqualified, frees him from his own version of 'the ancestor game'. As he tells Emily: '"Now that Mother's gone I don't have to dream of being my father any more"' (367). His Aunt Juliette, Madame Elder's older sister who has looked after her for many years, shares in this newfound feeling of freedom from the past: '"I've done my duty by Heloise as our father would have wished. She was always his favourite. Now I'm due for a rest"' (365). It is in this context that Emily rejects her own family obligations, deciding not to accompany Georges, her daughter Marie and their maid Sophie to Sydney, where he has been invited to supervise the building of the northern approaches to the Harbour Bridge, but instead to return to Tunisia to work with Olive Kallen. As they pack his father's books, Georges reads from the concluding section of Walter Pater's *The Renaissance: Studies in Art and Poetry* (1873): '*each mind keeping as a solitary prisoner its own dream of a world*' (370). Emily has a vision of the future, of Georges 'liberated from his past and from the onerous delusions of youth and ambition' (369). This is a future, with its echoes of her own father's and mother's lives, where she would be a prisoner dreaming of another world, and it is one she does not wish to share. Her experience of motherhood, she believes, has given her new insights into the mystery of Perpetua. As she writes to Olive Kallen, 'To understand why she sacrificed her motherhood—a far more elusive enterprise—will be to hear her story at last, as she surely hoped we would hear it when, condemned to the beasts, she wrote her desperate journal in that cell beneath the arena. Who did she write it for except for us?' (379).

As in *The Ancestor Game*, then, it is through the writing of the story of the other—in *Conditions of Faith*, an other of the same gender but from another time and race—that Emily makes herself at home. As well as writing Perpetua's story, Emily embarks on a journal of her own, addressed to her daughter. Believing Perpetua has been silenced by male authorities like Tertullian because 'she broke the chain by which mothers are compelled', Emily looks forward to a future in which 'there will be another way to be a mother, another way to be a daughter', one in which 'we shall be friends' (402).

Relationships between husband and wife, parents and children, are also central to *Lovesong*, which has other echoes of *Conditions of Faith* in its Paris and Tunisian settings, and its focus on a woman's attitude to motherhood. Like *The Ancestor Game*, however, it has a novelist as narrator, and much of the woman's story comes to us at two removes rather than more directly as with Emily's. Over a series of meetings with the unnamed novelist in a Melbourne café, John Patterner, an Australian, tells him about Sabiha, the Tunisian woman he met and fell in love with in Paris many years earlier, and 'the beautiful and terrible story of their little daughter Houria' (11). As in *Conditions of Faith*, the driving force of the narrative is something no man could have direct experience of: the desperate desire of a woman for a child, specifically a daughter. Sabiha has been very close to her own father, who, recognising her special qualities, sends her to Paris to help her recently widowed aunt run a little café. When she falls in love with John, Sabiha is convinced she will soon have a daughter to take back to El Djem and place in her father's arms. But the years pass without any child and when Sabiha's father falls seriously ill she becomes desperate. Inspired by some of the old songs of her grandmother, she takes the radical, though it is suggested also traditional, action of trying to get pregnant by another man. Like Emily's with Father Bertrand in the Chartres cathedral crypt, Sabiha's encounters with Bruno Fiorentino, in the much more prosaic setting of his market van, are marked by an elemental passion that results in a betrayal of their former state. In this case, however, it is the man rather than the woman whose world is turned most upside down, eventually resulting in his death.

A structurally simple story, though one involving complex emotions, *Lovesong* again demonstrates Miller's skills in portraying the other, especially the thoughts and desires of the passionate and resolute Sabiha. Her story is nicely set off by the humour of the framing narrative, as the novelist finds himself far from happy over his own daughter's choice of lover, and discovers that John is also planning to write a novel about his and Sabiha's lives. But he knows that John's story will inevitably be different to his; it is hard not to read the final sentence as Miller's direct address to the reader: 'Sabiha's story had come out of her and been carried to me; now, after I had lived in it jealously myself for a while, I would carry it to others, and in the end would let it go and be done with it, like all the other stories I have carried' (354).

In 1993, after the success of *The Ancestor Game*, Miller had written: 'The novel retells again and again the story of the person who is marooned on some kind of island of metaphor and who comes upon the tracks of another self... But always it is the story of the isolated self seeking to transcend its isolation by becoming the other, the other self, through the communication of the subjective reality of the self' ('Chasing', 6).

As readers, we are also seeking to transcend our isolation by entering imaginatively into the lives of others. Through the stories he has shared with us since 1988, Alex Miller has enlarged our understanding of the human condition, providing new insights into both age-old and contemporary dilemmas, as well as creating many memorable characters with whom we can emphathise.

WORKS CITED

Broinowski, Alison. *The Yellow Lady: Australian Impressions of Asia*. Melbourne: Oxford University Press, 1992.

Esau, Erika. *Images of the Pacific Rim: Australia and California, 1850–1935*. Sydney: Power Publications, 2011.

Miller, Alex. *Lovesong*. Sydney: Allen & Unwin, 2009.

——. *Conditions of Faith*. Sydney: Allen & Unwin, 2000.

——. 'Chasing My Tale'. *Kunapipi* 15.3 (1993): 1–6.

——. *The Ancestor Game*. Ringwood, Vic.: Penguin, 1992.

Pierce, Peter. 'The Solitariness of Alex Miller'. *Australian Literary Studies* 21.3 (May 2004): 299–311.

- 9 -

CONTINENTAL HEARTLANDS and ALEX MILLER'S GEOSOPHICAL IMAGINARY

ELIZABETH McMAHON

ALEX MILLER HAS COMMENTED that the world of his fiction is 'international'; it is the 'fractured modern one' (Caterson 'Playing The Ancestor Game', 10). His central characters commonly perform what Georg Luckás famously termed a 'transcendental homelessness', the desire to be at home everywhere, which ironically indicates an absence of real attachment to anywhere at all (*Theory of the Novel*, 41). These wanderers travel across the modern world, but remain locked within the boundaries of the self. This dilemma is a highly conventional feature of the modern novel. Miller's intervention into this map of the self is, however, multi-layered and deeply original. This chapter will examine how the alignment between geography and subjectivity operates in four of Miller's novels to identify his refiguration of the inherited map of modern identities.

The four novels focused on here are *The Ancestor Game* (1992), *Conditions of Faith* (2000), *Journey to the Stone Country* (2002) and *Landscape of Farewell* (2007), and are grouped together for their shared troubling of the modern quest. Specifically, this chapter argues that each of the novels deploys the conventional figure of man-as-island only to worry it out of its tired boundedness. In each novel the wanderer is only truly located when they enter into the centre of another, which is figured as being within a continental diversity. Crucial to this transformation is the leap from the abstraction of metaphor into the grounded realities of history and culture—and back again. For it is this awareness of the mutuality of imaginary and real cartographies that enables the radical refiguration of modernity's man-island in the imperatives of the 'fractured' present.

This slippage between the man-island as metaphor and as reality was determined by its original articulation. The declaration from John Donne's seventeenth meditation, that 'no man is an island', has become axiomatic of the Western subject in modernity. The aphoristic potency of the metaphor of man-as-not-island relates to its paradoxical complexity, wherein the interdiction against isolation contains the implicit admission of precisely that condition. According to Donne's axiom, we are each as irredeemably bounded as an island—as islands operate in the Western imaginary—and yet we need to reach beyond the borders of self to the continent, to culture and community, and reattach the fractured segment of self to the whole.

The year Donne published the seventeenth meditation, 1624, was the same year Britain established its first island colony in the New World on St Kitts in the Caribbean. This coincidence of poetics and politics, a complicity of figure and ground, highlights the complex interconnection between the figurative economy of the (masculine, Western) subject and the new coordinates of space and history in modernity. It enables us to read 'no man is an island' as an overdetermined and defining utterance of the European Age of Discovery and colonisation, poised between an older cosmographical understanding of harmonious correspondences between man and the world, and the new fractured global geography of the modern era. Further, we can see how this moment of transition, a statement made into, and carried by, the winds of change, creates the new space by which to circumscribe its man-islands within itself. These real and imaginary man-islands include a spectrum of circumscriptions: slavery and convict colonies, opportunistic utopias, fantasies of self-invention and containment, drives and delusions of autonomy and possession—all of which betray a desire for what Gilles Deleuze describes as the island's promise—and subsequent refusal—of a complete alignment between the imagination and geography ('Desert Islands', 10). Implicit also from the moment of its utterance, and played out as the man-island folds into the shifts and flows of this real and imaginary geography in modernity, the anthropomorphic overlay of man and island alters from a representation of the man-island as a cosmos to a single, fractured, isolated ego (Gillis, *Islands*, 26).

At our own juncture in late modernity—what island historian John Gillis has termed 'the second great era of globalisation' after the European Age of Discovery (38)—the Western subject remains constrained in this psychic cartography. Postmodern relations of self and geography map alignments and misalignments of fractured terrains, overlaid and overlapping but nonetheless separate and shut off: the movement and incarceration of refugees; the opportunistic movement of national borders; islands sinking in the rising oceans of climate change. At this juncture it is questionable whether the isolated island-ego can reattach to the main, or even whether the continental 'main' of community and shared culture remains. His undoubtedly privileged position is bounded by the fear of losing this presumed centrality. The links from island to continent are broken and the continent is itself fractured by borders of irreconcilable difference.

Jean-François Lyotard's formulation of the *differend* theorises the possibilities of relation and connection in the context of these absolute differences, in which we are closed within the boundaries of respective beliefs and disbeliefs that disregard or fail to recognise the premises, terms and languages of others. In Lyotard's terms, it is the absence of shared ground which results in an impossibility of connection or communication across the bounded, walled territories between one territory, culture or individual and another. Seeming debates between these parties may be staged as if communication is occurring but when the reality of one party cannot be articulated in the language of another, real, unassimilable difference is neutralised. Lyotard writes:

> I would like to call a *differend* the case where the plaintiff is divested of the means to argue and becomes for that reason a victim. If the addressor, the addressee, and the sense of the testimony are neutralised, everything takes place as if there were no damages. A case of differend between two parties takes place when the regulation of the conflict that opposes them is done in the idiom of one of the parties

while the wrong suffered by the other is not signified in that idiom (*The Differend*, 7).

Lyotard develops this idea to propose that notions of justice and injustice can be sustained in postmodernism despite the refutation of a single absolute authority. One of his proposed solutions is figured in terms of islands: he suggests that we need to become voyagers moving between islands, taking news of one island to another, without the assurance or fixity of a stable ground of our own (131).

Unlike Donne's era, however, we are no longer in an epoch of islands and seas but of continental power (Gillis, 124)—indeed Halford Mackinder's 1904 theory of continental heartlands re-mapped the globe in the twentieth century.[1] In Lyotard's terms, the question arises as to how we are to negotiate the undoubted legacy of island separateness in an era of continents. The question applies specifically to Australia, the sole island continent, where we overlay the desire to align ego and landscape, which characterises the island imaginary, onto the monumental scale of the continent; hence the monstrous hubris of Patrick White's Voss, who seeks an alignment of space and self over a whole continent. A similar colonialist conflation of island and continent is presented in the opening pages of Alex Miller's novel *The Ancestor Game* when the protagonist, Steven Muir, briefly returned to his English family home, reads a description of Australia by Colin MacInnes, included in the 1961 catalogue of Sidney Nolan paintings Steven had sent to his father years before: '*Australia is an Asiatic island that Europeans inhabited by accident*' (7). And yet the description continues by asserting it is a 'kingly race' of Europeans who inhabit the 'continent': the initial and forced occupation of the land is thereby diminished as an island accident, yet its secured possession of place is 'kingly' and continental.

Miller's fiction characteristically rehearses the complexities of this geosophical, geopolitical imaginary, and his novels repeatedly redraw the anthropomorphic map of self and space across global and regional interconnections to negotiate irreconcilable differences. Miller's world is the 'fractured modern one' (Caterson, 10) of late modernity and the novels explicitly perform a destabilisation of imagined centres, especially the certainties of the metropole and the modern metropolitan subject. Miller identifies Australian cities as far more decentred and pluralistic than European cities, which are organised around the spectacle of what Michel Foucault termed 'sovereign power', a centre of absolute and singular authority (Caterson, 10). Yet Miller's fiction is also structured and organised around centres, journeys to the heartland, to the interior, to the originary intensity of the core, which Steven refers to in *The Ancestor Game* as an 'internal homeland', the 'extensive and complex landscapes' deep inside the self (10). In another figuration of the centre in the same novel, Gertrude Speiss describes her sense of security in her father's love as always knowing herself 'to be at the centre of his concern' (19). The relation between these various understandings of centrality, as they are mapped across characters and continents in these four of Miller's novels, is the motivating question of this chapter.

Each 'pilgrim' in Miller is a kind of man-island. By his own account, *The Ancestor Game* 'retells again and again the story of a person who is marooned on some kind of island of metaphor and who comes upon the tracks of another self' ('Chasing', 6). Viewed in terms of the relationship between self and geography, recurrent patterns and ethical processes come to view in Miller's work that involve the pilgrim figures—the island maroons— breaking out of their insularity. However, this is not achieved according to Lyotard's model of voyagers moving between islands but by their often-reluctant foray into a continental interiority. This interior may be an internal homeland but it is always, paradoxically, located in the centre of another; a non-monological, non-homogenous centre. Gertrude's certainty that she is 'at the centre of [her father's] concern' is one such instance of Miller's new and transformative centre. Gertrude's father, a German living in China, takes the unexpected *arrivant*, his baby daughter, into his 'centre', crossing gender, culture and age in an act that recentres both parties.

This recentring process is firmly located in the psychic and spiritual lives of Miller's characters but it is also resolutely located in the historical realities of time and place, including the circumstances of the modern diaspora and the legacy of dispossession and displacement in late modernity, especially postcolonial modernity. Miller has said that he believes we can only understand and sympathise with the broader brutalities of history via the stories of individuals, and certainly his novels enable personalised access to monumental concerns (Caterson, 7). This is not to suggest, however, that his characters are somehow allegorical or representative, for part of the dilemma rehearsed in the novels is the necessity of each island maroon to be forcibly removed from the condition of metaphoricity into history and cultural otherness, a process that requires the decentring of self into the centre of another.

A concept and experience of the centre also organises Miller's novels at the level of structure and teleology and, by extension, determines the experience of the reader. In his recent essay, 'John Masefield's Attic', Miller writes, 'With a novel, as with the exploration of a maze or a labyrinth, it is not a matter of reaching a conclusion, but of finding a centre. It is the centre that satisfies us. When it is reached the novel is abandoned. It may look finished but that is artifice, craft' (263).

Here Miller distinguishes centre from conclusion and suggests a quality of depth to the centre, created in part from the act of circling around it: outward, inward and downward to the core. So, too, this core is vital and dynamic—unlike the stasis and deadness of conclusion. We may reach the centre but it is the identification of a generative engine of idea, self and text, not an endpoint. Here, too, at the level of form and process, we are presented with the centre that is inconclusive and unfinished, a fractured, modern form like the world of which Miller writes, but which moves towards a centre nonetheless.

The interaction of these various centres undergirds Miller's novels and we can often track a double movement that simultaneously disavows and claims centrality. The flow between the decentring and centring movements, and from insularity to centrality, is, I suggest, usefully understood through the trope of interchange—in its range of meanings from dialogue and transaction to replacement and substitution, and junction or crossing point. For it is in the networked resonances of the interchange that Miller locates his shifting centre. Central to this discussion is the concept of friendship, and the attendant slippages across self, other and *polis,* and between the domains of fantasy and facticity. These bonds and slippages recall both the classical scholars on friendship and Freud's formulation of the melancholic subject, who has lost a repressed version of himself only to recognise it in another.[2] In drawing the threads of these connections, I wish to suggest that Miller's fiction performs a complex operation of Lyotard's *differend*, achieved in terms of the continental interior where, above the clamour of bounded difference, one truly listens to the strange idiom of another.

In each of the four novels I focus on here, the questing protagonists are positioned at the very outset at a junction of monumental change, which also involves radical geographical dislocation. *The Ancestor Game* opens with a closure, that of family and birthplace in England, which casts Steven back to Australia. *Conditions of Faith* opens with a family framed in a painterly beach scene reminiscent of Charles Condor or Tom Roberts, which marks the beginning moment of the young heroine's departure from Australia for France. *Journey to the Stone Country* opens with the breakdown of Annabelle Beck's marriage, which leads her to leave Melbourne and return to her childhood home in North Queensland, which is described as 'another country' (9); the opening scene of *Landscape of Farewell* presents an overdetermination of departure in which we are introduced to Max Otto in the grip of grief at his wife's recent death, about to deliver the final lecture of his academic career and then carry out a planned suicide. His encounter with the Australian academic Vita McLelland results in his interconnected series of decisions: to live, to revise his work to ethical purpose, and to travel to Australia.

Each of these junctions and moments of change proves to be simultaneously meaningful and inadequate. While this first journey serves as the pivot of change, it proves to be only the first in a necessary series of displacements. Further, these displacements or progressive dislocations are revealed to be pilgrimages to alternative centres in truly foreign places, as the title of *Landscape of Farewell* makes explicit in its reference to Muhammad's pilgrimage to Mecca.[3] Further stages of journeying are necessary to break down the monad's 'island of metaphor', and the formation of interiority as insularity that binds them there. Hence in *The Ancestor Game* Steven moves from England to Australia and then via narrative to Shanghai and Hangzhou. In *Conditions of Faith*, Emily Stanton mistakenly anticipates that her move from Melbourne to Paris will be the transformative experience she desires, but it is only when she moves from Paris to Tunisia that the full weight and cost of transformation and a creative inner life is revealed to her. In *Journey to the Stone Country*, Annabelle imagines she is returning home to the Townsville of her childhood, and in a way of course she is, but once there she embarks on a second journey to the more distant past of her family and Bo Rennie's family. And in *Landscape of Farewell* it seems that Max could be no farther from his native Hamburg than when he goes to stay with Dougald Gnapun in Mount Nebo. But in this narrative, too, the consciously chosen journey, which seems to have reached its destination, is only the beginning point in the real pilgrimage into the unknown, which occurs in the terrain of the Expedition Range, Dougald's people's home place.

In all these narratives, the characters and the reader are taken to the space of beyond: beyond the pale of charted ground into the domain of territory yet to be negotiated, where terms are not fixed. That which can be imagined is, by fiat, inadequate, for it does not exceed the limits of the self. Each pilgrim needs to be taken beyond the limits of an imagined home place, beyond the capacity to recognise coordinates and terms of orientation. Each of the journeys is figured as a return to the past—variously personal, tribal and cultural—and it is always to the past of another that is also, in a complex interchange, somehow also the past of the self. The space of beyond is the space of the return where one encounters oneself and the other as both utterly foreign yet truly close.

This complex relation in these novels between self and self, and self and other, is foregrounded by the terms of the key relationships which galvanise their narratives. In each novel, the initial closure that predicates the journey, the initial moment of interchange that sets the narrative in train, is the foreclosure of familial ties: Steven and his parents in *The Ancestor Game*; Annabelle and her husband in *Journey to the Stone Country*; Max and his wife Winifred in *Landscape of Farewell*; Emily and her parents, and then her husband and child, in *Conditions of Faith*. The journey ahead of the characters very decidedly rejects family structures even though the journey is always in part a return to an overdetermined site of the past, including family. The staging of this initial rejection is necessary, I suggest, to the process of defamiliarisation, but also as a way of foregrounding the ethos of friendship in the pilgrimage, friendship founded across and against familial and cultural ties. Hence the three friends in *The Ancestor Game* are presented as various kinds of orphans, the life-changing friendships formed by Emily, first with

Antoine in Paris and then with Hakim and Olive in Tunisia, in *Conditions of Faith*, the friendship between Annabelle and Bo in *Journey to the Stone Country*, and the friendship between Max and Vita and Dougald in *Landscape of Farewell*.

In Miller's novels it is the interchange of friendship across countries that is mutually enabling for the individuals, and which proposes a model of justice within the incommensurability of globalised modernity. From Aristotle's discourses and Cicero's letters on friendship, we are presented with the conflation of the friend as other and the friend as the self. Aristotle is attributed as asking, 'What is a friend?', to which he answers: 'A single soul dwelling in two bodies.' Cicero sets up a similar claim: 'For he, indeed, who looks into the face of a friend beholds, as it were, a copy of himself.'[4] Aristotle's model highlights the uniqueness of friendship by dividing the unity of one soul into two beings, which must then be made one in their relationship. Cicero's model operates by resemblance and recognition, so that friendship is born of mutual recognition and likeness. However, as the philosophers debate, this closeness must also contain absolute distance. For a relation of pure resemblance, of interchangeability alone, cannot allow for difference or freedom. In Miller's novels we recall the complex negotiation of sameness and difference in the friendships between the two old men, Otto and Dougald, in *Landscape of Farewell*, and between Steven and Lang Tzu in *The Ancestor Game*. Early in the latter novel, Steven observes Lang in an art gallery one evening and recognises himself: 'The scene before me was familiar. It was like a memory. Looking at Lang, I could have been looking at myself. As I once had been. Ages ago. On the bank of a river somewhere, waiting to attempt a crossing' (38).

Early the next morning, as Steven leaves Lang's house, he catches his own image in a mirror and 'could not resist the impression that I was becoming the person inhabiting the landscape within his mirror' (39). The great friendship between them is related to and signified by their acts of mutual creation, their artistic productions, in a thesis that sets up a great likeness between the interchange of imaginative sympathy in friendship and in art.

This web of connections between art and friendship, resemblance and distance, the self and another, is subject to a further paradoxical inversion in

Miller's fiction. For friendship cannot be forced but it is presented as utter necessity across a range of registers and contexts. Max Otto, for instance, would have killed himself if he had not formed the friendship with Vita McLelland; Dougald Gnapun would not have been able to return to his homeland nor pass on the story of his people without Max Otto. To broaden out this view to its historical implications, Max Otto would not have been able to confront his family's complicity in the Holocaust without the friendship of Vita and Dougald. So, too, Dougald's knowledge of the past and his complex admiration for his great-grandfather, the warrior Gnapun, and the story of the massacre, would have been unrecorded and unresolved. Yet these imperatives cannot be the purpose of friendship. In her discussion of Derrida's thesis on friendship, Sandra Lynch observes, 'Certainly we cannot guarantee the durability of a friendship, but nor can friendship be coerced. It cannot have a particular purpose in the sense of being an instrument of my desire. Friends must engage purposefully but without purpose and see what happens—much like the artist does in producing a work of art' ('Aristotle and Derrida', 105). In a similar understanding, in Miller's fiction friendship and art exist side by side, and often as interconnected creativities, but neither can be forced.

It is in this home space of the friend, of otherness unforeseen, that Miller's novels locate possibility for his island maroons. But their subjectivity is imbricated in and across so many other domains of experience. Crucially, in all these texts, this friendship is indissoluble from justice. As Vita McLelland tells Max, historical reparations are mandatory, but Miller's novels set out the complex mode of their realisation on the basis of friendships formed in the present. The reparation is thereby original, and hence vital, as the individual creative relations of two people. But such a process does not deny the difference and distance between the two parties, or else the putative friendship would privilege the interests, desire and vocabulary of one party over the other—the very condition of Lyotard's *differend*. Miller's fractured postmodern and postcolonial worlds, however, adhere only in 'the recognition of a common strangeness', by friendships formed among self-proclaimed exiles. This 'common strangeness' does not flatten out difference to assert that all are equally exiled and hence equal or the same. This is the concluding wisdom of Annabelle's decision not to accompany Bo and Arner to the playground of the old people in *Journey to the Stone Country*, for despite her closeness to place and people, the differences are profound and need to be respected. Indeed, Miller has explicitly stated that reconciliation between Indigenous and non-Indigenous Australians is important but insufficient. What is required, he writes, 'is the far more difficult question of the acknowledgement of difference' ('Sweet Water', 104).

The recognition of 'common strangeness' also recognises the specifics of each difference and the limits of understanding. The 'common' quality is that none is centred but all are presumed strange. Lynch refers to Maurice Blanchot's understanding of this common difference in his formulation of friendship: 'Friendship, this relation without dependence, without episode, into which, however, the utter simplicity of life enters, implies the recognition of a common strangeness ... the movement of understanding in which, speaking to us, they reserve, even in the greatest familiarity, an infinite distance, this fundamental separation from out of which that which separates becomes relation' (quoted in 'Aristotle and Derrida', 106).

This insistence and negotiation of difference and sameness—indeed the appreciation of this complexity—is a fundamental concern for queer representation, which has urgently explored the dilemma of sameness and difference in intimate relation for those too readily deemed interchangeable. Characteristically, the focal duo play out a chiastic exchange of fates. We see this same interchange often in Miller's fiction: Max Otto writes Dougald Gnapun's story more realistically than Dougald could, and Dougald lives the death originally planned by and for Max. Emily writes Perpetua's story on behalf of her friends in Tunisia in *Conditions of Faith*. Gertrude writes her father's story in *The Ancestor Game*. In each and all of these cases, as with queer representation, the swapping of fates and the embodiments of another's story always involve slippage between object-cathexis and identification (whether *to have* or *to be* the other) and an attendant negotiation of the real and the metaphorical, of ground and figure, by which one character might take on the imaginative life of the other, or one defined as more inclined to fantasy and abstraction may be forced into the facticity of history. In these relations, and in Miller's novels too, the intimate other is presented as a form of a lost self and/or a lost love object from childhood, and we seek him or her both for themselves and to restore our lost selves, whose loss we experience as melancholy for, as Freud defines the melancholic, s/he refuses to relinquish these losses and lives with the memory of the attachment (244–8). In Miller's terms, his protagonist is often 'a person who is marooned on some kind of island of metaphor and who comes upon the tracks of another self' ('Chasing', 6).

Miller's protagonists are often portrayed as melancholics in this formal sense: Max Otto refuses to accept the loss of his wife; Annabelle Beck has lost her husband—temporarily at least—to another woman. By his own admission he is only partly gone—he may return—suspending Annabelle in a melancholic state. The opening scene of *The Ancestor Game* describes Steven Muir and his mother at his father's funeral, a primal loss felt long before the actual death and not resolved by it. And Steven's admission that Lang represents an earlier version of himself (quoted above) makes this melancholic condition explicit.

This is the interchange negotiated in the space of beyond and the time of before in Miller's fiction. It is the space where the relations between self and self, self and other—and the other's own subjectivity—can be reshaped and reimagined. Crucially, this complex psychic process is poised between the domain of our phantoms and the broader facticity of history. When one views this process in one of Miller's novels, and especially when the novels are viewed collectively, we are presented with a modern fractured world where connection and interchange are occurring in and across the continents of postmodernity. For the island maroon who is the Western subject, the final doubling concerns their exercise of choice and then relinquishment of autonomy. Like Max taking up the writing of Dougald's story in *Landscape of Farewell*, or Emily writing Perpetua's story in *Conditions of Faith*, one must accept the invitation to enter into the centrality of another, in a foreign continent, enter into the creativity of art and friendship, and be prepared to become lost there.

NOTES

1 Halford's Mackinder's 1904 address to the Royal Geographical Society, 'The Geographical Pivot of History', is accorded the status of a foundational

moment in the study of geopolitics. In it he put forward his 'heartland theory', in which he divides up the globe by continents and argues that whoever rules the heartland of the main continent (Europe and Asia) will rule the world.

2   The classical texts on friendship include Book Nine of Aristotle's *Nichomachean Ethics* and Cicero's *On Friendship*, as well as the assertions attributed to Aristotle in *Lives of Eminent Philosophers* by Diogenes Laërtius.

3   Muhammad delivered 'The Farewell Sermon' on 9 Dhu al-Hijjah, 10 AH (632) in the Uranah Valley of Mount Arafat in Mecca, seventy-two days before his death, at the end of his final pilgrimage. Details and the text of the sermon are accessible at http://www.islamicity.com/articles/Articles.asp?ref=IC0107-322.

4   The astute reader of Alex Miller, Ronald Sharp, has recognised the importance of friendship in Miller's novels. See Ronald Sharp, 'More Than Just Mates', *Australian Literary Review*, 4.6 (July 2009): 18–20.

WORKS CITED

Aristotle. *Nichomachean Ethics*, Book 9. http://nothingistic.org/library/aristotle/nicomachean/index.html#b9. Accessed 8 May 2011.

Caterson, Simon. 'Playing the Ancestor Game: Alex Miller interviewed by Simon Caterson', *Journal of Commonwealth Literature* 29.2 (1994): 5–11.

Cicero. *De Amicitia or on Friendship*. http://ancienthistory.about.com/library/bl/bl_text_cic_friendship.htm. Accessed 8 May 2011.

Deleuze, Gilles. 'Desert islands'. In *Desert Islands and Other Texts 1953–1974*. Trans. M. Taormina. Los Angeles: *Semiotext(e)*, 2004: 9–14.

Freud, Sigmund. 'Mourning and Melancholia' (1917). *Standard Edition* vol. 14. London: Hogarth Press, 1957.

Gillis, John R. *Islands of the Mind: How the Human Imagination Created the Atlantic World*. New York: Palgrave Macmillan, 2004.

Laërtius, Diogenes. *Lives of the Eminent Philosophers*, Book Five. http://ebooks.adelaide.edu.au/d/diogenes_laertius/lives_of_the_eminent_philosophers/book5.html. Accessed on 8 May 2011.

Lukács, Georg. *Theory of the Novel*. [1920]. Boston: MIT Press, 1974.

Lynch, Sandra. 'Aristotle and Derrida on Friendship'. *Contretemps* 3 (July 2002): 98–108.

Lyotard, Jean-François. *The Differend: Phrases in Dispute.* Trans. Georges Van Den Abbeele. Minneapolis: University of Minnesota Press, 2002.

Mackinder, Halford J. 'The Geographical Pivot of History'. *Geographical Journal* 23.1 (1904): 421–2.

Miller, Alex. 'John Masefield's Attic'. *Best Australian Essays.* Melbourne: Black Inc, 2010.

——. *Landscape of Farewell.* Sydney: Allen & Unwin, 2008.

——. 'Sweet Water'. *Bulletin.* 16 December 2003–13 January 2004: 100–4

——. *Journey to the Stone Country.* Sydney: Allen & Unwin, 2002.

——. *Conditions of Faith.* Sydney: Allen & Unwin, 2000.

——. 'Chasing My Tale.' *Kunapipi* 15.3 (1993): 1–11.

——. *The Ancestor Game.* Ringwood, Vic: Penguin, 1992.

Sharp, Ronald. 'More Than Just Mates'. *Australian Literary Review* 4.6 (July 2009): 18–20.

Alex's father, Alexander McPhee Millar, with Kathy, Alex (with his hand to his eye) and Ruth, about 1940.

Alex as farm labourer, Exmoor, about 1951.

Alex's family at the beach after Alex had left for Australia. Alexander (Alex's father), Kathy, Ruth, Ross and Winifred (Alex's mother), about 1955.

Alex in Queensland, 1953.

A portrait of Alex taken in Brisbane in 1954.

Max Blatt with Anne Miller, Araluen, New South Wales, about 1971.

Alex with Ruth Blatt at the launch of *The Tivington Nott* at the Brunswick Street Bookstore, 1988.

Alex with the poet Barrett Reid (left) and the artist Rick Amor, 1992.

Alex at the offices of the *Age*, 1993.

Alex and Stephanie Miller, Rhodes, 2005.

Alex and his children Kate and Ross, and Erin Ritchie, 2005.

Kate Miller with Col McLennan, Frank Budby and Elizabeth Hatte, Miles Franklin Literary Award, 2003.

Frank Budby, Barada Elder, Mount Britton, 2009.

Col McLennan, Jangga Elder, Neblo, 1999.

Alex with Anita Heiss, Li Yiao and Kate Miller, 2007.

Alex in his study at Castlemaine, 2011.

Elizabeth Hatte, University of Sydney 2011.

Robert Dixon and Alex Miller, University of Sydney, 2011.

- 10 -

PERSONAL PERSPECTIVES on the CENTRAL QUEENSLAND NOVELS

FRANK BUDBY, ELIZABETH HATTE and ANITA HEISS

THIS CHAPTER IS A transcript of a panel session chaired by Anita Heiss at the Sydney symposium, *The Novels of Alex Miller*, on 13–14 May 2011. The participants were Liz Hatte (Northern Archaeology Consulting), Colin McLennan (Elder, Jangga) (not present) and Frank Budby (Elder, Barada).

Dr Anita Heiss: For those of you who weren't here last night I'm Anita Heiss. My mob's Wiradjuri and I pay my respects to the Gadigal on whose land we are today. My job is to introduce our special guests but I want to preface that by saying I think there's some confusion about whether or not I'm Vita. [Laughter] I just want to say for those of you who like Vita, I'm Vita. If you don't like Vita, I'm not Vita! [Laughter]

I was first introduced to *Journey to the Stone Country* by the late Andrea Stretton in 2004 when she asked me if I would speak with her about the novel to the New South Wales Jewish Women's Society here in Sydney. I made a point of not researching any reviews or reading the readers' notes on the publisher's website before I read it because I didn't want my reading of the novel to be influenced by other people's opinions. I wanted to have my own personal, and indeed critical, response to the novel.

I am an urban-based Koori woman, daughter of an Aboriginal mother and an Austrian father, and someone who is also a hopeless romantic. When

I read the novel, most of the story of Bo and Annabelle was plausible to me as I believe and have witnessed that love knows no boundaries, that real love is stronger than racial difference, even though personal histories and upbringings can influence the way we meet, the way we communicate and the way we function with others on a day-to-day basis. So apart from the story of the land I found much familiarity and appreciation in the story of the interracial relationships between Aboriginal and non-Aboriginal people. And that was a main focus for my reading of the work.

First and foremost I read *Stone Country* as a book by a whitefella writing about what is equally an Indigenous story as a non-Indigenous story. The first thing I did before reading the novel was seek out an acknowledgements page. How did this Miller bloke I hadn't met know so much? I didn't find an acknowledgements page and about eighty pages in I was thinking I've got to find out how he knows so much and then of course I found a dedication to 'the real Annabelle and Bo, whose story this is'. Since then I've spent a bit of time with the real-life characters who drive the story and they are Liz Hatte, who is here, Col McLennan, who unfortunately can't be here, and Frank, Uncle Frank Budby, who was the model for Dougald in the book. We have our apologies for Col, but I'm thrilled to introduce Liz and Frank who will share how life has changed in their Queensland since the release of the novel.

First I'll introduce the lovely Liz Hatte, who is a graduate in classics from Queensland University. She taught for some years overseas before returning to Australia and taking up a teaching position in Melbourne. In 1987 she returned to North Queensland to start up the first archaeological survey company in Townsville. Since then her company has completed hundreds of cultural surveys on behalf of Indigenous groups from the Cape to the hinterland of the Central Highlands. Liz was born and raised on a cattle station on the Suttor River, in traditional Jangga country. Liz will have a yarn about her response to the novel and the response of the local people as well.

[Applause]

Liz Hatte: I'm delighted to be here today and to be able to share in this wonderful celebration of Alex's works. Just in the next few minutes I want to present to you what are my personal reactions to Alex's novels, from my perspective and also, I include in that, from Col's, because he's asked me to say a few things and he has supported what I said I would like to say.

I feel like I'm in a very peculiar position because I was there for all of Alex's novels. I was present as a friend but I was particularly there as a model for one of his novels. During this talk I think it will become obvious that some of my reactions stem from the shock of seeing what are incredibly familiar landscapes and familiar people become part of Alex's wonderful writings. Just as importantly, for the first time, I believe the people in Central Queensland also have seen themselves reflected back in works of major literature

So, having said that, I, like the characters in the novel, especially in *Journey to the Stone Country*, did do the things that Alex talks about. We did drive at strange hours of the day and the night in four-wheel drives up and down the highway between Moranbah and Townsville, and we still do. I was present at that comic and embarrassing interchange with the mine engineer, Andrew, that is represented in *Journey to the Stone Country*. We did stay at that mining camp that looked like a concentration camp (it still does) and similar camps have since proliferated throughout the Central Highlands. I did camp in the beautiful Ranna Valley and it was like paradise. I did move to Townsville from Melbourne and I do have a bust of Dante on my mantelpiece. [Laughter] The comparisons go on.

But, I do realise also that I am not Annabelle. It's a very, very strange thing. But I feel as if Annabelle is like a twin sister and a very, very good and totally sympathetic friend. And one of the strange things, especially about *Journey to the Stone Country*, and one of the huge satisfactions, is that familiar and intimate things are reflected back through Alex's clarity of vision, language and his wisdom.

So, at times in the novel it's very strange to see that issues that confronted Annabelle are actually answers to problems that I haven't solved myself. Alex suggested answers to issues that I hadn't really resolved. I actually found them in the novels. [Laughter] If I sound confused it's because it is a bit confusing. It's a very strange position to be in. And a wonderful one. I'll tell you about two examples.

One is the transformation of Annabelle from that scientist who went up there from Melbourne and fairly cockily assumed that she could take things and that she could present things to Dougald and that he would respond and that she needed to know everything. It gradually becomes evident, particularly at the end after the meeting with Panya, that Annabelle realises she doesn't have the right to investigate everything, some things are better left unsaid, and some things are better left hidden, and so she decides not to go to the playgrounds of the Old People. Through working with Frank and Col at the same time I think I was undergoing that sort of transformation and that's continued until now. I'm probably not as much a scientific ideologue as a person who does cultural heritage, definitely not a scientific one anymore. Hopefully I'm far more sensitive to Aboriginal people's sensitivities. That's one answer that was provided for me by Alex in your novel, before I even realised it.

The second one is that wonderful episode between Bo and the mine engineer, Andrew. I'd just like to read you a few little sections of that. Several things struck me most strongly in reading this interchange. There is more than one way to express ownership or the owning of the land. Bo (and Alex) both accomplish it in wonderfully understated ways. The mine engineer, through the mine, has the title to the land but he knows nothing about it except where the coal might be. Then, in just a few simple sentences, without appearing to say much at all, Bo expresses an intimate knowledge of both the country and what is likely to be there, and the mine man has nothing left to do but go away embarrassed and very chastened.

There are two short extracts here that I'll read.

> He turned back to Bo. 'What do you think you'll find here Bo?' He looked at Annabelle. 'I know you people have your methods.'
>
> Bo toed the dust with his boot and plucked a strand of loose tobacco from his tongue. He looked up, narrowing his eyes as if he searched for a presence more elusive than the British breeds he'd hunted once. 'Well, you never know what you will find out here once you start looking, Andrew.' He waved his hand—that encompassing gesture, taking in the whole of heaven and hell and the world of men and of cattle; and of other things that would not be spoken of today, and perhaps would never be spoken of again but would become, after he was gone, the sediment of lost histories.

> The mine man said uncertainly, 'Our people have been over every inch of this country. We didn't find anything.' (37–8)

[Laughter]

Liz Hatte: We had that said to us on many occasions when we're doing cultural surveys. You know, 'We couldn't find anything, there's nothing here.'

Frank Budby: Thousands of artifacts later . . .

Liz Hatte: Yes. Thousands of artifacts, many scarred trees, lots and lots of things later we come back and say this is what we found.

> 'You fellers don't see it. Because you're not looking for it.' Bo spoke gently to the mine man, his smile easing the blunt passage of his words. 'But there's stuff here all right. And we shall find it.'
>
> 'Well good luck,' the mine man said. He looked into Bo's eyes as if he desired between them a strong meeting of men; a meeting he could reflect upon after he had left them and from which he might draw a reassurance of the substance of this encounter. 'I'm sure you will.' (38)

A little later.

> Annabelle reached in to the back seat of the Pajero and fetched out the map she had been studying earlier. She spread it on the bonnet. The mine man leaned and placed his finger confidently on the word TANK. 'We're here.' He looked up and pointed. 'The mine's through there.' He looked down at the map again. 'And that's the Isaac.'
>
> 'Through there,' Bo corrected him, gesturing as if he advised a driver to adjust his steering lock a degree or two. 'The mine's through there, Andrew.'
>
> The mine man laughed and looked at Annabelle. 'Well roughly,' he said. 'It's roughly through there.' It seemed he did not take kindly to being corrected by a mere degree or two.
>
> 'Not roughly. Roughly's no good to you out here. You'll get yourself lost in these scrubs following roughly. The mine's through there!'

Bo said firmly, squinting along his adjusting fingers, his hand steady, advising precision. 'She's right there.'

Annabelle rolled the map and put it on the back seat and she closed the door of the Pajero.

There was a silence. (39)

That is actually, almost word for word, how it happened. At the time it was an amusing scene but in retrospect I realise the significance of it and, by association, begin to grasp a little of the significance of European ownership of something they don't understand at all versus Aboriginal dispossession of a place they know absolutely intimately. I think one of the terrible results of this ownership of something you don't understand, and I'm speaking purely from a Central Queensland, Central Highlands perspective, is reflected in the landscape. The vast forests that once covered the whole of the Central Queensland highlands have mostly disappeared. They've been cleared in their broad-scale clearing for cattle processing and replanted with buffel grass. The beautiful landscape has been pockmarked with open-cut mines. The major rivers have been diverted, the arteries have been cut off from the land and basically the land is dying. They just don't get it. I won't say any more about that but it's one of the things that I've taken out of that little section. I had no idea of its significance at the time. So thank you, Alex.

One of the other things that has happened in Central Queensland and that I touched on before is that Alex's depictions of the landscape and the people have provided a validation for many ordinary readers who have read Alex's novels in Central and Northern Queensland. Just as one example: the year before last Alex was chosen as Townsville's writer and *Journey to the Stone Country* as Townsville's book. It was inspired by the Townsville librarians who purchased many copies, put them in their libraries and encouraged people to read them. Alex came up and gave several talks to the local people. They were really crowded events and they were attended by many of the people who came from the landscape that Alex talks about and that he describes. Many people had actually followed the trips made by Annabelle and Bo with the aid of a map and some of the people were from Mount Coolon, originally from around Mount Coolon. The delight and ecstasy on those people's faces as they talked about their country and about the properties they came from was something wonderful to behold.

And there is a large readership among the people who work in the mines, also the pastoralists, the descendants of the pastoralists and the people who came from that landscape. So I thought I'd share that with you.

I'd like to talk about my personal relationship and interaction with places and events in Alex's Central Queensland novels. One was fairly close to the setting for *Watching the Climbers on the Mountain* and also *Landscape of Farewell*. The other one is next to the property that is the setting for *Journey to the Stone Country*.

Our childhood reads like a lot of pastoral childhoods. We were voracious readers. We read anything and everything, so our reading was a total mishmash. Like the white-anted library on Ranna Station in *Journey to the Stone Country*, it was amazing that you could find around a property and, almost without exception, it had a European focus. There was a combination of the great novels, plays and poetry in the European tradition: volumes of Shakespeare, Dickens, the Russian writers, the Romantic poets. I found a copy of *Madame Bovary* when I was eight and I read that but I didn't understand it. [Laughter] I found it on the property next to the setting for Verbena in *Journey to the Stone Country*. We read history, stories of the great archaeological discoveries in Europe, Egypt and the Middle East (but nothing about Australia. Australian archaeology didn't exist at that stage because there was a belief that Aboriginal people hadn't lived here that long, another form of dispossession). There were scientific journals, there were steamy westerns, like Zane Grey, and romances by people like Carter Brown. And lastly there were trashy magazines like *Pix* and *People*. Apart from a reference in one of these magazines there was not a trace of Australian reference. This exception was a double-page special coverage of the Cullin-la-Ringo massacre. Reading it was a bit of a shock. It was a heavily biased story. We know the story; it has been spoken of by several speakers this morning, of the massacre of nineteen Europeans from Victoria near Springsure in 1861. It's the only reference to Aboriginal history that I ever found when I was growing up. Obviously it had significant reverberations as, at the time, my family owned a part of the original Cullin-la-Ringo station and we could see in the distance a place called

Murdering Gap through which the Aboriginal raiding party was said to have passed when they were on their way to kill the Europeans in an extremely well-orchestrated attack during the day as the Europeans went about their work. It was very close to us.

In Alex's wonderful fictional account, in *Landscape of Farewell*, the massacre is described as a righteous punishment for the settlers' dreadful and treacherous transgressions of sacred Aboriginal law in disturbing the 'playgrounds' of the old people. The version presented in the trash magazine was racist, it was sentimental, it was doctored, it was censored and it troubled me for many years because that was the only version that said the Aboriginal people didn't just give up their country and willingly go on to reserves and be our slaves, which is what we were led to believe in the school history books at that time. There are vast contradictions between these two versions of the so-called 'contact period' as the European frontier expanded across Queensland.

Henry Reynolds', I think, was the first account from the other side of the frontier that Robert [Dixon] mentioned this morning that presented the shock of the other side of history and the horrors of the European invasion that were visited on Aboriginal people. The only other explanation I think I've read of Cullin-la-Ringo was by the historian Raymond Evans,[1] who put it into the context of a payback for a massacre of people who were at a spring festival near Springsure and who were massacred by the owner of the neighbouring property. There was also the fairly widespread kidnapping of children that occurred in the years before the Cullin-la-Ringo massacre in that area. That account was satisfactory from a purely historical perspective but Alex's fictional account is the only really satisfying explanation, in human terms, that I've ever come across for the Cullin-la-Ringo massacre. It is one that places the event within the intensely personal realm, that presents us with a possible scenario that made this act inevitable and that lays a human face over the bones of history. And for me it has finally laid it to rest. As Alex said, the complex organisation that was required to accomplish such a deed should have been celebrated as the achievement of a great general. Instead it was pictured as a traitorous savage act.

I want to move on with a few comments about the same topic, the dreadful contact history in Central Queensland. In *Landscape of Farewell* Alex has put it into the European context of history, within the tradition of what we, as Europeans, know about what happened in this period. In *Journey to the Stone Country* he asks far more personal questions which I found extremely confronting.

Annabelle discovers in the confronting scene at Panya's house towards the end of the novel that her grandfather and George Bigges murdered the Aboriginal owners (including Bo's ancestors) and that Annabelle's beloved home was therefore stolen. Panya relates how she and Grandma Rennie hid inside a dead bullock's carcass for several days until it was safe to come out. In this way Alex addresses the nature of the reality in northern Australia where the European invasion was more recent. It's a fairly confronting thing. For those people who have lived in pastoral Queensland, especially in North Queensland, for several generations, we have to really ask ourselves what did our grandfathers and our great-grandfathers do? The memories and places of massacres are very much alive in the minds of many contemporary Aboriginal people. Just as painful must be the fact that descendants of both the perpetrators and the victims still live in the same vicinity. I know my ancestors arrived in Queensland in the 1880s. I remember stories as a child told by my father about massacres. That's all I remember, that he talked about massacres and he talked about particular places in western Queensland but nothing else. There's no personal record of any involvement in any deeds like this but they were there at the same time as the massacres and that is a very, very unsettling thing. Alex has really forced me to face that. I really can't say any more than that, except that the confronting is continuing.

The history of contact is almost within living memory in North Queensland and this situation is something that we really need to face. It is very close, much closer than it is in the south, as people who have lived in North Queensland know. There are a few examples I want to finish off with. A few years ago I was reading with several colleagues, one of whom told me a story about a man who died only a few years ago in northern Townsville. He didn't know how old he was, but possibly around about eighty when he died. When he was a little boy, he saw the native troopers come and they murdered his camp, murdered his family and he remembers seeing his grandmother tossed on the fire and burned. We estimated that it must have happened in the 1920s. It's absolutely, totally shocking. He's almost certainly not the last person to have a memory of contact like that.

On another occasion we were doing a survey when one of the owners came to meet us. One of the elders took incredible exception because she knew that her family had been massacred by his ancestors in the not-too-distant past, probably at the end of last century. Frank and I can both tell you that on many occasions when we go to properties to do cultural heritage surveys people say, 'Oh no, there were never any Aborigines here. They were on the next property but they were not here.' [Laughter] It happened to us last year.

So we go out to do the survey, as we said before, we find stuff everywhere. We find campsites several kilometres long, we find wonderful scarred trees that were canoes, we find permanent water full of fish and full of food and the people have said, 'No it would have been too hard for them to live here, they wouldn't have been able to make a living.' It's astonishing. Absolutely astonishing. Col really wanted me to emphasise this point. I think 'reconciliation' will never really happen until we have acknowledged this fact, unless we have confronted it, unless we face the guilt and allow people to tell their stories, for themselves. Because they still have yet to come out. I think most people would agree that a lot of Central Queensland contact history is still in the diaries and a lot of those diaries are still on the station properties. They have not yet been published.

Thank you very much.

[Applause]

Anita Heiss: That's great. Thanks for that, Liz, that challenge.

Now it's my great privilege to introduce Uncle Frank Budby, an elder of the Barada people. The traditional country of the Barada is situated between Moranbah and Nebo on the Central Highlands of Queensland. Frank lives on his property outside Nebo where he is the principal of his extensive consultancy business, Woora. In addition to his Nebo base Frank has a home near Mackay on the coast. A stockman in his youth, Frank has spent the past twenty years building up a major consultancy business which employs great numbers of his people, our people. Frank is also deeply involved in the repurchasing of traditional country and the managing of land claims on behalf of his people under the Native Title Act. Alex's novel, *Landscape of Farewell*, is dedicated to Frank, so please make Frank welcome.

[Applause]

Frank Budby: Good morning, everyone. First off I'd like to acknowledge the Gadigal people of this land and I hope they don't mind me coming onto their country.

Now, I'm just gonna talk off the top of my head. They wanted me to write something but I just couldn't get me head goin' but I'll talk about my upbringing for a start. My mother was born on a—we're not sure where she was born, but she was sent from a station called Tinnenburra down on the Queensland–New South Wales border. She was sent as a young child to Taroo mission. They lived there for a couple of years and then Taroo closed down so they built Woorabinda and her mother went to Woorabinda and so she and her brothers went up there.

She lived there until such time as she was old enough to work, probably twelve or thirteen year old they used to send them out. In them days they were under the Aboriginals Protection and the Prohibition of the Sale of Opium Act. I don't know what opium's got to do with it. [Laughter] But that's what the act was so if some station owner wanted to employ someone they had to go to the Protector of Aboriginals who was either the local policeman or someone in charge like that. They'd have to sign a memorandum of employment and they were allowed to go out onto that property then. They weren't allowed to leave the property while they were working there. My dad, he was born up at Nebo in the heart of our country, which is in the Central Highlands in the hinterland behind Mackay. He was a drover and had his own droving plant. He was highly renowned in the district for his abilities as a horseman and cattleman and buckjump rider and all those sort of things. He was, we have records of him being out working on the station when he was nine year old, mustering and that sort of thing. He told me they didn't give him a saddle. The boys just had to ride bareback to go out mustering.

That's a bit of my background. I grew up in Mackay. Our mother always said, 'You've gotta get an education,' so she made sure we were sent to school but all I wanted to do was get out in the bush with the drovers. That's what I did. But to cut a long story short Mum and Dad got married, the movement of people was starting to become more liberal. You didn't have to get a, well, I think you still had to get permission from the Chief Protector of Aboriginals to go somewhere. If you wanted to go from Mackay to Rocky, you had to have that permit. If they caught you without that it was straight back to the mission. Anyway, we won't dwell on all of those things. One thing though, Mother and Father, they never had any birth certificates. They were born back in 1912. There were no birth certificates given for them and it's very hard to find any records of where they were born, when they were born, but we do know from what they told us. So, there we are.

We saw a need, when the mines started up in our country in the seventies, and in those days, when we go back through the records one archaeologist used to drive around for two or three days, do enormous amounts of country and put out a report about it all saying, 'Yeah, there's plenty of artifacts here but there's no need to remove anything. There's so much here that it'll never be destroyed.' [Laughter] He was called Gallopin' Major. [Laughter] That's what we called him. Anyway we set off. My wife had passed away and I was at loose ends on what to do. This was at the start of the nineties wasn't it, Liz? And our first one was one of the mines was building a dam on the Isaacs River in this gorge and we knew of rock art sites there, and anyway a mate of mine who was a surveyor working up on the dam site come and saw me one day and he said, 'They're gonna build that dam up there where your rock art is.' So then I thought well I'd better do something about this. I rang nearly all over Australia before I found someone that I could listen to that would give me a contact to the right people. And that was Ian Owens and he put me on the right track. From there we spoke to the mining companies and told them we have to do this and that.

The Act back then was the Landscapes Cultural Heritage Act. It wasn't a very good Act. It didn't really acknowledge cultural heritage but now we have a new Act in Queensland that has been in for the last six years and we, well I believe, so far as Acts go, it's pretty good. It's workable for us. The major things it says is that the state doesn't own the cultural heritage, artifacts and that. Previous to that you had to send all the artifacts to the museum and they'd stick 'em in a corner somewhere.

So that's in the early nineties, when Liz started working for us. When one mining company heard about us then it just had to happen. So that was the start of that and I s'pose all of this ramble on is about how we got to meet Alex. Liz said to me, 'Our friend's comin' up here, coming up to visit. He's a writer from Melbourne.' Another one of these Mexicans comin' up. [Laughter] And a Pommie too. [Laughter] So this fella comes in and there are some people that you meet that you know you have an instant rapport with and Alex was one of those people.

The things I admire about *Stone Country* is he took one trip out on that mine stuff. I didn't go on that trip 'cause I was off doin' something else. My son was there. He was about eighteen I think. And me daughter, still a teenager, and Col and Liz. So they went out and did this job. But Alex was studying all the time and his perceptions of the people's mannerisms and his understanding of people is very uncanny because when you read *Stone Country* and you look at his description of each and every one of those. Arner, he was my son, but Alex had him down to a tee. Sittin' in that four-wheel drive, music blaring. I'm happy to say now he's finally got married. [Laughter] He's given away that music. We used to say 'What are you listening to that American rap music for?' [Laughter] My daughter was Trace. She's since grown up and she is exactly like the way Alex describes her. She runs the consultancy now and her nature and her mannerisms are down to a tee. A very determined young woman, she is. Alex had that down pat. With Col and Liz, Bo and—what was your name?

Liz Hatte: Annabelle [Laughter]

Frank Budby: Col. It's a pity that Col's not here so you could see and meet him. He is a unique sort of a character. In those days he used to smoke very heavily, which Alex had down pat. How he'd stand up there and roll them and roll it round his mouth. Alex had that. He got all this worked out and I thought that was great. There are so many things in *Stone Country*. There's the love story between Col and Annabelle, Bo and Annabelle. There's a steamy love scene on the couch or table, something about fish. [Laughter] And she's never lived that down. [Laughter]

Anita Heiss: It's all fiction, she says.

Frank Budby: It's all fiction. We were out on a mine and an environmental chap came up and he said, 'I was reading a book about you fellas.' And I said,

'No, no, that's fiction, that's not us.' [Laughter] 'But of course it's you,' he said. 'We worked it out straight away.' [Laughter]

But I think everybody in the mines up there have read it. So many people have read it, station owners, people in the mines. They picked up who it was straight away. Your fiction is not really fiction at all. [Laughter]

There's the love story and then there's Col's journey, Bo's journey from there back to the stone country. It seems like Panya was the one who drew him back to give to him her views on him having a relationship with the daughter of some of the people who had massacred their people. I saw into it that it was Arner who was probably Panya's messenger because everywhere that Col went Arner was driving for him and they finished up back at the stone country with Panya. So, I read into it that it was Arner who took Col back to the stone country to get his retribution. And that's what I saw into it, you know. Col had to know that and be told that by Panya, the things that she said to him. So that's that one and I think that's part of all this, of knowing Alex and all that. And we've been down to Melbourne and talking about Queensland or North Queensland the people up there are different. There's nothin' wrong with us, it's all these southern people. [Laughter]

For me and Col too, I s'pose, goin' from up there down to Alex's house, he invited us into his house with his lovely wife and his family, beautiful people, that was strange for us, you know. That don't happen too much up in the north. You gotta be on your guard all the time, you know. You get that way you can pick out the ones that have the racism. One time when we were younger we'd cringe away from it but now I confront it straight on, and tell 'em. They call me Cranky Franky but. [Laughter]

We have a lot of dealings with a lot of mining companies at a high level. At last count there were nearly twenty mines just in our traditional country, coal and coal seam gas, exploring and moving, drilling holes everywhere. It's a pretty controversial issue but the reason we're doing what we're doing is the cultural heritage. There is a little bit of archaeology in there. We've dated fireplaces and all those sorts of things.

My main aim is, and I'm trying to embody that into all of our people, is that we've got to make sure that our cultural heritage stays as intact as possible because that is the story of our past and the people who came before us and the things they suffered when settlement started. So we guard it jealously. We can get fairly aggressive about people who just want to ignore it. But we have a good Act now that will help us. If they do the wrong thing we can prosecute and there are very big fines. The mines have sort of, most of the big companies have thought we can't fight this, there's an Act there, we've got to do this, so they're more inclined to come to us. But we have built up a presence out there, we want to make sure that we do everything to the best of our abilities and do it right and to be honest about it and any gains that might be made we handle those funds in a very responsible manner. Like in cultural heritage at the moment we have about thirty people employed. We have teams of three or four and we have teams out there doing jobs all over these mining places.

That Alex took the time to write *Landscape* and *Journey to the Stone Country* just enforces things in my mind a bit. That we're probably doin' the right thing. Just to come down here also has broadened my horizons. I've never been to a place like this or a symposium before. I can stand up and talk in front of a crowd of people, usually our mob, wanting to fight each other. [Laughter]

Anita Heiss: Don't worry, these really want to fight each other too. You should have seen it last night. It was terrible! [Laughter]

Frank Budby: All of that has come about 'cause of Alex and the friendship that we've built up. He quite regularly comes up. When I say regularly, every couple of years he thinks, 'I'd better go see that old Budby, I s'pose.' He only comes for the billy tea that I make. [Laughter] And the barbecues. Inese and Ron [Sharp] came up there a couple a year ago. We had a barbecue cooked out on the coals. Wasn't bad, was it?

Myself, my nature is I'm good at logistics and organising things. I know everything, you know. And even if I am wrong, I don't admit it. [Laughter] Whereas Col, he's probably as good a bushman as you'll get because he'll study what's around. He'll watch the birds, he'll see these birds. We get these environmental impact studies that say this bird is extinct or in danger, Col will walk around, 'Oh yeah? There's some there.' [Laughter] He knows all the trees, all the herbs and what's for medicine, what's for food, all those things, and he is the expert on that. That's the way he does it. He's unique. It's a pity he couldn't come today to give you some enlightenment.

The other one I want to say is, Alex, were you talkin' about him givin' directions to the farmer about which way the storms go? That's true, we know which way the storms go, which ones come from where, which ones will land, 'cause you've got to know the country, where the watercourses are, the landforms, but the way Alex described Col giving directions was exactly right. He'll close his eyes and he'll ask himself which way to so and so. It's like he's on his horse, ridin', and he'll say that way and you haven't got a clue what he's talkin' about. [Laughter] So even if he doesn't know where he's going you still think he knows. [Laughter]

I've waffled on there on different things but I just wanted to give you a picture of what we do up there and the few little words I've said haven't really told the full story. I could ramble on here for ages. Anita and I could go on here for ages.

Anita Heiss: I'm not going to be the one to tell an elder to stop. I'm just wondering do we want to have some questions or would you like to have conversations over lunch? Does any one have any questions for Frank or Liz?

Elizabeth Webby: One of the things that has always intrigued me about these two novels, particularly *Journey to the Stone Country*—and I also want to thank Liz and Frank very much for coming down and sharing with us, it has been absolutely wonderful—but Frank mentioned the character of Panya and I did read it twice because I was on the Miles Franklin committee that year and every time I came to that chapter when Panya speaks it would just blow my mind.

Frank Budby: It's very confronting.

Elizabeth Webby: It's very confronting but it's also an incredible character. So is there an original for Panya? We've heard about the others.

Frank Budby: I think she's a conglomeration for want of a better word. I don't know all the fancy words like some academics. [Laughter] Yeah, a conglomeration of a lot of different people that Col has talked to Alex about around the campfire. I have an idea who it is but I can't sort of talk about it, she's passed on now.

Elizabeth Webby: I'm just being an ignorant white person who wants to get too much knowledge.

Alex Miller: Well, as one ignorant white person to another one, when

I wrote the Panya section, which took me totally by surprise, I said to Col, 'I don't know where she came from' and he said, 'The Old People gave her to you, old mate'. And I think that's as good an explanation as I'm going to get.

Anita Heiss: Can the Old People give me some characters for my books? [Laughter] We might break for lunch. First of all, thank you both for travelling so far and bringing a new dimension to the symposium. I know it's Alex Miller's thing but I think you're the star. [Laughter and applause] So, thank you.

[Applause]

NOTE

1   Evans, Raymond. *A History of Queensland*. Melbourne: Cambridge University Press, 2007.

- 11 -

The FRONTIER WARS:
History and Fiction in *Journey to the Stone Country* and *Landscape of Farewell*[1]

SHIRLEY WALKER

THERE ARE SOME STORIES that must be told lest 'none be left to think of them and shed a tear' (Miller, *Landscape*, 12). The stories Alex Miller is concerned with in *Journey to the Stone Country* (2002) and *Landscape of Farewell* (2007) are those of the Aboriginal massacres which accompanied the invasion of Australia. But he also reminds us, in *Landscape of Farewell*, of all such episodes of mass murder, including the Holocaust, but going back through history to the Trojan Wars and beyond.

The massacres on the colonial frontier have been the great secret in Australian history, the truth that dare not speak its name. What Miller's character, Professor Max Otto, says about the Holocaust in *Landscape of Farewell* could as well apply here: ' ... an evil beyond the reckoning of humanity was being done in our names and ... we were never to understand it or to recover from it. It has haunted my generation and the ghost of it will not be gone until we are gone' (227).

Few writers since Joseph Conrad have shown such a keen awareness of human complexity and historical process—what he has called the 'vast impersonal forces of culture and history'—than Alex Miller (Miller, email, 2008). He has ten novels to his credit and has won the Miles Franklin Literary Award, Australia's most prestigious literary prize, twice, as well as many other national and international awards. These include the Manning Clark House National Cultural Award in recognition of his 'outstanding contribution to Australian cultural life' and the 2008 Weishanhu Award for Best Foreign Novel in the 21st Century for *Landscape of Farewell*. Each of Miller's two great historical novels—*Journey to the Stone Country* and *Landscape of Farewell*—is concerned, in different ways, with massacres: both of Aborigines by Europeans and of Europeans by Aborigines.

The historical record of massacre has been fiercely contested. Professor Henry Reynolds, late of James Cook University, in his book *The Other Side of the Frontier: Aboriginal Resistance to the European Invasion of Australia* (1981), claims that twenty thousand Aborigines were killed in frontier violence. Keith Windschuttle, in *The Fabrication of Aboriginal History* (2002), labelled this as 'black armband' history, and has attempted to discount almost every massacre. The stand-off among historians has diverted attention from the real concern, which should be apology, reconciliation and reparation. At least some of these concerns were addressed by the former Prime Minister, Kevin Rudd, in his Apology to the Stolen Generations, delivered in the Federal Parliament, Canberra, on 13 February 2008.

Meanwhile two recent historical texts—Jonathan Richards' *The Secret War: A True History of Queensland's Native Police* (2008) and *Frontier Justice: A History of the Gulf Country to 1900* (2005) by Tony Roberts—are based on contemporary documents. These make it quite clear that mass murder of Aborigines accompanied the expanding frontier in Queensland and that the authorities turned a blind eye wherever possible. The native police, commanded as a rule by ex-army officers, were used, in the language of the frontier, to 'exterminate the blacks', and all sorts of euphemisms were used to disguise their activities. 'Dispersed', for instance, was a euphemism for mass murder, and 'the patrol was sent on ahead', in the officers' reports, meant that the patrol had been turned loose on a group of Aborigines or an Aboriginal camp (Richards, 76–81). In many cases the bodies were heaped up and burned to destroy the evidence. The relatively few killings of European settlers by Aborigines were followed by waves of panic, racism and quite disproportionate vengeance.

The 1857 Hornet Bank massacre of eight members of the Fraser family and three others is a prime example. So many Aborigines were killed in reprisal, according to some writers, that at least one tribe from the Upper Dawson became extinct (Richards, 23). And yet, it seems, the precipitant for the massacre was the rape of young Aboriginal girls by two sons of the Fraser family. Mrs Fraser, it is said, had repeatedly asked a member of the police to 'reprove her sons for forcibly taking the young maidens ... they [the sons] were in the habit of doing so, she said, notwithstanding her entreaties to the contrary' (in Richards, 23).

Given the conflicting historical accounts, it perhaps remains to the fiction writer to unblock the past, to stir our compassion so that we can move forward. Yet, as Inga Clendinnen's 2006 essay, *The History Question*, suggests, any writer of historical fiction in Australia can now expect conflict with the historians who, despite the fact that they cannot agree, consider themselves to be the sole guardians of the 'truth'. Kate Grenville is a well-known casualty, not only for her award-winning novel *The Secret River* (2005), which won the Commonwealth Writers' Prize, but also her more recent *The Lieutenant* (2008). One of the main problems is that Aboriginal history, which is almost invariably oral history, has been consistently dismissed as evidence by our historians and lawmakers.

What can the novelist do that the historian can't? Alex Miller, in a recent exchange of emails, gave this opinion of the relationship between history and its fictional representation: 'I don't claim ... that fiction gets *closer* to the truth than history, and I would never claim this. But I do claim that fiction has its own peculiar kind of truth. There is, in my opinion, no one dominant truth but many, just as if you apply light to a prism the seeming singleness of its colour breaks up into a spectrum of colours, but each related in some intimate way to the other.' He goes on to make a fundamental distinction: 'The truth of fiction, it seems to me, lies in the moral and emotional confusions of the interior lives of "us", whereas the truths of history lie in the cultural and social issues and conditions in which people of any given age live (Miller, email, 2008).

The fiction writer is obviously able to individualise history, to enter the minds of all participants, to experience the motivations of the killers as well as the suffering of the victims. Fiction also allows the reader to experience violence and bloodshed as if present. This is a long way from the analytic prose of the historian.

The two novels I'm about to discuss—*Journey to the Stone Country* and *Landscape of Farewell*—are closely concerned with the 'moral and emotional confusions of the interior lives of "us"', which Miller writes about. Each has as its central concern a hidden or half-forgotten Aboriginal massacre. In the first, the victims of massacre are Aborigines; in the latter a large group of settlers is murdered by Aborigines. Both novels are set in Central Queensland, in country that was settled—even the word 'settled' is ambiguous here—by pastoralists in the middle of the nineteenth century. As the many accounts cited by Richards and Roberts confirm, this 'settling' was brutal, accompanied by random acts of violence as well as, in some cases, wholesale slaughter.

Miller is nothing if not even-handed. The psychology of massacre, whether carried out by one side or another in the frontier wars, is obviously his prime concern. Moreover, each novel has the same overarching pattern: the journey to the heart of darkness, the contemplation of mass slaughter in all its bloodthirsty horror, and its psychological as well as practical consequences. As well, Miller questions the recurrence of massacre in human history and what it tells us about human nature. It is no accident that the central motif in *Landscape of Farewell* is the stirring quotation from Homer in which Agamemnon urges his brother Menelaus to destroy the Trojans: 'We are not going to leave a single one of them alive . . . down to the babies in their mothers' wombs—not even they must live. The whole people must be wiped out of existence, and none be left to think of them and shed a tear . . .' (12).

In the first novel I'm discussing, *Journey to the Stone Country*, Aunt Panya, an old Aboriginal woman, is the sole survivor of an Aboriginal massacre which has been covered up while the pastoralists have grown rich on the land of her people, the Jangga. Panya tells her story in a burst of passion and Miller places it, for maximum effect, at the end of the novel, when we have become accustomed to polite discourse between the two races.

Up to this point, the novel has presented a wide panorama of Aboriginal/white relationships in Central Queensland, compounded by the activities of multinational companies eager to exploit the coal in the Bowen Basin. A dam is to be built in a river valley, land that had once belonged to the Jangga people. Some Aborigines oppose it because of the cultural significance of the land and the presence of sacred sites; some approve because of the jobs the project will provide. Others, more bitter, approve the dam because it will wipe out and submerge all traces of the pastoralists: 'To obliterate memory of them and sink their pitiful remains beneath the waters of Ranna Creek, risen upon them so unimaginably in these new days!' (210).

Annabelle Beck, a disaffected academic from Melbourne, on the run from a failed marriage, returns to this country where her grandfather had established his station. Her deep emotional commitment to her childhood country is matched by her complete lack of understanding about how it was acquired. There she meets Bo Rennie, grandson of a beautiful Aboriginal girl married to one of the few sexually honourable white station owners. In his will, Ian Rennie, Bo's grandfather, left Verbena Station to his Aboriginal wife, but she has been tricked out of it. Bo Rennie intends to get it back for his people. He plans to take Annabelle to the stone country, the sacred place of the Jangga people, but first he must take her to visit his Aunt Panya.

They find her in a derelict shack, slumped on a sagging sofa in a darkened room, 'the cold blue light of a teevee playing over her features' (335). The 'shit-bucket' as she calls it, is beside her. She chain-smokes and coughs her gobbets of phlegm into the bucket. The fetid air is swarming with blowflies. Bo expects a welcome but Panya is affronted that he would dare to bring Annabelle Beck into her presence.

Annabelle's grandfather and his mate had murdered her people. Panya only survived because she was hidden in the hollow carcass of a old scrubber bull: '"Me and your Grandma was all curled up inside that carcass looking out through the old bull's skullholes watching them men murderin' our people in the moonlight ... We stayed in that old bull for three days like we was goannas livin' there and then we come out and walked the scrubs all the way back to the Suttor"' (338–9).

She continues:

> 'I seen that Louis Beck ride down my little brother across that clearing and bust his skull wide open with his stirrup iron ... That grandfather

of hers hunted us through them scrubs till we had to stop and rest. Then he shot the grown people and he rode down the children and clubbed them to death with his stirrup iron . . . Every day I weep for them murdered people . . . To me it just happened yesterday'. (339–40)

The novel concludes with a number of responses to Panya's story. Annabelle and Bo will continue to be lovers but after this revelation it is impossible for her to accompany him on his journey to the stone country. Yet there are positives. Bo will get Verbena Station back. It will combine the best traditions of each race: the hospitality to all Aborigines, who will be welcome to come and camp there, to work there with the cattle, and the best practices of the white pastoralists. Miller makes it quite clear that this reconciliation of the two traditions could only have occurred after the truth had been brought out into the open and acknowledged.

I spoke earlier of Alex Miller's deep awareness of the complexities of history, what he calls, in his email to me, the 'vast impersonal forces of history and culture'. *Journey to the Stone Country* is deeply elegiac, its subtext the passing of all historical eras, including both the Aboriginal and the vast nineteenth-century pastoral appropriation of Central Queensland. Even though their passing is accompanied by violence, if not massacre, something survives: the beauty, the quietness of the Australian bush: 'a persistent virgin quality in the bush that had not yielded to their presence and would close over once again after their departure and retain no trace of them' (140).

Miller writes of the Aboriginal stockmen moving the cattle through this quiet beauty, the unspoken understanding and rapport between them, their respect for one another and for the cattle in their charge. Yet, even at the same time, a dried-up riverbed in the bush reminds him of the long and tragic processes of history, as if these processes are indeed part of nature itself. The riverbed cuts through the sunlit timber 'like an abandoned highway from some unnamed metropolis of antiquity whose population had been dispersed and murdered long ago, the scattered survivors dreaming their time would come again and the great wheel of history turn once more upon another unimaginable revolution of their fate' (46).

Two monuments to lost civilisations are opposed to one another. The first is the abandoned homestead of a once-great pastoral family on land that was acquired through the massacre described by Aunt Panya. Its library—a storehouse of European culture starting with Gibbons' *Decline and Fall of the Roman Empire*—has been eaten out by white ants: 'millions of white ants at their blind work, recycling the world and returning it to some kind of cosmic dust' (181). All that is left of European culture is a procession of empty leather spines.

The other monument is the stone ground of the Aboriginal people where the labyrinth of the generations is set out: 'lying there on the bare ground, polished by the wind and gleaming white in the moonlight like rows of skulls laid out in a secret pattern' (192). The implication is that the playground of the stone people, the Jangga, will survive; European culture will not.

Miller's more recent novel, *Landscape of Farewell,* is based on a real event in Australian history, the massacre at Cullin-la-Ringo Station. On a fine October day in 1861 every member but one of a group of settlers was set upon and killed by the Aborigines in whose country they had sought to settle. And yet they were one of the strongest and best-armed parties of white settlers ever to enter the Central Highlands of Queensland. In the settlers' view, the massacre was achieved by treachery and there were nineteen deaths in all. There were no Aboriginal casualties that day but revenge was swift. The police 'overtook a tribe of natives, shot down sixty or seventy, and ceased firing when their ammunition was expended' (Richards, 66). And of course that was not the end of it. The massacre of whites provided an excuse for continuous slaughter of Aborigines throughout the district, and far and wide beyond it for years to come (Richards, 24; Miller, *Landscape*, 277–9).

Miller first encountered the story when he was working as a stockman on a Central Highlands cattle station close to Cullin-la-Ringo. Born in London in 1936, he came to Australia at the age of sixteen and hitchhiked from Sydney to Queensland in search of the outback. He recalls the 'dramatic escarpments of the Central Queensland ranges and the fast-flowing streams and open ironbark forests . . . I fell in love with the country' and 'the impulse to write about that massacre was enormous; it remained with me and haunted me all my life'. Its appeal, he says, was that of 'a huge massacre . . . which was so bloody well organised. They obviously had somebody in charge who was an extremely gifted and persuasive leader ... It doesn't reconcile with the stuff you usually read, which describes Aborigines as a band of wild savages running around and waving their arms about' (Miller, quoted in Perkins, 'Journey').

In *Landscape of Farewell* he finally found the right characters around whom to tell the Cullin-la-Ringo story. The moral dimension of the novel is intense. It concentrates on the inner life of three characters, and three characters only, all historians of one kind or another.

The first is Max Otto, an aged and disillusioned German professor of history. He is devastated by the recent death of his wife and has suffered all his life from a sense of guilt-by-association. He has good reason to believe that his father took part in the atrocities of the Second World War, yet he cannot bear to investigate it, even though his main research interest is the historical study of massacre.

He plans one last gesture—delivering a conference paper on 'The Persistence of Massacre in Human Society' at an international conference in Hamburg—then he intends to go back to his apartment and kill himself. He knows that his paper is second-rate, patched together from a mouldering heap of old notes, but he begins with the stirring Homeric quotation on massacre concluding with, 'The whole people must be wiped out of existence, and none be left to think of them and shed a tear.'

His lecture is challenged immediately. An Aboriginal academic from the University of Sydney, Vita McClelland—she's the second historian in the novel—springs to her feet, calling Max to account before all the audience: '"How can this man presume to speak of massacre," she asks the enthralled gathering, "and not speak of my people?"'(15). Vita is passionate with pity for her own people. She is not interested in the recurring cycles of history; instead she insists on the uniqueness of Aboriginal massacre: 'For her the wheel of history ... had come to a stop at her generation's door' (15). In a calmer mood, she invites Max to a conference in Sydney, presumably to re-educate him, then on to Queensland to visit her Uncle Dougald Gnapun, an Aboriginal elder. '"The time to kill ourselves,"' she tells him, '"is after we've paid our debts, not before"' (51), and Max Otto still has a debt to history.

So he begins his journey to Mount Nebo in Central Queensland. This is also a journey towards the truth, towards moral clarity. Here he will meet Dougald, an oral historian, the guardian of an Aboriginal story of massacre. So there are, basically, only three characters, all historians. Each of the three represents a different approach to history and their differences alert us to the slippery nature of historical 'truth'.

Dougald's fibro cottage is in a desolate little mining town on the edge of nowhere. Mount Nebo is now almost deserted, the mining boom having moved on. The abandoned machinery in the paddock behind the house—three huge yellow bulldozers, overgrown with creepers, looking vaguely like rusting dinosaurs—suggests the relentless cycles of change and decay, for the European settlers as well as the Aborigines.

Dougald is desperate to tell the story of his great-grandfather, the heroic warrior Gnapun who led the Aborigines at the Cullin-la-Ringo massacre. Like Aunt Panya, he alone knows the 'truth' of a massacre, handed down orally through three generations. It must be written down before he dies. Now he will entrust this task to Max Otto, the historian of the written word. But before Max is fit to be trusted with Dougald's story, he must come to terms with his own complicity in massacre.

Max recalls an episode in Germany during the war when he is sent to stay on his uncle's farm for his own safety. One day, returning from the fields, he is accosted by a gipsy girl whose parents have just been killed—for not only the Jews were exterminated in the Holocaust. She asks for bread; he denies it. This is the image of personal complicity which he comes to see, towards the end of his life, as crucial.

He must also learn something of unintended guilt, of careless complicity. The death of a goat, perhaps a scapegoat, is a particularly brutal and significant episode in the novel. A small goat, having been rescued from its dead mother by Vita and hand-reared, is now tied up in Dougald's backyard. Because of Max's carelessness—he hasn't hammered its peg in properly—the goat wanders off, slips on a muddy bank and is hung from a tree branch high above a slimy pool. Swinging like stinking carrion in the wind, the goat is tangible proof of Max's guilt. In the middle of the night, in his night attire, the old professor crawls out along the quaking tree root to release the goat's body, intending to give it a decent burial.

This brave but precarious act of atonement must be followed by punishment. Max slips and falls with the goat into the filthy pond below, and has to be dragged from the slime by Dougald. It is only when Max has taken part in a ritual act of atonement for the death of the goat, risking his life to free its body, and ending up in the slime, that the author, and Dougald, consider him fit to write the story of the old massacre in all its ambiguity, seen by the settlers as an act of savage treachery, but by the Aborigines as a ritual cleansing of their sacred places.

Laid up with a damaged ankle from his fall, Max writes, at white heat, his version of Dougald's account of the massacre. For the first time Max is writing history with personal passion and involvement, so moved has he been by Dougald's account. He writes it as heroic epic. Gnapun will be the warrior hero his grandson wishes him to be. The Aborigines are neither savages nor victims; they are warriors defending their sacred sites. They have a just cause.

Gnapun will also have the supernatural qualities of the warrior hero. Before the battle he is subject to visionary seizures, like a shaman. He is able to identify with the opposing leader—whom he sees as his 'other', his double, his brother—and experience his very being, even his coming death. This enables Max to narrate both sides of the story.

The European leader has his own plans, not just the acquisition of the land. He envisions a harmonious multi-racial community; the passionate justice and the beauty of it. There 'the sons and daughters of our mingling shall people a new Eden'; black and white will 'live in equal fellowship and not as master and slave'. It is, he tells his son, 'God's great plan' (183).

But in their ignorance, the settlers have committed a great crime. They have collected the stones of the sacred playgrounds of the old people, the Aboriginal ancestors, and used them to build their walls. The fabric of Aboriginal spirituality has been destroyed. Now 'Time has been brought to the stones ... They have lost their position in the sacred Dreaming and their power to sustain the ... people can never be restored to them' (189–90).

The massacre is sudden, savage and complete. Each Aboriginal warrior marks his man and, at Gnapun's signal, the raucous cry of the black cockatoo, each one slaughters his opponent as Gnapun slaughters the leader whom he sees as his brother:

> Gnapun ... slips the fierce quartz blade into the cringing flesh of the leader and he bears on the shaft with all his weight and cries again with the cry of the great black bird of his spirit and the spirit of his fathers, lodging the hungry point deep in the bone of the leader's pelvis, so that the leader is flung violently to the ground ... the Book flying from his hand as he strikes the hard-packed earth ... his spectacles flying from his face and catching the morning sun in their flight ... And still Gnapun bears on the groaning shaft. Then, with an abrupt flinging action of his hands, as if he is disgusted and wishes to rid himself of something distasteful, he relinquishes the shaft and steps away from the dying man. The man, who is himself. (204)

Gnapun burns all the weapons in the settlers' camp and, most importantly, the Bible, the book which contains the great plan for the destruction of his people and their sacred places. Then he turns again to the dying leader, his brother:

> Between them there is only the bewildering mystery of their brotherhood: *Thou has driven me out this day from the face of the earth; and from thy face shall I be hid; and I shall be a fugitive and a vagabond in the earth; and it shall come to pass that everyone that findeth me shall slay me.* Gnapun caresses the leader's hand and lingers beside him. Then he lays the leader's hand on the desecrated ground of the messengers' Old People and stands ...
> ... The strangers lie where they have been felled, the men, the women and the little children. The ground is soaked with their blood and the air is filled with the hot stench of it and of their burning dwellings ... (206–7)

There are no winners here. The settlers and the strangers are all dead. The warriors will all be hunted down and ignominiously killed. Gnapun will become an outcast.

The account of the massacre having been written, there remains one more step: the journey to Dougald's ancestral country and the search for the warrior

Gnapun's final resting place. For Max Otto this is the mythic journey into the wilderness under the guidance of a wise elder, and the confrontation with the darker aspects of both self and race. The terrible climb up the escarpment in the Expedition Range almost destroys him but, having survived, Max is now free to return to Hamburg and begin his investigation of that other massacre, the Holocaust, and his father's part in it.

Another of Miller's preoccupations in *Landscape of Farewell* is the relationship between land ownership and massacre. Both novels suggest that a deep and spiritual connection with the land can exist across all racial divisions. For instance, the passion of Max's uncle for his ancestral German farmland approaches mania. It is 'an indissoluble aspect of his innermost sense of who he was, that source from whence he had his origins' (97). Likewise Dougald's attachment to *his* country is 'an ancestral knowing grappled into the roots of his being'(89). But each vision is individual; nothing is permanent. The sacred soil of Max's uncle's farm is now a suburban wasteland, block after block of post-war apartments. And so great have been the changes to Dougald's homeland in the Expedition Range that his only reliable guide to it is the 1845 *Journal* of the German explorer Ludwig Leichhardt. All visions of personal ownership, of a spiritual link with country, are delusive in a world of relentless and cyclical change. This is probably what Miller meant when he wrote that once the Sacred Places were destroyed, the Eternal was lost. All the Aboriginal people and places were now 'the victims of Time, the terrible thing that has been set free among them like a pestilence and will devour their souls' (206).

I need to return now to the notion of historical 'truth', and the contrasting claims of history and fiction. Such are Miller's storytelling skills that it is only in retrospect that we, and Max, realise the ambivalence of his account of the massacre. Can a massacre ever be justified? Can history ever be objective? Is it possible for the historian to enter into the passion of the event, as Max does, yet maintain any objectivity? After Max passes his version of the massacre over to Dougald, the doubts flood his mind:

> I was under the shower and was singing the Beatles' song, 'All You Need is Love' . . . when the obvious struck me and I fell silent. It was

> the superior voice of my knowing other self, of course, and it rang like a bell in my head: *So you have identified yourself at last with the perpetrator of a massacre*... But it had not occurred to me... Not once during those long nights struggling to bring Gnapun's story into being, those long nights of being him, the joy I had felt, the kindred intensity of my feelings, not once had I ever experienced the remotest touch of guilt-by-association with the terrible crimes of that day... By what knotted confusion of my unconscious reasoning... had I considered myself to be in the clear with Gnapun? He and I were both members of this same murdering species. It was a puzzle to me how I could have composed his story with such a sense of innocent detachment from the crimes, and yet with such an intense belief in the emotions of the motives that had brought those crimes about. Clearly the massacre of the strangers had been for me more than just the telling of a story. For once in my life I had not been constrained by the severe discipline of history, but had been at liberty to invoke the dilemmas inscribed in my own heart, inscribed there during my childhood, and which had haunted me ever since. (215–16)

There, he has said it. Any attempt to fictionalise history must, of necessity, be contaminated by the subjectivity of the writer.

Landscape of Farewell, then, has a rare level of wisdom. It has profound things to say about historical truth, colonial violence and the need for atonement. It is, in the author's words, a novel about 'such things as guilt and innocence and the unreasoning persistence of evil' (Miller, email, 2008). As well, it brings together Australia's anxiety about its Aboriginal history and the anxiety of contemporary Germans about what happened in the Second World War. The book is, in fact, the dramatisation of a fundamental question: How does the good and just person come to terms with the obscenities of history without being complicit in them? Or, to put it another way: How does the writer, of history or historical fiction, tell the uncontaminated truth?

NOTE

1 An earlier version of this chapter was delivered as the Ninth MacDermott Lecture, Centre for Australian Studies, University of Barcelona, 26 February 2009.

WORKS CITED

Clendinnen, Inga. *The History Question: Who Owns the Past? Quarterly Essay* 23. Melbourne: Schwartz Publishing, 2006.

Grenville, Kate. *The Lieutenant*. Melbourne: Text, 2008.

———. *The Secret River*. Melbourne: Text, 2005.

Miller, Alex. Email to Shirley Walker, August 2008.

———. *Landscape of Farewell*. Sydney: Allen & Unwin, 2007.

———. *Journey to the Stone Country*. Sydney: Allen & Unwin, 2002.

Perkins, Corrie. 'Journey into the Heart of a Massacre'. Interview with Alex Miller. *Australian*, 16 February 2008.

Reynolds, Henry. *The Other Side of the Frontier: Aboriginal Resistance to the European Invasion of Australia*. Sydney: UNSW Press, 1981.

Richards, Jonathan. *The Secret War: A True History of Queensland's Native Police*. St Lucia: University of Queensland Press, 2008.

Roberts, Tony. *Frontier Justice: A History of the Gulf Country to 1900*, St Lucia: University of Queensland Press, 2005.

Windschuttle, Keith. *The Fabrication of Aboriginal History*. Vol. 1. Sydney: Macleay Press, 2002.

- 12 -

OLD TESTAMENT PROPHETS, NEW TESTAMENT SAVIOURS:
Reading Retribution and Forgiveness Towards Whiteness in
Journey to the Stone Country

LILIANA ZAVAGLIA

In *Journey to the Stone Country* (2002), Alex Miller explores a national history in a regional setting, mapping a literary path towards reconciliation between black and white on what we may consider—and what he himself has described—as a place sacred to both Indigenous and European dreaming ('Sweet Water', 104). Yet *Journey to the Stone Country* is not only a literary journey. Contained within the literary of Miller's intricately drawn fictional world is the literal, the lived experiences of the characters' real-life counterparts, whose stories inform the reconciliatory movements of the novel. On the power of stories which may inform a novel, Miller has noted:

> The novel is often ... the voice of those unremarked women and men who slide into the dark and leave scarcely a trace of their passing. But we all leave some trace, no matter how slight, and it is often this trace that the novelist goes in search of. This sense in the novel ... of the private and the unofficial, the unrecorded and the silent, finding its voice is one reason we are so powerfully drawn to the genre. (*The Book Show*, 2006)

These traces—this literal of the literary, as it were—render Miller's novel a multivocal one, and my reading of it sets out to reveal the self-recuperations inherent in the redemptive longings of whiteness in the novel, while also taking into account those 'traces' of the truths—the 'unofficial' and the 'private'—of the women and men upon whose stories Miller has drawn in *Journey to the Stone Country*. This reading then, like the novel itself, is a polyphonic one, and invokes a Bakhtian vision of the novel, which is 'characterised by the multiplicity of voices present in it, none of which are subject to the authoritarian control of the writer himself' (Forgacs, 'Marxist Literary Theories', 195). This reading registers the limitations of the Christian redemptive narrative as voiced by a white discourse longing for closure, while also admitting its possibilities as experienced in the individual lives of those 'unremarked'-upon people who are the real-life counterparts of Miller's characters, and whose experiences inform his novel. Finally, into the mix of voices which authorise the narratives within the narrative, my reading attends to the self-revelatory traces of the author himself, whose interventions also interrupt the notion of a single unitary truth by his unveiling of what Elizabeth Hatte has called 'the shock of history' (Budby et al, 'Personal Perspectives', 00), that rare space of unsettlement where the past turbulently unfolds and remains transfixed in the mind of the reader, well beyond the world of the novel.

In his essay 'Sweet Water', Miller distinguishes between 'European dreaming' and 'Indigenous dreaming' as a marker of difference that complicates his understanding of what reconciliation might involve: 'it is not a question simply of reconciliation, important as that is, but is the far more difficult question of the acknowledgement of difference' (104). Miller's references in this essay to the sacred and to European dreaming refer us to familiar cultural narratives sourced in Christianity. While the moral and religious authority of Christianity has receded in the Western imaginary, the promise of redemption offered by its grand narrative of fall and salvation is still deeply attractive, a powerful physic to a settler culture weighed down by its violent history. That narrative, however, may also offer a facile exit from the burdens of the past—burdens which more appropriately require ongoing mourning, without the possibility of the closure and new beginnings that the Christian narrative mode authorises. When dealing with the literature of trauma and of a troubled colonial history, the quest for Eden reclaimed as the solution to the violent past may therefore become a problematic one. In his work on historical trauma, American historian Dominick LaCapra questions the function of the Edenic myth, locating it as the result of a foundational metaphysical absence, rather than a loss that is situated on a historical level. 'The conversion of absence into loss,' LaCapra argues, 'gives rise to both Christian and Oedipal stories... When [paradise is] understood as lost... because of some sin or fault that could be compensated for in order for redemption or salvation to occur... Paradise Lost could be regained' ('Trauma', 702). It is when such absences are conflated with the very real losses of the victims of traumatic history that the 'significance or force of particular historical losses... may be obfuscated or rashly generalised' (712). For LaCapra, these conflations forestall a necessary 'working through or acting out' for the victims of trauma. He argues that what is required in response to historical trauma is, rather, an 'empathic unsettlement' (699, 722–3) in the listener and, with it, 'a refusal to seek facile uplift, harmonisation or closure' (723).

In her own work on mourning, Gail Jones has noted that there is in Australia a 'historic refusal to mourn' ('Sorry-in-the-Sky', 160), and she refers to Jacques Derrida's notion 'that we must be revisited, as it were, by represented claims' (166) to allow the condition of being ethically haunted. One aspect of 'ethical haunting' might be the scriptural entry of the Aboriginal dead, wounded and lost into the pages and memorials of white Australian memory and history, there to be honoured and recognised along with the other (white) losses memorialised in the Australian nation. In *Telling the Truth About Aboriginal History,* Bain Attwood argues that: 'In the case of Australia... it has remembered and mourned only those who fought wars elsewhere... It has not developed ways of remembering and mourning the victims of wars here, particularly the Aboriginal people who lost the most as a result of these wars... indeed, the settler state has never acknowledged that they are worthy of recognition' (194).

In *Journey to the Stone Country,* Edenic returns and opportunities for revisitings proliferate for both Indigenous and non-Indigenous characters. The novel begins in crisis when Melbourne academic Annabelle Beck arrives home to discover that her husband has betrayed her. She retreats to her childhood country in North Queensland, which brings her once again into contact with Bo Rennie, an Aboriginal ringer and elder of his people, the Jangga:

> Annabelle recognised in him the style of man who had worked for her father... Independent, gracious and modest horsemen. Silent for the most part. Respecting the mysterious ways of the scrub cattle... Leaving you with the impression that although they were hired hands they worked for themselves, seeking some higher purpose of the brotherhood to which they belonged and acknowledging their equals only in each other. (18)

'Brotherhood', 'higher purpose' and 'mysteriousness': these words gesture to the religiosity of the outback myth of the bushman and to a particular tradition of national literature. Bo Rennie emerges as the bushman from the sacred stone country of the Jangga, with a cultural authority that calls out to whiteness from the site of blackness. He is full of knowledge, full of grace—a revelation to Annabelle—telling her that they have already met:

> 'Grandma Rennie defied your old granddad. He wouldn't have our mob on Haddon Hill, but she always told us the Suttor was our own country and she took us kids over to the swimming hole and defied him... it was before you was old enough to remember. But I remember... Grandma Rennie and your mother used to share a picnic back in them days... We tumbled naked in the water together... We met... I knew you was gonna come back one day.' (23–4)

The childlike tumble of nakedness and innocence, the foretelling of return and the black and white sharing of food in an Aboriginal idyll gestures to a mythically shared Edenic site of origin, an imagined beginning as it might have been when white and Aboriginal cultures first came into contact. However, I want to juxtapose the romance of this Edenic beginning with the historical realities of the settler-colonial project, which conducted its enterprise on the basis of land acquisition for the material gain of empire. It was done at the cost of excluding the first inhabitants from land to which they had a legitimate prior claim and it begat, to use another biblical term, the *terra nullius* myth on which the white nation was founded. The romantic idyll of Bo's remembrance is also further troubled by the necessary furtiveness in this Eden, where women eat and children play in secret, beyond the gaze of Grandfather Beck, the white patriarch whose forbidding presence necessarily menaces the portrayal of an innocently shared Edenic space.

Apology and the admission of the Aboriginal dead into the pages of white history have been difficult prospects for Australians. Though the HREOC report *Bringing Them Home: Report of the National Inquiry into the Separation of Aboriginal and Torres Strait Islander Children from their Families* was tabled in Federal Parliament on 26 May 1997, it took until 13 February 2008 for a parliamentary apology to be offered by Prime Minister Kevin Rudd to the members of the Stolen Generations. For Annabelle, who experiences these events in the turbulent years of the 1990s, confronting the horrors of the past proves almost unbearable. Her shocked response to the possibility of what her white forebears may have done accurately reflects the historical trends of recent Australian discourse on race relations and its (re)discoveries of the bloody history of the frontier. Responses to these revelations range from sorrow and horror, like Annabelle's, to the disassociation and outright disavowal that characterise historian Keith Windschuttle's polemical book, *The Fabrication of Aboriginal History* (2002). At one point, after unthinkingly removing an Aboriginal artefact from the landscape during a cultural survey, Annabelle notes the discomfort of her Aboriginal colleagues and it causes her to wonder: 'Maybe they all hate us ... Deep down. For what we've stolen from them. For what we've done to them. It was the first time she had considered such a possibility and she was a little shocked by the implications of it. To be hated, after all. It was unthinkable ... Not to be forgiven by the people one lived among' (94).

Miller is registering a moment where the Western desire for knowledge—what he describes in 'Sweet Water', following Husserl, as 'the passion to know' (103)—violates not only the Aboriginal numinous, but also rebounds upon European culture itself: 'One enormous impoverishment that European culture has suffered because of the unbridled passion to know is a loss of the idea of the sacred' (104). Annabelle's realisation also marks a moment when she is made aware of what colonisation has cost 'her kind' (211). It is the traumatic utterance of a descendant of the perpetrating culture. As Graham Huggan (drawing upon the work of Dirk Moses) observes, 'perpetrator trauma', the delayed consciousness of the crimes one's forebears have committed, "continues to haunt the perpetrator-collective until it changes sufficiently to narrate it into a new legitimating story as a constitutive part of its self-understanding... Perpetrator trauma, like other forms of trauma, blocks the past to which it seeks access in a narcissistic process driven by the inability to mourn"' ('Nazis', 9). Here is a space where Gail Jones's idea of a revisiting might apply—a space where we might consider how the primary trauma of the historical victims of colonisation has produced this possibility of hatred. Yet the narrative reaches only the impasse of a traumatic blockage and retreats from such a haunting, moving instead towards the comforts of the salvific trope. What is needed, and what is longed for by Annabelle, is an Aboriginal voice which offers not hate or retribution, but forgiveness and new beginnings, and this is what she finds in Bo Rennie.

Bo is Miller's messianic riposte in an Aboriginal world of civil rights-style activism, which insists on justice by way of treaty, material recompense and sovereignty. Bo requests no recompense beyond what he himself works for and attains. His solutions for his people differ markedly from the activism of earlier decades. On noting the similarities between Annabelle's father and his own, Bo says 'our two old fellers got along all right. Neither one of them liked to see anyone have a day off... All they ever knew was work' (43). In contrast, speaking of his friend Dougald Gnapun's children, Bo remarks, 'They've got that mission attitude. Where'd they get that from? They didn't get it from their dad. Till he got sick, Dougald only ever had two days off in his life... What's the idea of sitting in that truck all day? What's that gonna do for them?' (45).

'They've got that mission attitude': it is a line Bo repeats a number of times in the novel. It has become a familiar refrain in Aboriginal political discourse, most often heard from the Indigenous leader Noel Pearson. In 2007 in the *Griffith Review*, Pearson outlined his reasons for pursuing an individual rights platform over and above the civil rights platform of his earlier activism. In particular, he took issue with the left of Australian politics:

> The moderate left... would probably argue that neo-liberal dominance increases the number of disengaged people and the difficulties

of returning them to the working mainstream ... The problem is that it is assumed that the life chances of the disadvantaged depend on the other-regard of the successful—either a precarious dependency in the absence of state institutions, or an institutionalised dependency which my people have come to know as passive welfare. In reality, *what is needed is an increase of self-regard among the disadvantaged*, rather than strengthening their belief that the foundation for their uplift is the welfare state and the other-regard of the successful. ('White Guilt', 4–5)

Pearson and Rennie share similar views in this respect. In a discussion with some relatives regarding the flooding and building of the dam in the Ranna Valley, Bo says:

'That dam's not gonna make nobody free ... If you wanna be free you gotta get out and do something yourself ... You may as well have stayed on missions as get yourselves tied to the government and them banks ... you'll never get to be the boss of what you are doing. Not with them people. Your kids neither. That dam's not gonna be an economic base for them, it's gonna be another chain round their necks.' (331–2)

When the question of reclaiming the Verbena property arises, Bo's solution is not to go through the Land Council, but to buy Verbena back himself. Just how is later clarified by Elsie, Les Marra's sister: 'Bo don't want the Land Council getting mixed up in Verbena. He don't want that country for the Murris ... Bo wants it for his grandma and for old Iain Rennie' (326).

Bo Rennie, therefore, does not believe in the collectivist action of Aboriginal corporations in land acquisition. His answer to freedom is an individualistic one, grounded in his Edenic remembrance of his grandparents' past. It also slides seamlessly into the great Australian dream of private land ownership: the small Edens that were apportioned, in Justice Brennan's words in the *Mabo* decision, parcel by parcel, and by which Aboriginal people were disinherited of their country. Bo Rennie's Protestant work ethic coalesces with Pearson's. In his depictions of collectivism versus individualism, Miller therefore records the reality of Aboriginal politics as a site which is as riven and contested as its non-Aboriginal counterpart. Indeed, the only remarkable feature of this political divide is the way in which the dominant white culture feels the need to fetishise the divisions each time they appear publicly for consumption, a fetishisation which is absent from the novel itself.[1] The more pertinent question in *Journey to the Stone Country* is whether the rhetoric of self-advancement through hard work espoused by Bo and his family has the capacity to overcome the structural racism of white culture, as Bo appears to believe. In response to that question, the narrative—with its mix of the literal and the literary—provides only a conflicted and provisional answer. While Bo's notions are admirable (for they seek to sew up the rents of violent colonial history by locating a shared black/white dreaming on a site sacred to both), they are also problematic. Verbena is a site which has already been lost once through settlement, and then lost again, when the freehold rights which protected white people were not applied to black people, regardless of Bo's rhetoric of hard work and self-advancement. Bo explains:

> 'Grandma Rennie was a traditional Jangga woman . . . She was took over to Ranna Station on the Broken River when she was a kid and she grew up there with them white Bigges girls as one of their family. That's where my granddad, Iain Rennie, met her and they was married soon after. When he was killed off his horse, Iain left the Verbena Station to Grandma . . . That's how a Jangga woman come to have a cattle property out this way . . . she was an unusual woman. She had them store people in Mount Coolon deal with her and us kids just the same way they dealt with the other station owners and their kids . . . There was never no distinctions made while Grandma was alive.' (25)

Here, Bo characterises Grandma Rennie as unusual, so unusual that, by sheer force of her personality and presence she, along with her white husband, is able to dismantle the structural racism which inheres in white culture. Yet this is a romanticised telling by Bo, which grows only starker with the narratorial silences on the precise nature of Grandma Rennie's arrival in the Bigges household as a girl: 'She used to tell us them Rennies come over there and took her and her sister May down to the Ranna when she was eight years old. They had her helping in the laundry at first. Then when she got a bit of age on her they promoted her up to the house to take care of them three girls' (106). Bo also explains that when his grandfather, Iain Rennie (himself sixteen years her senior), asked permission for Grandma Rennie's hand in marriage at sixteen, 'Grandma's mother hadn't seen her daughter for seven or eight years' (109). The nature of Grandma Rennie's removal from her family, which makes her and her sister members of the Stolen Generations, goes unremarked in this vignette. What is emphasised by Bo here, rather, is how a member of that same Rennie family, which removes the child at the age of eight, has returned to ask for her hand in marriage at the age of sixteen.

This inexplicable elision and the foregrounding of the romance in its place become less perplexing when considered as an outworking of transgenerational victim trauma. If trauma comprises, as Anne Whitehead suggests, 'an event or experience which overwhelms ... [and] resists language or [adequate] representation' (*Trauma Fiction*, 3), then Bo's passing over of the colonial practice of Aboriginal child removal reveals the nature of such traumatic history, which is defined by repetitive amnesic turns and minimisations, until such a time as it is finally admitted into the script of public memory. This inscription finally does take place, latently arriving with Panya's revelations at the close of the novel. The narration's passing over of the powerlessness of Grandma Rennie as an Aboriginal woman in colonial society again occurs when Bo explains how her sister and nephew swindle her out of her land:

> 'When Grandma went and seen a solicitor in Mackay about it he advised her to take her share of the sale price and count herself lucky she was getting anything at all. He pointed out that according to the Protection Act she'd never been legally entitled to have her name on any title deeds to freehold country anyway, or even for that matter to have had a legal marriage to Iain Rennie, as the Act prohibited Murris from holding title to freehold property and from marrying into the white community'. (256)

The power of personality, dignity and hard work, along with the story of an individualised black and white love union as the chief means of overcoming colonial racism, is thus revealed here as a chimera, as a longing for what never was. It may be read as an attempt at wish fulfilment. In the novel, history has shown that Eden shared is a precarious prospect in the stone country. It is granted and maintained only under the auspices of benevolent whiteness.

And yet—because of those traces of the literal in the literary—this reading is also troubled, complicated by other voices. I began with the observation that the 'literal' of *Journey to the Stone Country*—the traces of lived experience contained therein—must necessarily be considered in any critical analysis of its literary discourses. The imperative to acknowledge the historical truths contained within the fictive of the novel is undertaken not only to scripturally mark the page with these oral testimonies (for that is what Miller's traces are) and not only to allow them into contention with the critical readings of the self-recuperating repairs of whiteness in the novel; it is also to acknowledge the self-revelations of the author. Of his own writing, Miller has noted: 'As a novelist, I have been not so much a liar as a re-arranger of facts ... The purely imaginary has never interested me as much as the actualities of our daily lives, and it is of these that I have written ... not autobiography in the conventional sense, it is nevertheless deeply self-revealing of its author' (Quoted in McPhee, 'Shadows that Cross Our Souls').

It becomes apparent, therefore, that while one reading of the novel locates Eden shared as wish fulfilment attempting to repair history for the benefit of whiteness, the real-life counterparts to Bo Rennie and Annabelle Beck, Col McLennan, an elder of the Jangga, and his partner, the archaeologist Elizabeth Hatte—and Alex Miller himself—have another story to tell, another position from which to speak. They emerge to challenge this unitary reading by attesting in their own voices to the lived reality of new beginnings on their sacredly shared land. These voices operate as what French critic Gerard Genette calls 'epitext', those devices and practices located in the social space outside the book, such as interviews, promotional dossiers and weblogs, that 'mediate a book to its readers, ensuring its presence in the world' (Dixon, 'Tim Winton', 246). In this respect, the epitext of *Journey to the Stone Country* authorises a literal reading of the narrative. Elizabeth Hatte has affirmed the deep regard and affection with which Lorna Clark (the fictionalised Grandma Rennie of Verbena Creek) was held by both black and white at a time when such interracial unions were all but impossible. A church was indeed packed to the brim when the couple married and it was filled with both black and white in celebration (Miller, in conversation, 2011). When Annabelle Beck acknowledges 'Grandma Rennie was a legend in the district' (25), it is a remembrance drawn from the memory of Elizabeth Hatte. Col McLennan has also spoken of his grandmother's ability to transcend the racist policies and practices which were part and parcel of Aboriginal people's daily lives, so that her grandchildren were treated as equals with the white children of the district (Zavaglia, telephone conversation, 2011).

If on the discursive level of whiteness, the Edenic childhood tumbles in the water of the Suttor reveal a white longing for a shared beginning as it might have been—a sense of loss for that which, in LaCapra's terms, may be only a foundational absence in disguise—then there is also the lived truth, in Hatte's words, 'that the dream was also realised in the life of Lorna Clark' (Zavaglia, telephone conversation, 2011). Here, then, are Miller's traces—oral testimonies encased within the fictive—of the lives of the black and white women and men who lived in union on what they regarded as Edenic land, each voice speaking with an authority which collapses the possibility of a definitive unitary reading in the novel.

While some of the real-life counterparts of *Journey to the Stone Country* have emerged to attest to the possibilities of the redemptive narrative, other more shadowy characters in the stone country are to date contained solely within the fictive realm. Les Marra is a 1970s-style fire-and-brimstone civil rights activist whose collectivist work is juxtaposed with Bo Rennie's ethos of individualism, which is associated with more recent trends in Aboriginal advocacy. Together they represent the shifting grounds of Aboriginal politics in Australia. Unlike the fetishising gaze of whiteness, which dramatises the spectacle of such political divides, they understand each other's intentions, even if they disagree with their methods. There is no sense of hatred between them. Bo Rennie is equivocal about Les Marra. 'He's a smart feller,' he tells Annabelle. 'He's doin' it for the young people. But I never seen no good come of the way him and Steve operates' (68). Susan Barrett, an anthropologist engaged to survey the Ranna property for significant occupation, is less equivocal:

> 'The Land Council bought back this incredibly beautiful station for them. It's enormous . . . Now these elders, Les Marra and Steve Punaru . . . they've signed an agreement for the valley to be dammed. They say the sale of the water to Bowen and Mackay will provide an economic base for the next generation. But it won't. It'll just become another source of handouts . . . You give them back their Eden and they drown it.' (87)

But it is not a black Eden that Les Marra wants to drown; it is the notion of the white Eden the Bigges pioneers planted on Aboriginal land that Les would destroy. Retribution towards whiteness is to be found here, in Marra's insistence on the drowning of the Ranna. He erupts onto the pages of the novel in a helicopter, with the sound of the chopper blades 'shattering' Annabelle's illusion of isolation on the Ranna. Marra is described as wearing 'a black shirt, black jeans and a black cowboy hat with theatrical yellow and red feathers stuck in the band . . . his feet apart, hands on hips, as if he were the chevalier of a masterful order visiting his presence upon an outlying fiefdom of his domain' (197).

He is characterised in melodramatic strains of manic laughter, uttering prophetic Old Testament announcements of impending destruction while clothed in the attire of a feathered Grim Reaper. Annabelle feels he has 'an insistence, malevolent and without forbearance', that makes her 'fear him instinctively' (197–8). Marra announces the Ranna's drowning with glee:

> 'She's all gonna be drowned.' He watched them, something expectant and exultant in him, the pupils in his eyes . . . vitreous and nocturnal, as if he saw into their hearts . . . His hatred. His black shirt and black jeans, the red and yellow feathers trembling in his hat . . . An entranced prophet . . . He might have announced to them: *I have returned not to reclaim this country for my children today but to visit the apocalypse of my retribution upon it!* (210)

This is the judgement of the Old Testament numinous being visited upon a corrupted whiteness. Marra's hatred is deeply threatening to Annabelle, who realises that 'Les Marra's vision of the future would never be reconciled to her existence ... There could be no place for her, or for her kind, in the victory he envisaged' (211).

The most melodramatic gothic figure of Aboriginality, however, is Panya—Grandma Rennie's last remaining contemporary and the last stone woman:

> An old woman sitting ... Her eyes set deep in her head ... The skin of her features jowled and folded down over her cheeks as if it would slough and leave the naked white bone of her skull ... There was a strong smell of excrement. An open pail standing beside the settee. Blowflies humming around inside the pail, coming out and batting against the teevee screen ... She coughed, gasping and choking and bringing phlegm into her mouth. She leaned forward and spat the goblet of phlegm at the pail. It hit the side and slid down, the flies rising with a hum at the impact. (334–7)

The characterisations of Panya and Les Marra create instinctive aversions for the reader. Panya herself is drawn with such repulsive strokes that her obvious trauma as a victim of history is obscured by repellent visions of bodily expulsions. 'Empathic unsettlement' (LaCapra, 699) is difficult here. Panya is angry with Bo for bringing Annabelle into her home and for his intent to take her to the stone country. Bo remains silent, 'as if he had been called before the ancient dark of this old Jangga woman's judgement to answer for all the wrongdoing of his life' (336). Yet what is Bo Rennie's wrongdoing? He has been at all times a graceful and dignified figure. Indeed, in an earlier reflection, Annabelle has already revealed his messianic status by intuiting that

> He seemed to hold the key to all their fates. But it seemed that they must wait for it. He would not be hurried. Perhaps he did not even know he held such a key and was untroubled by his possession of it. She did not think she was being entirely fanciful. Too many aspects

of her past and present life were linked in him for her to dismiss her
thought as fantasy. She was prepared, rather, to believe it . . . (169)

Annabelle is correct in her intuition, for it is by his union with her that he will bear the stripes for the sins of whiteness—sins which are traced through Annabelle's own bloodlines back to Grandfather Beck. Panya unveils 'the shock of history', the massacre of her people:

'[Annabelle's] granddad was huntin our families up through them scrubs . . . Me and your Grandma was . . . watching them men murderin our people in the moonlight . . . Where are my sisters and brothers, Bo Rennie? . . . Where did them kids go to? . . . I watched them bein murdered! . . . I seen that Louis Beck ride down my little brother across that clearing and bust his skull wide open with his stirrup iron . . . You bring that Beck woman here so she can apologise to me?' (338–41)

As for forgiveness, she notes: 'No one never come here and asked me to forgive em . . . All they wanna do is forget. They want us to believe the bad times is over and we all gotta be friends now. Only they got everything for themselves, and they not giving it back. That's what the white man want now. Peace for himself. And that's what you gonna give him. But that's not what I'm gonna give him . . .' (344).

Panya's words are electrifying. Miller's inscription of them across *Journey to the Stone Country* should indeed be celebrated, for they fracture the totalisation of the redemptive narrative, which attempts a closure for whiteness. Even though he anoints Bo Rennie the messianic hope for whiteness in the novel, he has not silenced its historical victims. When Panya says that no one asked her forgiveness, she speaks the truth. At no point in *Journey to the Stone Country* is there an apology. There is a shattering silence in the novel on the matter of apology and of address to the victims of history.

In 2002, when the novel was published, no official apology had yet been made to the Stolen Generations. Panya's hatred (and Les Marra's desire for vengeance) are both 'the acting out' of trauma, and require an 'empathic unsettlement', from Annabelle. Yet the narrative of white redemption cannot sustain such unsettling. It requires some kind of resolution to Panya's revelations, and retreats to the succour of the Christian tropes that have sustained it. Recoiling from the belated arrival of traumatic history, Annabelle wonders if 'Surely, there would have to be an atonement in blood for such horrors... What amends could there ever be for murder?' (347). At this moment, Annabelle looks to Bo Rennie, depicted in a Christlike suffering solitude. This is the eschatological conclusion to the novel. Bo himself is the sacrifice for white redemption, as he stands 'in the bottom of the gully... a forlorn and solitary figure in the dried up broken landscape' (347).

Journey to the Stone Country is therefore an intricate text that registers ambivalent cultural desires which both shift towards and away from the discomforts of historical trauma. There are many voices speaking their stories, from the literary voices of the novel to the literal traces encased within them, from the self-revealing authorial voice to 'those other voices... who slide into the dark and leave scarcely a trace' (Miller, *The Book Show*, 2006); and then there are the contestations of the Aboriginal political voices, each with its own solutions for the future advancement of Aboriginal Australia.

With the inclusion of all these voices in a polyphonic register, the 'harmonising closure' (LaCapra, 723) of the Christian redemption narrative, which relies upon a monologic voice to succeed, is ultimately refused. The totalising narrative of fall and redemption in *Journey to the Stone Country* fractures beneath the weight of the voices of the traumatised and the lost. It is Panya's voice, which refuses easy resolutions, and it is the hate in Les Marra's voice, which trouble an easy exit for whiteness. By allowing all the voices of the text equal authority along with his own, Miller registers his own ambivalence towards a redemptive closure, allowing the reader an ethical haunting which is difficult to put aside. There is no unitary truth offered, only this haunted note on which the novel pivots: 'No one never... asked me to forgive em' (344), says Panya. Her complaint rivets our attention long after the pages have closed, particularly when one glances retrospectively at the 2008 National Apology to the Stolen Generations. While the hopeful conclusion of Bo and Annabelle at the point of a new beginning is also to be had, via Miller's intervention, we are brought to that space of 'empathic unsettlement' where we are reminded that just as there is no simple closure for history's traumatised victims, nor can there be for the rest of us, who must learn as a nation to both recognise and memorialise their losses, and then to mourn with them for what was lost.

NOTE

1   An example is the media event that erupted over an inappropriate tweet by Larissa Behrendt in response to Bess Price's comments about the Northern Territory Intervention on *Q&A*, ABC TV, 11 April 2011.

WORKS CITED

Attwood, Bain. *Telling the Truth About Aboriginal History*. Sydney: Allen & Unwin, 2005.

Bringing Them Home: Report of the National Inquiry into the Separation of Aboriginal and Torres Strait Islander Children from Their Families. [Commissioner: Ronald Wilson] Sydney: Human Rights and Equal Opportunity Commission, 1997.

Budby, Frank, Elizabeth Hatte and Anita Heiss. 'Personal Perspectives on the Central Queensland Novels'. In Robert Dixon, ed. *The Novels of Alex Miller*. Sydney: Allen & Unwin, 2012.

Dixon, Robert. 'Tim Winton, *Cloudstreet* and the Field of Australian Literature'. *Westerly* 50 (November 2005): 238–53.

Forgacs, David. 'Marxist Literary Theories'. In Anne Jefferson and David Robey, Eds. *Modern Literary Theory*. London: Batsford, 1988, 166–203.

Huggan, Graham. 'Nazis, the Holocaust, and Australia's History Wars'. *Australian Studies* 2 (2010). Canberra, Australian Capital Territory: National Library of Australia.

Jones, Gail. 'Sorry-in-the-Sky: Empathetic Unsettlement, Mourning and the Stolen Generations'. In Judith Ryan and Chris Wallace-Crabbe, eds. *Imagining Australia: Literature and Culture in the New New World*. Cambridge, Mass.: Harvard University Press, 2004. 159–71

LaCapra, Dominick. 'Trauma, Absence, Loss'. *Critical Inquiry* 25.4 (Summer 1999): 696–727.

McPhee, Hilary. 'Shadows that Cross Our Souls'. (Review of *Landscape of Farewell*). *Australian*, 7 November 2007.

Miller, Alex. In conversation at The Novels of Alex Miller: A Symposium. University of Sydney, 14 May 2011.

——. *The Book Show*. Ramona Koval, Presenter. ABC Radio, 30 November 2006.

——. 'Sweet Water'. *Bulletin*. 16 December 2003–13 January 2004: 100–4.

——. *Journey to the Stone Country*. Sydney: Allen & Unwin, 2002.

Pearson, Noel. 'White Guilt, Victimhood and the Quest for a Radical Centre'. *Griffith Review* 16 (May/Winter 2007): 1–39.

Whitehead, Anne. *Trauma Fiction*. Edinburgh: Edinburgh University Press, 2004.

Windschuttle, Keith. *The Fabrication of Aboriginal History*. Sydney: Macleay Press, 2002.

Zavaglia, Liliana. Telephone conversation with Elizabeth Hatte and Col McLennan, 15 June 2011.

- 13 -

DOUGALD'S GOAT:
Alex Miller and the Species Barrier

DAVID BROOKS

I WOULD LIKE TO open with a proposition, a theory if you like, that, in a great many narratives, there is a place, a site, where they confess, or at least pay some acknowledgement to, the stories they have not followed in order to follow the story that they have. Their roadkill, one might facetiously term it, their *rejectamenta*, their abject. And it is not just stories, it is concepts as well, even or perhaps especially ethical positions: places, sites, where they acknowledge all that has had to be set aside in order for those stories, concepts and ethical positions to come to be. I do not say that they in any way specify or itemise them, or that this acknowledgement is anything but the vaguest symbolisation—indeed, it is so much a matter of the subconscious that it is hard to see how it could be—although in some cases they can take a pronounced and almost indisputable form.

In one of the bold philosophical projects of which I sometimes dream, I would in fact go further and attempt to demonstrate a collateral premise that much of our human ethics are based upon a separation from and rejection—abjection is a better term, since this is a matter of our identity and what we do to shore it—of the animal, and that the animal therefore always haunts, unacknowledged, our ethical reflections. Miller's texts, I suggest, are ethical reflections, and so are haunted in this way.

But back to that place, that confessional locus. I do not have a name for it—this site that is like standing at the edge of a pit—but for the time being, thinking of Plato's *Timaeus* and discussions thereof by Julia Kristeva and Jacques Derrida, I am inclined to call it choratic. I could digress into an account of Plato's concept of *chora* here, and even digress, within that digression, into its curious relations to Cora or Kore (Persephone), forebear of Eurydice, in order to establish an Orphic dimension, but that is subject for a different essay.

If I were to attempt to identify the particular character and strength—the *virtu*—of Alex Miller's writing I would talk immediately about its intuitive quality, an opening it comes so repeatedly to, not a border crossing necessarily, but certainly a border viewing. As if he were to take us over and again to a figurative door, somewhere within his subject, which, whether or not he or his protagonists accept to do so, the fiction itself then challenges its readers to pass through. It takes various forms—the transcultural in *The Ancestor Game* (1992) (where, in fact, there is a very literal red door), the ekphrastic in *The Sitters* (2003)—but the intuitive engine, the propensity within them is the same. For now, and because it is of particular concern to me, I would like to look at the form—the particularly choratic form—it takes in *Landscape of Farewell* (2009) and, briefly, in *Journey to the Stone Country* (2002).

Landscape of Farewell is a book about mourning. Each of its central male characters—Max Otto, a German historian from a university in Hamburg, whom we find on the point of his retirement, and Dougald Gnapun, an Aboriginal elder from Central Queensland—is mourning the death of his wife, Dougald's five years before, Otto's only very recently. And beyond this deep personal grief, each is involved in a kind of cultural mourning: Otto for a childhood and cultural innocence shattered by the activities of the Third Reich, and for the love for his father, a former SS officer, that has been so complicated by it; and Dougald, perhaps predictably, for the suffering brought to his people by white invasion, but also (like Max) for complications thereto in his own family history.

I could be more accurate and specific about these mournings but, while they are very germane to it, they are not the principal focus of this paper. I want, instead, to talk about a particular scene in *Landscape of Farewell*, to prepare for which I need to present a brief synopsis, at least to the point where this scene occurs. Max Otto has decided to commit suicide. His career seems to him a failure. His beloved wife is dead, and the recent history of his nation and his people has forced upon him a kind of silence and guilt-by-association that have blighted his life. Before he takes his pills, however, he will give a valedictory paper to mark his retirement, although he feels that in fact it will only confirm his incapacity, since its subject, the continuity of massacre from classical times to the present—the subject of a book he has long wanted to write—has defeated him. He gives the paper—a disappointment, as he had anticipated—and as he is leaving, to scant applause, a young black woman, a Professor Vita McLelland, halts him with a diatribe, the only point of which Miller gives us is that Professor Otto has omitted to mention the massacre of her people.

The applause for her is far louder than for him. Drinks and canapés are served. He leaves as soon as possible. Before doing so, however, he has a moment of realisation, not just as he subsequently puts it, that hers is the voice and perspective of the future, but of something of the extent to which his own generation has let her generation down. He goes to her and apologises. Vita is taken aback. Max leaves. She follows, demands that he take her for a drink and, when he declines, assumes that he must needs go home to his wife. When he tells her that his wife is dead, Vita is embarrassed and apologises. Although it is true that Max makes his apology first and alone, it is also true enough that apologies are easier to make when both sides are somehow complicit. It is a minor point, but it does leave something about the nature of saying sorry open to some further questioning, and so it is important to register it.

Max and Vita do, then, go for a drink, and drink on. She stays, quite innocently, in his apartment overnight. They become friends. She instructs him to come to Australia, to a conference she is organising. She needs his prestige, but mainly, as she tells him, he needs to meet her uncle Dougald. Max doesn't commit suicide. Although he attends the conference, we are told nothing of that, and next meet him arriving at Dougald's house at Mount Nebo, a mining town in Central Queensland.

But now for the scene. How do I describe it? A harrowing scene. A naked woman hanging from the exposed branch of a tree part-way down a cliff behind Dougald's house. A woman, with her tongue blackened, her neck broken by the fall.

Those of you who have not read the book are perhaps suddenly alert. Those who have read it are either momentarily confused, alarmed or amused, perhaps all three. What is going on? Perhaps you want to protest that there is no naked woman in that scene. That in fact it is Dougald's goat. But in wanting to correct me—to *specify*—you of course *specify*. Yes, it *is* a goat, a nanny-goat, whom Max, interrupted by Dougald's return after a few days away, has failed to tether properly. But if you are also thinking '*only* a goat' then I have either failed in my mission or, more likely (that image of the naked woman might linger), my arrow has not yet hit its target. On the wall behind me as I write—the wall of an artists' house lent to me by the Broken Hill City Council—someone has written out that famous line from Theodor Adorno: 'Auschwitz begins when people look at a slaughterhouse and think "They're only animals."' A bit too heavy for a paper of this kind? Perhaps. It is my contention that, in any case, this scene is choratic, in the sense just described.

But I am getting ahead of myself. Several pages before this scene there is another, of Max's arrival, and a description of Dougald's backyard:

> He led me back through the kitchen and out onto the square of concrete behind the house. He indicated an enclosed water-tank stand. 'The shower's in there. She's not too bad this time of year.' He turned and pointed towards the back of the yard. A path through the grass led to a wire enclosure in which a dozen or so brown hens and a rooster were penned. Beside the hen run there was a narrow shed constructed of timber slabs with a door at the front. The door of this modest building, like the door of the wardrobe, hung open. 'That's the toilet,' he said. Behind the toilet, beyond the back fence, was an open field in which three large yellow bulldozers, rusting and overgrown with creepers, had evidently been abandoned. 'See them tall trees? The river's down there,' he said, pointing. 'She's not much just now. We haven't had any decent rains this year.' . . .
>
> A ground mist hovered like a softly levitating bed sheet above the open field beyond the hen run, the abandoned bulldozers a looming family of dreaming pachyderms. All was silent, except for the distant

throbbing of the mine. Dougald and I were at the back fence. He had fed the hens and I had collected seven warm brown eggs from their boxes.

'We'd better shift her peg,' he said. His voice caressed the words, as if he spoke in order to listen to himself, in order to hear a human voice in this place. Lifting his hand, he pointed at the freckle-faced nanny-goat. She had cropped almost to the earth the growth of weeds and grasses within the compass of her tether. (68–70)

These passages and the components from which they are assembled seem innocent enough, perhaps, but in literature there is not a great deal that is innocent. Everything is *choice*. Let's start on the periphery of this scene—with two aspects only—and then tighten the focus. The toilet door open like that of the wardrobe in Max's monk's cell-like room in the house behind them, a fairly familiar image of the proximity of and access to the subconscious, reinforced—I'd say put beyond doubt—by the mention of the proximity and throbbing of the mine. And the way this yard space has been feminised, even maternalised: the nanny-goat, the hens, eggs warm in the hand, the particular and very significant caress of Dougald's voice (caressing not the goat but the words themselves, as if to emphasise the barriers they represent and create); even the family of pachyderms. Put them—the unconscious and the feminine/maternal—together and one might venture the Orphic dimension I mentioned earlier. But that, I think, would be a lyrical seduction, a sleight of mind. There is too much more. Not unsurprisingly for a book which harbours so robust a dream of reconciliation, the passage/space gives on to, for example, the river, site of blessedness, baptism—access, if one can cross it, to the Promised Land (and Miller has mentioned the Promised Land only three pages before). But again I'm ahead of myself.

There are other things here, less appealing and likely of notice. The hens are caged. The goat is tethered. There are varieties, orders, of animals in literature just as there are out of it—the domesticated as pet, the domesticated as food source, the exotic as entertainment, the exotic as source of awe, the exotic as feral/pest, wildlife to be protected, wildlife to be controlled, to name only a few—and each has its own semiotic, its own logic of use and representation.¹ And these, the hens and the goat, are animals of use, tethered or confined—why should one hesitate to say imprisoned?—accordingly. The scene might be idyllic for Max, for Dougald, and for the reader, but it is doubtful that it is idyllic for those they are at this point looking upon.

When we come, not many pages later, to the scene first mentioned, of the goat whom Max did not 'properly' tether—who, as she has slipped down the cliff-face, has been strangled, in fact hanged, when her rope caught on an exposed tree root, we might legitimately ask just who it is in this book who is most or first attempting to get to the Promised Land? And there are some logical, if conceptually uncomfortable, implications—Dougald as gentle farmer, mournful over but not vindictive concerning the effectual decimation of his race, is also, from this perspective, and I put it as gently as possible, a gaoler. The point, and there *is* a point here, is to do with the complicated root-systems of apology—for some, such a clear and obvious thing to do, to say, but for others—how can the white invaders *not* apologise?—well, perhaps that is the door Miller wants to lead us to.

These complications could well be the subject of a paper by themselves. There is not the space to go far into them here, and yet, as already mentioned, they are deeply pertinent. For all its immediate ethical concerns, *Landscape of Farewell* conveys the feeling of containing further complications—ethical complications—that I think Miller wants us to notice and consider. I will sketch only a few.

Max gives a paper in Hamburg. The paper—its failure and inadequacy—is the subject of Vita's immediate and devastating attack. The paper, on 'The Persistence of the Phenomenon of Massacre in Human Society from the Earliest Times to the Present'—is on a subject of profound concern to the book—Miller's book—which follows. And yet, aside from the fact that its list of massacres did not include that of Vita's people, we are given no idea whatsoever of its argument or of the nature of its failure. So, too, Max—reformed and rehabilitated, or at least revitalised, having acknowledged so dramatically his own shortcoming—then goes to Sydney and gives a second paper. This, surely, is of even greater relevance, given what has come and is to follow, but this time we are not even given a title, let alone told how it went; indeed, aside from giving him the excuse to be here, it seems to slip entirely from the book's attention. And as to the matter of apology itself, Max's apologies, I will readily admit, are unconditional, and that, of course, is the way they should be. Conditional apologies are not apologies at all. This may be why Miller gives us Max's first apology so quickly and dramatically. But a book, while a plot may unfold within it, is also a synchronic thing. Max's apology is followed almost immediately by an apology from Vita herself, just as, later, Max's second, for the death of the goat, is followed by Dougald's account of the massacre conducted by his great-grandfather. Max may be able to offer an unconditional apology; Miller may be able to offer an unconditional apology; but it seems the book needs to balance them, as if one can't happen without the other—although why this must be is largely unstated. And beyond this, as I have already intimated, since it is very much an ethical investigation, the book has an entire ghost- or shadow-economy of the animal, of which Miller seems conscious and of which he wants to encourage our own awareness. Again I can't do much more here than sketch: it might be enough to say that Vita's protest, that *her* people don't get into *his* history of massacre, could all too readily be also the goat's stifled cry. There are elisions here, segues between orders of signification, a game—but it is never a game—of snakes and ladders.

There is a feeling, that is, that a number of crucial matters have had to be set aside—to be relegated—in order for apology to become possible. This is no surprise, of course: it has been part of our recent national experience. Perhaps it is why the Apology took so long. Perhaps we could say that in any situation where what Freud called the narcissisms of minor difference[2]—the *agonising* narcissisms of minor difference—come into play there has to be a great deal of such repression and relegation. Indeed I might go so far as to suggest that in any such process of the reconciliation of two deeply entrenched parties, a third party is likely to be involved.

It is now time to look at the scene itself. To prepare for it you need merely to remember that Dougald has been away, and that at the moment of his return—interrupted *by* that return—Max, shifting the tether peg of the goat, had only half-hammered it into its new position. The scene itself occurs in the early hours of the next morning:

> The moment we reached the riverbank we saw her. The ground fell away abruptly at our feet for ten or twelve metres in a near-vertical cliff. It was a dangerous and precipitous place. The elaborate root structures of the great trees had been deeply undermined by erosion, and the mesh of their intricate lattice exposed to the air. Except for a stagnant scum of green algae, which glowed in the cold morning light with a faint and eerie sheen, the riverbed was dry. The exposed tree roots formed the matrix of an elaborate trap. She was hanging by her tether rope, her wooden peg lodged in the fork of a root two or three metres below us. Her tongue lolled from the side of her mouth, purple and swollen, and might have been her disgorged stomach. She hung there, spinning slowly, grinning up at us, her teeth glinting in the rictus of death, her intelligent antique eyes no longer shining with her secret interior life, but bulging blindly, the pupils dull. She was a hideous sight. Her death must have been slow and terrible, for her hoofs had scored the bank deeply in her helpless struggle to free herself. (114–15)

A brief scan of the imagery will tell us what kind of place we have come to. There is the proximity of the river, and we have spoken of its significance already. And there is the emphasis placed upon exposed roots that might remind us of Derrida's remarkable, poetic, representation of deracination in *Of Grammatology*.[3] And there is the fact that the dead goat, as placed here, comes *between* Max and Dougald and the river, as if something about her and/or what she represents threatens to prevent them from ever reaching it (at least until Max *falls with her*, as he does a few pages later, but that scene, and the complications and complicities of it, is an essay to itself).[4]

But although this scan may tell us what kind of place we have come to, it does not tell us why. So, too, a scan—if we can call it that—of the goat herself will give us some intriguing vectors, but will not offer up her deeper significance so readily. Let's look at her. She is a nanny-goat, in which capacity she carries not only the maternal but an additional inflection of the disciplinarian and the teacher (in a sense both Max and Dougald are infantilised before her). But she is also mute (her tongue, her strangulation). She is also subject (collar; rope; peg).

Clearly she has been killed (or, rather, her death has been *brought about*)—if I read this secret but nonetheless timeless imagery aright—by some mesh in our thought, or perhaps it would be better to say some confusion, some entanglement (we are actually given the word *fork*, and that will do) in the roots that subtend it. I am not overreading. Careful emphasis is placed here. We are not just given 'exposed roots': we are given 'The elaborate root structures of the great trees'; we are given 'the mesh of their intricate lattice' ('lattice' is used several times and in several contexts in this book, as if a kind of clue); we are given 'the matrix of an elaborate *trap*'.

She is abject. She is an embodiment of (our) abjection. Indeed, abjection could be seen to be quite consciously adduced—folded back upon itself—in the reference to her tongue appearing to be her disgorged stomach. And she is, of course, and quite literally, a *scape*-goat, of the kind described in the Old Testament, where the Lord details to Moses the process by which animals are to be offered up in sacrifice for the expiation of sin. A bullock for a sin offering, a ram for a burnt offering, and two goats, over whom lots should be cast, to determine which one should be slaughtered and which one loaded up with the sins of the people and sent into the wilderness, 'unto a land not inhabited' (Leviticus 16.22).

It is, of course, and as already admitted, of the nature of the abject—of this relegation into the Other—to be difficult to name. Is it, in this case, some thing or things we need to set aside in order to think that we, any of us, have stewardship, let alone ownership, of this or indeed any country? Is it that deeply repressed awareness in us that the other side of apology for massacre is complicity in massacre, in the forked sense that this book offers us: that is, both in the sense that, as Miller presents it, each side, Indigenous and invader, has engaged in human massacre, and in the sense that, forgiving—apologising to—each other, they are glossing over the fact—awareness—that even as they do so they are still engaged in, are mutually complicitous in, that vastly wider massacre that Isaac Bashevis Singer called Eternal Treblinka? and that great paradox of our deeply divided behaviour, which I have elsewhere called our wound:[5] that, in order to be merciful, we have to turn our backs upon our continuing mercilessness; that, in order to be compassionate, we have to turn our backs upon our continuing lack of compassion.

The nanny-goat's throat is constricted; her tongue swollen and purple: she is an image at once of the voiceless and, perhaps, of the unspeakable. My point is less to attempt such specifications of the abject than to point out a site—a site, and perhaps a process. Choratic, I have called them, but you may wish to use other terms. And, of course, to encourage a kind of reading *for* such sites and processes. Even when they cannot be found—even if my opening premise is a kind of wild hope and exaggeration—it is surely worth our while to look for them since doing so galvanises the issue of the unspoken, which is not, after all, so much the unnecessary of our lives (and narratives, and ethical positions) as the matter from which those lives and positions have been carved.

In case my reader might be inclined to think such findings contrived or fortuitous, I'd like to glance, in closing, at another novel of Miller's, *Journey to the Stone Country*, and a similar choratic scene, in Bo Rennie's account of the scrub bulls of Zigzag Station:

> 'These ridges are full of old scrub bulls. They eat them poison zamia nuts when the feed cuts out in the winter, then when the heat comes on in summer the rickets come out of their limbs. They go down in the hindquarters and get themselves snared up among that shattered basalt. When we'd ride up on one of them, the wild dogs would be sitting in the shade close by, watching him die, taking it in turns to jump in for a quick bite every now and then ... I've lain there plenty of times in my blankets in the moonlight listening to one of them trapped bulls bellowing. That high-pitched bugling sound they make. You'll know it when you hear it. The trumpet of the angel, my dad used to call it. Carries all up and down these ridges ... I used to lie there at night thinking that old angel was out there turning the stones over looking for me.' (137–8)

Eloquent enough by itself, the passage becomes even more so, and more destabilising to the ostensible ethics of the novel, when we realise that the house in Townsville of the parents of Annabelle, Bo's white co-protagonist—the house in which Annabelle is temporarily staying—is on Zamia Street, that a whole chapter takes its name from this street, and that a chapter soon to follow, curiously titled 'A Plague of Dogs', contains the following lines—and oblique acknowledgement:

> 'My dad used to tell us you people fought like wild dogs over there at Verbena.'
> 'Wild dogs? Well we fought when we needed to fight, that's what we did. We had some real good fights out in front of that big tamarind tree of Grandma's.' (226)

But, to the sceptical, even corroboration needs corroboration. Look then at the curious paradox, elsewhere in the book, by which, although they note the roadkill, even count it, as if in sympathy for the creatures thus slaughtered, Miller's protagonists drive the country roads carelessly and at high speed, even at dawn and dusk, the peak danger times for wildlife, doing little or nothing to avoid contributing to the toll.

This paradox seems to concentrate, if not in any way resolve, much of what Miller seems to be wrestling with in these texts: the way the ethical resolutions we struggle for, while other, far deeper and far more difficult business remains unaddressed, will seem like guilty rhetorical platitudes, matters less of forgiveness than mutual complicity, fragile, vulnerable not, like our other human constructions, before any tsunami or flood or earthquake—those nice available metaphors—but before something far more damaging to our own senses of ourselves, the return of which, like the return of anything too long repressed, can be devastating. I'd like to call it our own deep moral conscience but I'm not sure that wouldn't in itself be a platitude. In truth I don't know what to call it, or whether it even has a name.

Let me try to approach it from a different angle. In the roadkill trope just adduced, you could be forgiven for thinking that Miller is looking at his own characters with a measure of scepticism, even disdain, a disdain there again in the novel's closing pages. Bo takes Annabelle to see Panya, an old Aboriginal woman with first-hand experience of a massacre in which Annabelle's own grandfather participated (the grandfather who in his senility befriended—became the constant companion of—a bull). Disgusted that Bo has brought

Annabelle into her house, Panya unleashes a diatribe of truth and of horror that neither Bo nor Annabelle has any answer for, and leaves the reader uncertain as to how, at last, to regard them. Certainly any ethical resolution they represent—and I do think they are intended to represent one—looks hollow indeed, based upon a turning one's back on, rather than a facing of the past. Yet these are characters lauded—beloved—by critics and author alike. What is happening here? It is as if a door has been left open—Panya's door—and a chill, choratic wind is withering the human landscape. Where has it come from? Panya? But she herself is victim, not origin. Even her message is messenger. To get the beginnings of a better idea, look at how it was that Panya, as a young girl, survived the massacre in the first place: 'Your grandmother's old lady hid us two kids with her in the hollow carcass of a old scrubber bull that was layin out in the open ... Me and your Grandma was all curled up inside that carcass looking out through the old bull's skullholes watching them men murderin our people in the moonlight' (338–9).

Then go one rather obvious step further.

NOTES

1 There are other animals in this book, for example, even in the scenes we have been discussing: Dougald's beloved and deeply faithful 'pale-eyed wolf-like bitch' (72); the two younger dogs, 'her offspring and members of her tribe' (72), who attach themselves to Max, the bulldozers who, as if pointing up one of the book's redemptive dreams, are caught mid-metamorphosis.

2 In *Civilization and Its Discontents*, for example, where he argues that the human impulse toward aggression is so deep that, in any coming together in *love* there must be a commensurate redirection—scape-goating—of violence.

3 'We know that the metaphor that would describe the genealogy of a text correctly is still *forbidden*. In its syntax and its lexicon, in its spacing, by its punctuation, its lacunae, its margins, the historical appurtenance of a text is never a straight line. It is neither causality by contagion, nor the simple accumulation of layers. Nor even the pure juxtaposition of borrowed pieces. And if a text always gives itself a certain representation of its

own roots, those roots live only by that representation, by never touching the soil, so to speak. Which undoubtedly destroys their *radical essence*, but not the necessity of their *racinating function*. To say that one always interweaves roots endlessly, bending them to send down roots among the roots, to pass through the same points again, to redouble old adherences, to circulate among their differences, to coil around themselves or to be enveloped one in the other, to say that a text is never anything but a *system of roots*, is undoubtedly to contradict at once the concept of system and the pattern of the root. But in order not to be pure appearance, this contradiction takes on the meaning of a contradiction, and receives its "illogicality", only through being thought within a finite configuration—the history of metaphysics—and caught within a root system which does not end there and which as yet has no name' (*Of Grammatology*, 101–2).

4   As—to introduce yet another of the intersecting loops of interpretation here—may be the fact that she is not actually Dougald's goat—my title is misleading here—but (and although arguably she is no one's) is presented as Vita's, or rather as a goat whose mother has been killed on a country road and whom Vita has rescued, a tale which brings even greater shame to Max and Dougald's subsequently taking so long to bury her.

5   'The Smoking Vegetarian' (*Angelaki*, 129–37).

WORKS CITED

Brooks, David. 'The Smoking Vegetarian'. *Angelaki: Journal of Theoretical Humanities*, 14.2 (August 2009): 129–37. Reprinted in *Best Australian Essays 2010*. Ed. Robert Drewe. Melbourne: Black Inc., 2010.

Derrida, Jacques. *Of Grammatology*. Trans. Gayatri Chakravorty Spivak. Baltimore: Johns Hopkins University Press, 1976.

Derrida, Jacques, and Peter Eisenman. *Chora/Works*. New York: Monacelli Press, 1997.

Freud, Sigmund. [1930] *Civilization and Its Discontents*. Trans. Joan Riviere. Revised and newly edited James Strachey. London: The Hogarth Press, 1982.

Kristeva, Julia. *Revolution in Poetic Language*. Trans. Margaret Waller, Leon S Rudiez. New York: Columbia University Press, 1984.

Miller, Alex. *Landscape of Farewell*. Sydney: Allen & Unwin, 2007.

——. *Journey to the Stone Country*. Sydney: Allen & Unwin, 2002.

——. *The Sitters*. Ringwood, Vic.: Viking, 1995.

——. *The Ancestor Game*. Ringwood, Vic.: Penguin, 1992.

Patterson, Charles. *Eternal Treblinka: Our Treatment of Animals and the Holocaust*. New York: Lantern Books, 2002.

Plato. *Timaeus and Critias*. Trans. Desmond Lee. Penguin Classics. Harmondsworth: Penguin, 1972.

Singer, Isaac Bashevis. [1968] 'The Letter Writer'. *The Collected Stories of Isaac Bashevis Singer*. London: Jonathan Cape, 1982.

- 14 -

The RUIN of TIME and the TEMPORALITY of BELONGING:
Journey to the Stone Country and *Landscape of Farewell*

BRIGID ROONEY

> To get beneath the impermeable barrier of present reality, I believed my writing would have to acknowledge the existence of the barrier. My writing would have to contain the barrier. It would have to *be* the barrier itself. Verisimilitude, on at least one of its operational levels, I considered vital to the enterprise. (Miller, *The Ancestor Game*, 151)

In *Journey to the Stone Country* (2002) and *Landscape of Farewell* (2007), his sixth and eighth novels respectively, Alex Miller appears to offer his readers more accessible, straightforwardly linear narratives than was evident in his third book, *The Ancestor Game* (1992). With characters displaced yet sensuously located, at odds with nationalist borders but at home in their exile, *The Ancestor Game* offers a labyrinthine, non-linear and reflexive postmodern novel that pursues the self–other encounter across time and place. It seems paradoxical, therefore, that Steven Muir—the novel's narrative 'I', who is also engaged in writing a book, *The Chronicle of the Fengs*—signals the necessity of 'verisimilitude'. For his writing to pierce the 'impermeable barrier of present reality', he believes he must recruit at some level, counterintuitively, realist techniques. Presumably this equates to a form of writing that aims at intelligibility, that engages in mimesis of the surface of things, and that incorporates the conventional, linear causalities of chronological storytelling—elements that Miller's postmodern text both includes and complicates. In *The Ancestor Game*, the operation of verisimilitude—its verisimilitude *of* verisimilitude—helps to achieve a mirroring surface-as-depth effect, exactly as articulated. The writing *becomes* the barrier it cannot penetrate.

Does Miller abandon such a project in his later, apparently realist, Central Queensland novels, *Journey to the Stone Country* and *Landscape of Farewell*? How, if at all, do these texts continue to work the seam between verisimilitude and reflexive composition, and probe present reality by situating writing *as* barrier? Or do they merely refer, with less aesthetic sophistication and with (arguably) diminished ethical sensitivity, to some external 'present reality'? Miller's recent fiction has attracted general praise, and probably a broader readership, yet also strong criticism in some quarters. This divided reception may be partly contingent upon his later fiction's increased accessibility and more explicitly national orientation. For both novels actively address 'present reality' by referring readers towards contemporary Australian debates about injustice and colonisation, Aboriginal dispossession and identity, and contemporary settler desires for reconciliation and belonging. In addition to some overlapping characters and settings, the two novels are thematically interlinked. *Landscape of Farewell* has been read as coda to *Journey to the Stone Country*, or its rewriting (Bennie, 'The Dirt That Lies Within', 32; McPhee, 'Shadows', 5). The journeys of their respective protagonists into Queensland cattle country, and towards ancestral Aboriginal homelands, provide a clear chronological scaffold in both texts. *Landscape of Farewell* is shorter and seems more distilled. With fewer characters it is less epic in its canvas than *Journey to the Stone Country*, yet it incorporates, as I will argue, an artful layering of temporalities. *Landscape of Farewell*'s more explicit artfulness—along with both its disarming, first-person, elderly male narrator and Miller's detailed concluding acknowledgement of Indigenous collaborators—has perhaps worked to deflect critical objections otherwise levelled at *Journey to the Stone Country*. Yet in my reading, both texts are more reflexively layered than appears from their surface conformity to verisimilitude. Examining the treatment of time and the self through the layering of narrative temporalities, my aim is to think from this angle about the scope and character of Miller's address to ambivalent questions of settler identity and belonging.

While it is important not to overstate the cleavage in its reception, Miller's Miles Franklin Literary Award-winning *Journey to the Stone Country* has been the focus of some academic criticism. These criticisms draw on postcolonial and whiteness studies to highlight problems with the way settler narratives may translate 'desire for the indigene and the land into ... desire for native authenticity' (Johnston and Lawson, 'Settler Post-Colonialism', 37). Accordingly, white settler narratives—even when sympathetic—run the risk of annexing an autochthonous Aboriginal identity for the settler. Or, more threateningly, they may prescribe and confine the terms in which Indigenous people might seek to imagine themselves. Hence *Journey to the Stone Country* has been criticised, firstly, for its romanticisation or exoticisation of its Aboriginal characters. These characters are seen as 'imbued with either an ancient, mysterious, "timeless" wisdom or an intensely erotic quality', and from this angle, the novel's reconciliatory politics appear as a messy convergence of older settler desires for indigenisation 'with new-age wish fulfilment' (Johnston and Lawson, 37–8). This especially applies to the depiction of Arner, the young son of Aboriginal elder Dougald Gnapun, who accompanies Annabelle Beck and Bo Rennie on their journey, and who sits impassively in his separate world. Arner reminds Annabelle of a prince, or a graven image: 'He was golden in the wash of sunlight, modest, serene, enigmatic and beautiful, as if he possessed a thousand years and more and might await the moment of his destiny without the anxiety of time' (54). Arner certainly functions here as unknowable other, as object of desire for Annabelle and, arguably, for non-Indigenous readers. Associated with this criticism is the view that Miller's text implicitly invests its hope in the Rennies (Bo and Grandma), who seem to point towards a reconciled, creolised, shared future for settlers and Aboriginal people, based on an ethic of individual responsibility and self-reliance—whereas the narrative's furious political resisters, Les Marra and Panya, whose separatist agenda is driven by an unassuageable hatred and desire for retribution, are ultimately sidelined. This implicit valuing may constitute a dubious intervention into sensitive questions of contemporary Aboriginal cultural identity (Zavaglia, 'Old Testament Prophets'). Lastly, critics show unease about Miller's central female character, Annabelle Beck, and question her positioning and choices. The ethical restraint shown by

Annabelle in finally relinquishing her journey to the country of Bo's ancestors does not, it is suggested, deflect the novel from reprising 'the oldest settler fantasies about otherness: sexuality, land, timelessness, and the dual allure and revulsion engendered by difference' (Johnston and Lawson, 38). Even for critics who read *Journey to the Stone Country* more sympathetically, the text seems equivocal, thwarting efforts to decide whether it finally 'endorses the notion of the Aboriginal sacred as a legitimate challenge to western understandings of time and the land, or . . . safely corrals the Aboriginal sacred as exoticism' (Ashcroft et al, *Intimate Horizons*, 178).

Some of the above criticisms are themselves not immune from the perils of binarism attributed to Miller's novel, binarisms that structure broader cultural discourses of Aboriginal identity as autochthonous and sacred and that lead to ambivalences theorised, for example, by Ken Gelder and Jane M Jacobs (*Uncanny Australia*, 1998). Whether the 'Aboriginal sacred' functions as a site of legitimate resistance or as safely corralled exoticism, Aboriginal identity in each formulation is firmly yoked to place and space. Place is indisputably paramount in Aboriginal high culture, but the relation between place and Aboriginal culture ought not be regarded as fixed, static or homogeneous. Tony Swain, for instance, has argued that certain Aboriginal groups engaged in modifications of place-centredness following episodes of contact with people from other cultures (*A Place for Strangers*, 1993). These groups began to admit forms of temporal consciousness that realigned (while maintaining) place-centredness. In the post-colonisation era, the strict confinement of 'Aboriginal identity' to 'geography' seems on the one hand crucial for survival and continuity, yet on the other hand risks reducing the access Aboriginal people might otherwise have to the freedom and mobility of identity enjoyed by non-Indigenous Western subjects. In a carefully considered analysis of current cleavages in Indigenous cultural politics, Dirk Moses has suggested that necessity has driven Australia's Indigenous intellectuals to found claims to sovereignty and land upon an ontologically distinct, autochthonous Aboriginal identity. The survival of this tiny minority group within a dominant culture intent on assimilation has made such an identity strategically indispensable. Yet, he suggests, in light of a critique mounted by Achille Mbembe in the admittedly different context of the African postcolony, this equation may foreclose on the possibility of agency and autonomy for Aboriginal people, making it difficult for Indigenous intellectuals to espouse alternative cultural identities or futures freed from the entrapping categories of a victimhood locked in the trauma of colonisation ('Time, Indigeneity', 18–22). The challenge, as Vicki Grieves puts it, is for settler societies like Australia to begin to '"decolonize by the decolonizing of the mind ... by developing new understandings and appreciations of Indigenous culture and society, new respectful ways of relating to Indigenous Australians and the incorporation of their lifeways into the idea of the nation"' (Quoted in Moses, 20).

It is neither possible nor appropriate to do more than register here the immense complexity of these cultural and political questions. Yet I hope to hold Grieves's formulation in mind, with its implications for respectful inclusivity and reciprocity, when asking in what sense, and with what ethical awareness, Miller's fiction negotiates this terrain—given that both his Central Queensland novels are so observant about Indigenous 'lifeways'. In turning to matters of style and composition, and to the temporalities of Miller's narratives, I suggest that such elements, inherent in self-consciously literary works, are deeply constitutive of the fullest range of meanings in play. It is therefore not surprising that we should find curious turns, equivocalities and 'implausibilities' in *Journey to the Stone Country* (Ashcroft et al, 180–1). Ashcroft et al suggest that fiction per se may not be adequate to this sensitive terrain (187). This may be because, as Gelder and Jacobs point out, the medium of fiction (the novel) is neither collaborative nor community based but is 'unauthorised' in its operations. As such, fiction often transgresses the 'sacred', entangling public and private boundaries (102). Yet there are several productive ways in which both *Journey to the Stone Country* and *Landscape of Farewell* seem aware of and work with these contradictions, never quite dispelling or resolving them, but rather foregrounding the question, for settler Australians, of ethical living, and perhaps ethical modes of writing, in circumstances of complicity. At the same time, it is important to recognise that both novels serve non-Aboriginal purposes, not least the writer's own aesthetic project, reproducing and reworking Miller's abiding fictional preoccupations (see Gorton, 'Company of Ghosts'; Pierce, 'Solitariness'). Even so, it is through the swerve away from the literal and referential that fiction may constitute its most potent address to 'present reality'.

Time, place and selfhood in *Journey to the Stone Country*

Journey to the Stone Country certainly evokes settler fantasies. Yet these are reflective of Annabelle Beck's point of view, and much therefore depends on whether we see her character as fixed or in process. A significant dimension of Annabelle's journey, including its romantic elements, concerns her (necessarily partial) induction into the presence and world of Indigenous others, and her reflexive engagement with discursive constructs of the other. Thus Annabelle considers at one point that she is 'in danger of misreading [Arner] in the light of her own hopes for his tribe and her own. To see in him Dryden's noble savage, the ecological saviour of a disintegrating world' (184). Her wry modulation through tropes of noble savage and ecological saviour permits her a modicum of self-awareness. It later occurs to Annabelle that Arner is simply a shy and awkward boy. She realises he is utterly devoted to Bo, something Bo himself does not recognise, anxious as he is about the young man's indifference and apparent deracination. These details are consistent with protagonists in process rather than fixed. Cultural stereotypes are registered, but shift, opening the space for other views. With its inward focus, the narrative presses upon the reader to move, with Annabelle, through romanticising of the other towards a more complicated encounter.

Attention to style, composition and temporalities, and to the narrative's phenomenological effect on the reader, suggests how *Journey to the Stone Country* does not just describe but simulates the journey towards the other. Narrative pace and rhythm prioritise inwardness and reflection, qualities arising in part from the equivocations, hesitations and reflexive turns in Annabelle's consciousness. This becomes continuous with the way various pasts, more or less distant in time and place, are recessed within the narrative's 'present reality', inscribed in the details of Annabelle's actual journey. With the harshly arrested time of broken marriage, Annabelle's swift relocation to Central Queensland marks a shift in pace and entry into a different temporality. In the first 'moment' of the novel, Annabelle stands at the front door of the Melbourne house, facing inwards to its cold, empty space, looking at her reflection in the 'bevelled mirrorglass of the hallstand' (1), and instantly intuiting that Steven has left her, that all their habits, special intimacies and routines have been consigned to an irrecoverable past. Stillness attaches itself thereafter, with variable yet cumulative effect, to an intensely realised series of rooms that seem to spatialise time and emphasise interiority. The slowing of narrative temporalities, through this series of rooms, works in tension with the linear progression of Annabelle's journey, and cuts across colonial time, like the termites feasting, continuously and audibly, on the abandoned Bigges' library at Ranna Station.

It is in the Zamia Street home of Annabelle's dead parents in Townsville, indeed in their bed, that Bo Rennie and Annabelle first make love. The sensory inscription of particular details knits together the contrasting space-times of the Melbourne and Townsville houses: emptiness and silence, memory and loss, the spectral presence of absent loved ones, the smell of fish cooking, the weight of a displaced stone illicitly souvenired from an ancient site,[1] the painfully recalled faux-erotic language of Annabelle's marriage—'his honey-gold skin, his gilded, café au lait', refunctioned here as banalities mockingly unequal to her encounter with Bo. The progression from cold to warmth occurs within a contiguous chain of spaces, moving from the kitchen of Dougald's house (between road and cane field), to a 'servo' café on the road, to Zigzag Station (twice), to Ranna Station, to Yacamunda, to May's place and thence Panya's house, finally fetching up amid the callously wrecked remains of Verbena Station.

The narrative's restriction to Annabelle's viewpoint is one means of intensifying inwardness. Miller's fiction is characterised by 'solitariness' or 'aloneness' effected through the singular consciousness of protagonists (Pierce, 307). This solitariness, however, by no means excludes otherness. Rather, solitariness is the condition of approach to the other. If the inwardness of Aboriginal others is not broached, it is nonetheless attributed through respectful notation of bodily comportment, gesture and silence. Likewise, the third-person narration, though relaying only Annabelle's perspective, is offset by long passages of direct speech—mostly Bo's—as he gently instructs and narrates, requiring of Annabelle, and the reader, preparedness to listen. Bo and Annabelle are in turn silenced, and forward momentum is stalled, by the searing curse of Panya, the last surviving stone woman. Time is arrested with Panya's traumatic revelation of massacre. With Bo, Annabelle stands mutely, the occasion and object of Panya's curse, hapless beneficiary of the deeds of her murderous grandfather whose carcass now appears to her 'as white-anted and as empty of portent as the books in George Bigges' library' (348). Panya's curse bleaches the very landscape of memory, meaning and hope, and in its wake they stumble out into 'the bleached light of day' (346) where Bo is a solitary figure in 'the dried up broken landscape' (347). This constitutes both a moral and aesthetic impasse: the narration focuses intently on Annabelle's broken, desperate thoughts, and on the strain of reconciling Panya's 'terrible song' with Bo's more benign, inherited story of the past—a story linked to the recovered photo of a youthful Grandma Rennie sitting with poise and equanimity on the Bigges' veranda, among the colonisers (some, it transpires, erstwhile murderers of her people). Beyond Panya's house, falteringly, the narrative resumes, moving tentatively to meet, without fully resolving, the question of ethical recovery, of what hope, love or meaning can possibly survive this ruin of time.

There are at least two ways in which *Journey to the Stone Country* sustains commitment to the possibility of a shared future. One resides in the way Miller's prose works to slow down hasty or precipitate reading. It promotes listening and dwelling, and does so through its cumulative registering of prosaic elements integral to the observation of place, and character *in* place, down to the noting of each cigarette Bo rolls or the grilling of sausages and eggs. Miller's consistent registering of otherwise extraneous detail is not a counter-literary logic. Rather, these notations anchor characters within homely routines, rituals and rhythms that suggest intersubjective accommodation. Their gestural presences and their implied but not broached interiorities constitute an insistence on dwelling alongside or with the other. Perhaps this is verisimilitude, working on one of its operational levels—as it also subsequently works for Miller's artist figure in *Prochownik's Dream* (2005), Toni Prochownik, who had 'never striven after an originality of style' (100). Stylistic mimicry of tangible rituals of interpersonal relations correlates with Annabelle's calm anticipation of her life with Bo: 'his arrival was not a surprise but a fulfilment of their orderly expectations of each other' (243).

This prose style conditions apprehension of Annabelle's relinquishment of the journey's last stage. Ashcroft et al. read Annabelle's decision as oddly unilateral, but in my view it defines the mode and limit of her claim to belonging. This curtailing of the desire to know is founded on respect for the other through a necessary self-containment—a restoration of personal balance that, while not at all commensurate with collective historical justice, is perhaps its precondition. This is encoded in a final repetition and inversion: the couple's wordless, companionable gathering of the scattered remnants of the Verbena house, their creation of a provisional camp, recalls but inverts the wreckage of coupledom that hollows out the museum-like space of the Melbourne house. Houses and rooms, I am suggesting, are extensions or emblems of the self's interior landscape. On the last part of their drive to Verbena, Bo and Annabelle pass the turn-off to her childhood home, Haddon Hill (a name, not coincidentally, that alludes autobiographically to Exmoor in England). In electing *not* to visit Haddon Hill, Annabelle shrugs off the fetishism of childhood memory that has already been unmoored by Panya: 'That old road of her memory was somewhere else. It possessed no reality. The return had already erased it' (154). For the novel's settler protagonist, as is the case elsewhere in Miller's fiction, to revisit in order to repossess past homelands hollows out their meaning. Instead, homelands and belonging are cast inwards, constituting interior landscapes that mediate the time of the self. A provisional self-possession emerges as the only viable mode of possession, made possible through acts of relinquishment, of surrender. If, therefore, the recurring motif of displacement from home in *Journey to the Stone Country* signals a search for belonging, this accedes to surrender *in* time, through a quietening of self, and an adjustment to the temporality of the other through circumspection, receptivity and acts of relinquishment.

Temporal crossings in *Landscape of Farewell*

I have been suggesting that Miller's characters locate themselves not simply with respect to geographically located spatial coordinates but also with regard to the temporal coordinates of daily ritual, deeply inculcated 'lifeways', and the precarious intergenerational transmission of story. This remains true of *Landscape of Farewell*, a narrative characterised by a profoundly concentrated set of crossings in space and time. As in both *Journey to the Stone Country* and *The Ancestor Game*, crossings in *Landscape of Farewell* evoke the rhetorical figure of chiasmus, a structure of parallel inversions that can be discerned in Miller's careful patterning in the order and direction of narration. Miller's use of chiasmus seems to signal an ethical demand to route the approach to the other through an examination of self.[2]

The temporal design of *Landscape of Farewell* only *seems* linear and conventional. The present time of narration is sourced in Max Otto's prologue, located in Hamburg, in 2004. Max immediately turns to the events of an earlier time when, in a state of despairing bereavement, he delivers his perfunctory valedictory address, 'The Persistence of the Phenomenon of Massacre in Human Society from the Earliest Times to the Present', planning to go home afterwards and commit suicide. His life-changing encounter with Vita McLelland ensues, leading to his stay with Vita's uncle Dougald Gnapun in Mount Nebo. Max's first-person narrative, in spare, clear prose, takes us through a succession of landscapes, in a journey that, once again, provides the novel's chronological scaffold. Yet this linearity is complicated by an extraordinary set of temporal and intersubjective crossings comprised of memories, dreams and fictional texts.

Mount Nebo appears as a silent, colonised landscape, with its grey monotonous scrubs, its rusting machinery and its heat haze. Redolent with death, the landscape is co-extensive with the ruin brought by an imperial modernity that is itself now subject to ruin. The narrative renders disparate landscapes of farewell as simultaneous—the near and far, past and present, physical and metaphysical. Max's recollections of his marital life with Winifred and of his childhood visits to his uncle's farm in Germany are interwoven with Dougald's landscape. This simultaneity encompasses the body's landscape of physical old age, with the swelling of grief, the ebbing of faith, and futility and loneliness following the death of the beloved. The fusion of physical and moral terrain in Mount Nebo is potently realised in the novel's eponymous chapter, 'Landscape of Farewell'. Through Max's moment of inattention, Vita's little nanny-goat escapes, and Dougald and Max soon find her hanging, caught by her tether in tree roots, and suspended in a grotesque rictus of death over a stagnant pool in the drought-ravaged Nebo River. Dougald's admission, 'This is not my country' (117), 'Nothing's ever going to work out up this way' (120), following Max's disastrous effort to atone, propels them on a mutual journey to Dougald's ancestral country. Yet, in an indicative interlude, an anxious, guilt-stricken Max enters briefly into Mount Nebo's grey monotonous scrubs and encounters there the small miracle of the yellow robin. Amid otherwise overwhelmingly bleak images, this scene confounds the potential *othering* of both the terrain and its living creatures, amplifying a grace note Max also finds in his daily domestic rituals with Dougald and their companion animals.

Perhaps the most searing landscape of farewell in Miller's novel is embedded in Max's fictional transformation of Dougald's story of his grandfather, Gnapun the warrior. Summoned by the messengers of a neighbouring tribe, Gnapun beholds with his own eyes the destruction that the colonisers, or strangers, have wrought upon the playgrounds of the tribe's old people. Gnapun's vision constitutes a significant episode in the novel, and returns me to questions about settler representations of the other:

> For the strangers have collected the stones of the sacred playgrounds of the messengers' Old People and have built walls from them ... everyone knows that to restore the stones to their places would not restore them to their power. Having been taken from their places, Time has been brought to the stones and they are lost to the eternal present of reality. They were there, now they are not there. They have lost their position in the sacred Dreaming and their power to sustain the messengers' people can never be restored to them. Set once again in their old places, the stones would themselves only belong to the past and would be merely history, there to remind everyone of what had once been and has been lost. The messengers' people, Gnapun sees, as he stands there weeping beside the tall man, cannot survive this but have been made exiles in their own country. They have been rendered capable of suffering from their past, an evil previously unknown to them, and a punishment no people has ever had imposed upon it before this day. For as everyone knows, to suffer from one's past is a punishment without remedy. It is the end of belief. To sing, after this, would be a

> blasphemy. After this there can be no innocence. The Old People of the messengers have been banished and humiliated. How will anyone ever bring them back? (190)

The colonisers shatter an Edenic and pristine Aboriginal world, irreversibly disenchanting the magic of the old people. Recalling the Burranbah stone taken by Annabelle, the removal of the stones from their rooted place destroys the continuity of Aboriginal time. The stones become museum pieces rather than living ancestors. The strangers unwittingly consign Aboriginal culture to the past, to history, ushering in a fallen world of exile and dispossession. It is at once the primal scene of the colonial frontier and a rehearsal of the biblical narrative of the fall. This vision is prelude to the fratricidal narrative of Cain and Abel; to massacre, the ultimate landscape of farewell.

But in according Time a capital T (along with capital D Dreaming), the terms of this powerful passage may revive concerns that here again we see settler colonial ascription of timelessness to a premodern, safely vanished Aboriginal culture. Does the novel reinstate an autochthonous Indigenous identity organically tied to the territory of the premodern? Does it affirm the colonising culture's present, and deny the coeval status of contemporary Aboriginal people, constraining the space for an Indigenous imaginary? These, as suggested earlier, are complex questions that ineluctably frame contemporary debates about the status of Indigenous culture vis a vis settler nationhood, from land rights to the Northern Territory intervention—a heavy burden for a work of fiction. Yet *Landscape of Farewell* withstands scrutiny in these terms. The above passage stands at the heart of an exactingly plotted temporal sequence, at the reflexive intersection of the narrative's highly nested design. This design is marked at its outer limits by 'Agamemnon's Edict', as Shirley Walker reminds us ('Agamemnon's Edict', 43), as it is also, finally, by the text's framing dedications, its Steiner epigraph and Miller's 'Acknowledgements'. By the time we reach the 'Massacre' chapter we are positioned to apprehend multiple meanings. It simultaneously fulfils Dougald's request and channels Max's moral search—functioning as both therapeutic consolation after Max's bereavement and negotiation of his guilt-by-association with his father's crimes. The parallels are audacious and risky, for Miller blends incommensurable historical acts of genocide. In recognising that 'To sing, after this, would be a blasphemy', Gnapun seems to ventriloquise Adorno's famous words that there is 'no poetry after Auschwitz'.

Nonetheless, an ethical engagement with the other, via the limits and failures of the self, is suggested through chiasmus, through the crossing and inversion of Miller's narrative temporalities. Analepsis (retrospection or flashback) crosses over with prolepsis (prospection or flashforward) in the course of Max's story of Gnapun. Accorded the omniscient power of an author to access the consciousness of another, Gnapun enters proleptically, in a dream-vision, into the mind of the missionary he will slay. This prolepsis runs athwart and inverts Max's own analeptic (retrospective) narration of the primal scene of frontier violence (referencing the Cullin-la-Ringo massacre), a scene laden with traces of the loss of Winifred, and Max's father–son complex. This cluster—threaded into the fatal consequences of the good coloniser's blindness—is enigmatically refracted in Max's recurring memory of his boyhood failure to help a gipsy girl who survived the massacre of her family, just as it is also prefigured and played out in the lapse in Max's attention that results in the death of Vita's goat. Myriad crossings in place and time work as a frame for the massacre story and amplify it.

How, then, does the narrative hold its ethical balance? It does so precisely through the reflexiveness afforded to Max's narrating consciousness, a power that Max, as we have already seen, has in turn afforded to his character, Gnapun. It is most significant that it is Max himself, retrospectively and analytically, who grasps the implications of his own narrative. Max is alert and awake to his own psychic processes. This denies the reader any position of ironic superiority over Max, making the reading as well as the writing of story collaborative. His shocked recognition of what drives his transformation of Dougald's story of Gnapun—his identification with the perpetrator of a massacre that allows the recuperation of his own father—deflects us from anxious fixation on the referential content of his story, and directs us instead towards metanarrative questions, to the intersubjective uses to which story is put—as gift, therapy, legacy, as tentative and necessarily risky cross-cultural exchange.

Max's massacre fiction enacts a chiastic, cross-cultural return. It is only through the appropriation of Dougald's ancestral story, a conversion into story that implicates and exercises the self, that the other can begin to be approached. And this process extends beyond Max as protagonist. Max's fiction folds in key elements from Dougald's extended recounting, just preceding the massacre chapter, of his boyhood bond with his violent father, whose abuse Dougald met with his own gaze, in an act of witnessing and taking into himself his father's pain. Here, with empathy rather than presumption, Miller's narrative threads into the fabric of Max's fiction perhaps the most painful strands of postcolonial Aboriginal identity. Moving back through time, through the line of fathers, the massacre story grafts its intergenerational narratives onto those machines that lie rusting in the ravaged cultural landscape of the Western imaginary—the biblical fall and the fratricidal story of Cain and Abel.[3]

Both *Journey to the Stone Country* and *Landscape of Farewell* confront the impasse wrought by settler complicity, but they neither avoid the implications nor submit to despair. Both focus on modes of conduct and comportment, working towards the temporary recovery of self and meaning. If there is resolution, if there is a vision of settler belonging, it is located in receptivity, in being and dwelling, and in a stance of openness to the other. In this context, Miller's fiction seems less interested in converting time into space ('nativising' settler identity in alignment with geographic territory) than in transforming space into time by foregrounding narrative process. The narration figures itself as a processual reworking of events. In the closing pages of *Landscape of Farewell*, running through his decision to include his meeting with Vita in his account of their journey to Gnapun's cave, Max draws attention to the deliberation, the purposeful decision-making, that characterises his act of composition. His closing words reprise the figure of chiasmus. A subtle loop in narrative time returns us to the beginning, yet simultaneously comes to rest upon its opposite, the discontinuous fragment, recalling also the scattered remains of *Journey to the Stone Country*'s Verbena house. Max describes watching an old Greek film, one that he had first watched with Winifred: 'Although I had forgotten much of the story, I enjoyed the broken fragment of the film as greatly as I had once enjoyed the whole of it. But there, it is all fragments, and in the midst of it we may know this sense of completion' (275). With this bare detail, the trace of Agamemnon returns. Such chiastic crossings—narrative temporalities that align, I have argued, with an approach to the other through the examination of the self—inscribe Miller's text at every turn. It is not until the epilogue, which returns to the narrative present, that we learn that Max's story has been told in the wake of Dougald's death, and that all along his primary addressee has been Vita herself. Max's final crossing thus recasts the entire narrative as his return of Vita's initial gift: the gift, that is, of life, and perhaps of an incitement to song, even—and especially—after all that has transpired.

NOTES

1   In Steven's study in the Melbourne house, Annabelle reflects on a 'grey wedge of antique marble' that he had once souvenired from the Foro Romano (4); in Zamia Street, she places the Burranbah stone on a table in the centre of the room and ponders its implications uneasily (94).
2   The ethical dimension I am suggesting here loosely correlates with Merleau-Ponty's use of chiasmus in *The Visible and the Invisible* as a figure for reversibility, for the constant oscillation in the self–other encounter that militates against fixed or dualistic separation.
3   Max embeds traces of Dougald's recounted father–son struggle within Gnapun's brotherly love for his victim, a complex that resonates with Mbembe's comment, cited by Moses: '... insofar as postcolonial theory has considered the struggle between Father and Son—that is to say, the relationship between coloniser and colonised—to be the most significant political and cultural paradigm in formerly colonised societies, it has tended to overshadow the intensity of the violence of brother towards brother and the status of the sister and the mother in the midst of fratricide' ('Time, Indigeneity', 12).

WORKS CITED

Ashcroft, Bill, Frances Devlin-Glass and Lyn McCredden. *Intimate Horizons: The Post-Colonial Sacred in Australian Literature.* Hindmarsh, SA: ATF Press, 2009.

Bennie, Angela. 'The Dirt that Lies Within Our Blood'. (Review of *Landscape of Farewell*). *Sydney Morning Herald,* 17 November 2007: Spectrum, 32.

Gelder, Ken and Jane M Jacobs. *Uncanny Australia: Sacredness and Identity in a Postcolonial Nation.* Carlton South, Vic: Melbourne University Press, 1998.

Gorton, Lisa. 'In the company of ghosts' (Review of *Landscape of Farewell*). *Age*, 10 November 2007: 23.

Johnston, Anna and Alan Lawson, 'Settler Post-Colonialism and Australian Literary Culture'. In David Carter and Wang Guanglin, eds *Modern Australian Literary Criticism and Theory.* Qingdao, China: China Ocean University Press, 2010, pp. 28–40.

McPhee, Hilary. 'Shadows that Cross Our Souls' (Review of *Landscape of Farewell*). *Australian*, 7 November 2007: Australian Literary Review, 5.

Merleau-Ponty, Maurice. *The Visible and the Invisible: Followed By Working Notes.* Claude Lefort, ed. Alphonso Lingis, trans. Evanston, Illinois: Northwestern University Press, 1968.

Miller, Alex. *Landscape of Farewell.* Sydney: Allen & Unwin, 2007.

———. *Prochownik's Dream.* Sydney: Allen & Unwin, 2005.

———. *Journey to the Stone Country.* Sydney: Allen & Unwin, 2002.

———. *The Ancestor Game.* Ringwood, Vic.: Penguin, 1992.

Moses, A Dirk. 'Time, Indigeneity, and Peoplehood: The Postcolony in Australia'. *Postcolonial Studies* 13.1 (2010): 9–32.

Pierce, Peter. 'The Solitariness of Alex Miller'. *Australian Literary Studies* 21.3 (2004): 299–311.

Swain, Tony. *A Place for Strangers: Towards a History of Australian Aboriginal Being.* Melbourne: Cambridge University Press, 1993.

Walker, Shirley. 'Agamemnon's Edict'. (Review of *Landscape of Farewell*). *Australian Book Review* (November 2007): 43–4.

Zavaglia, Liliana. 'Old Testament Prophets and New Testament Saviours: Reading Retribution and Forgiveness Towards Whiteness in *Journey to the Stone Country*'. In Robert Dixon, ed. *The Novels of Alex Miller: An Introduction.* Sydney: Allen & Unwin, 2012.

- 15 -

TRUSTING the WORDS:
Reflections on *Landscape of Farewell*

RAIMOND GAITA

When Robert Dixon invited me to speak at the conference that formed the basis of this book of essays I wondered whether to accept. Alex Miller is a dear friend whose writings I admire as I love and admire him, but I didn't know what I could contribute. As a philosopher, I'm not necessarily competent to offer critically appreciative comments of the kind a literary critic would; not at length, at any rate.

Nonetheless, for two reasons I chose to take a risk and to try to say something about *Landscape of Farewell* (2007). It was the first of Alex's books to be published after we became friends. That we should be dear friends was settled only months after we met when I asked Alex to help me shovel some mulch and to bring a gate to the property on which my wife and I had built a house eight years ago, less than half an hour's drive from Castlemaine where Alex and Stephanie Miller live. The pleasure we took in shared physical labour enabled us to recognise something in each other that has been fundamental to our friendship. Our house is in the country of my boyhood, in a part of Victoria that is spiritually important to me and has shaped my intellectual and moral sensibility. The importance that love of country can have in a life—how it can nourish and how it can corrupt it—has preoccupied my thoughts for many years. The same is true of Alex. His conversation and writings—especially *Journey to the Stone Country* (2002) and *Landscape of*

Farewell—deepened my understanding of it. I am grateful that it deepened in and because of our friendship.

Love of country in its many forms—in the many meanings of *country*—as Max Otto, the protagonist of *Landscape of Farewell* reminds us—is, one might be tempted to say, one of the things the book is about. I am, reluctant, however, to say that it is about that or really—I hope this doesn't sound carping—*about* anything. There is a plain enough sense in which one would say in response to the question, 'What is *Landscape of Farewell* about?', that it is about Max Otto, a German history professor who comes to learn, first through a young Aboriginal scholar, Vita McLelland, and then through her uncle, Dougald Gnapun, whom readers met in *Journey to Stone Country*, things he never dreamed he would, including things about what it means to write history. And so on. But to say that is just to sketch the story.

It would, of course, be pedantic to correct someone who asks what the book is about by saying that it is not about anything, but that one will nonetheless tell them some of the story. Why then do I make the distinction? Because the book gives us so much to meditate upon and because it is so reflective about its own themes, that to say it is *about* those themes invites the inference that Miller set out to write about them in order to express his opinions—about love of country, about the murderous impulses that appear to be part of human nature and that often issue in massacres and worse, about old age and about what it means to belong to a generation, to be between past and future, answerable to both. And much more. That would make the book vulnerable, in the wrong way, to correction by this or that academic discipline that is also concerned with such matters—by moral and political philosophy, anthropology, psychology, and of course history and the philosophy of history. Had the book been didactic in what it offers for mediation, then it would have been answerable to those disciplines. But it is not. I marvel at the fact that though one could spend a lifetime thinking about the book, there is not even a trace of didacticism in it. Just as Miller was drawn into his story, finding there and in its characters so much that surprised him, so this master storyteller draws the reader into the world of his story.

Max says that a good book is worth reading twice. *Landscape of Farewell*, I think, needs to be read at least three times. Or perhaps I should now speak only for myself. Reading it the first time, the suspense of the narrative so enthralled me that I skipped passages here and there, impatient to know what would happen. My eyes raced across the pages that told of Max's tragi-comic misadventures with Vita's goat, of the massacre of the white missionary family by the warrior Gnapun and his 'messengers' and of Max's journey with Dougald to his country, where the bleached bones of Gnapun, his great-grandfather, lie under an overhang and where Dougald becomes whole again before he dies. But, of course, in a novel as fine as *Landscape of Farewell* some passages compel one to stop. Some are short, as when Gnapun takes the fingers of the man he has slain 'gently in his own' (206). Some are longer, as, for example, Dougald's heartbreaking narrative about his father, deracinated and an alcoholic, who beat him almost every night because he knew that, of all his children, only Dougald could withstand the beatings, and that had it not been so, his father might have killed one of the other children in his rages. Or later in the novel, when Dougald tenderly expresses his need and gratitude to Max for writing the story of the massacre and for going with him to his country, to which 'his soul belongs' (260). One point of arrest constitutes a chapter in the book. It is called 'Winifred's Naked Shoulders'. In it Max remembers his dead wife, Winifred, undressing before she comes to their bed. She is a woman whose beauty developed as she grew older. The chapter is one of the most beautiful expressions of middle-aged erotic love that I have read.

Coming to the book a second time, I filled in gaps left in the first suspense-driven reading and, to a degree, took up the invitation to dwell on the many themes it offers for reflection, not yet fully aware of the gift I had been given.

Almost everyone who reads *Landscape of Farewell*, will, I am certain, be wonderstruck by how much it offers for meditation on the great matters of life—on sensuality, on the relations between human beings and animals, on spiritual relations to soil, to nation and to what Aborigines call country, on old age and its vanities and pathos, on the terrors of a child who wonders whether his father is guilty of terrible crimes. And, because the protagonist is a German academic historian who, through a series of accidents that he came to see as destiny, writes the story of a massacre by Aborigines of white Christian settlers who, with no thought or understanding, violated what was sacred to the Aborigines, we reflect on fate, on storytelling, on fiction and on history. But none of that is offered as though Miller intended it to be a contribution to debates about history and fiction as they were conducted when, for example, Kate Grenville wrote and then commented on the writing of her historical novel, *The Secret River* (2005).

The third reading took me to a more reflective appreciation of Miller's craft in the service of his art, but consistent with my opening disclaimer about my competence to comment on such matters I will say only that I often marvelled at his attention to detail and admired the way that enabled me to enter fully into the world of the novel. But to put it that way is to step back from the experience of reading. When I read the book for the first and the second time I didn't think of the detail as a gift from a superb craftsman to his reader: I felt as though I had been given new eyes and ears to appreciate a world I had never before encountered or to experience anew the world I had.

Landscape of Farewell is a reflective novel. It is reflective about the themes I mentioned earlier, and about literature and its relations to the discursive disciplines that are taught in universities. Miller is well read in many of those disciplines—in psychology, history and philosophy, for example—but his instinct against didacticism means that reflection within the novel is constrained by the disciplines of the novel. The novel cannot, in pursuit of a line of reflection, go into the details of political, philosophical or literary theory. But, of course, that is not true of the reader, who will take into her life the themes upon which Max and, differently, Miller as the author, meditate, and go wherever reflection appears to require her to go, caring only for the answers to the questions that it throws up for her.

That Miller is fully aware of this shows in Max's thoughts about what he did when he wrote his 'fiction' on the massacre for Dougald and about its relation to what he failed to do as a historian. Questions about the role of more discursive modes of thought are raised explicitly only in regard to history, but one takes them to have more general import for all the discursive disciplines that bear on his project to write about what it means for him to belong, as the German writer Bernhard Schlink puts it, to 'the second generation'. That generation grew to intellectual maturity in the aftermath of the Holocaust and, in the 1960s and 1970s, became fully aware of the political crimes and evils perpetrated by their parents and grandparents, and became entangled in their guilt. The 'second generation' defined itself by what it took to be its distinctive problem: how to respond clear-sightedly, politically and morally, to the discovery that someone you love or admire is guilty of the crimes of the Holocaust or was, in one of many possible ways, complicit in them.

Nothing about this, it is important to note, is resolved in *Landscape of Farewell*. Far from being a defect, this is one of the novel's cardinal virtues. Max doesn't know how he will write the book that he was all his academic life unable to write and is now liberated to try to write, having written the story of the massacre of the missionaries. One knows, though, that he will not find the answer by reading specialist texts on fiction and truth, or on fiction and non-fiction, or directly in the texts of any of the discursive disciplines. He will find it—if he does—only when he writes, or, as may happen, when he understands why he cannot write. He will succeed only if he finds the voice that shows that he has faced fully, with severe lucidity, the likelihood that his father was a Nazi war criminal. If he succeeds, what he will write will be different not only from the banal products of his academic career, but also from what he wrote about Gnapun. In both he wrote about massacres. The Holocaust was not a massacre, though many massacres occurred during it.

In *Landscape of Farewell*, there are two instances where a warrior speaks these chilling words: 'We are not going to leave a single one of them alive, down to the babies in their mothers' wombs—not even they must live. The whole people must be wiped out of existence' (12). The first time, they are spoken by Menelaus when he addresses the Greek troops before the sacking of Troy. The second time they are spoken by Gnapun. The massacres that were obedient to that chilling imperative were perpetrated for different reasons and in different spirits. Gnapun's merciless massacre of the missionaries—the spirit in which he enacts those terrible words—is consistent with his declaration that the leader of his victims is his brother and with the tender gesture when he takes the fingers of the leader of the slain missionaries in his own. It is inconceivable that Menelaus could be capable of such a sentiment or such a deed. Even so, his words and the deeds that expressed them resonate now for us in a different moral universe from the one in which the Wansee Conference announced the 'Final Solution' to 'the Jewish Problem'.

The Holocaust was different from massacres, partly because it was genocide, a crime different from mass murder—'the crime of crimes', as it has sometimes been called. Never, I think, has contempt for a people been expressed with such single-mindedness as during the Holocaust. Never before the Holocaust and never after it has there been such a relentless determination to wipe a people from as much of the earth as possible. That is one reason why the Holocaust is unique and why it is our paradigm of genocide. The Jews were murdered as though they were vermin, pollutants of the earth, and the nature and political enactment of that contempt distinguished it from the transitory hatreds that motivated other massacres, including the pogroms of Eastern Europe and Russia, and other genocides, such as the one perpetrated in Rwanda, where the Tutsis were murdered in the spirit of ridding the land of cockroaches. The Holocaust expressed a civic ideal, which, though it originated in war time, would have continued after the war if Germany had won it. Survivors of the Holocaust suffer the knowledge that the Holocaust originated in perhaps the most civilised nation in Europe, and that other great European nations were in different ways accomplices to it. That is different, I believe, from the terrible pain that comes from knowing, as the Tutsis came to know some years later, that those same civilised nations and others abandoned them to their murderers. It is different, I think, because more than all other genocides and persecutions, the Holocaust destroyed, or radically undermined in its victims, a sense of being at home in the community of nations and, indeed, in the world.

Max learns that the Holocaust is more than the worst of massacres by coming to understand the changing nature of his dread about what he might discover about his father: it changes from the boyhood fear that his father might not have 'acted decently' to the adult horror that he might have been involved in 'an evil beyond the reckoning of humanity' (227), evil beyond the reach of our conceptions of the ways people could fail to be decent. Max knows this, but even at the end of the novel he doesn't fully understand it. Miller makes clear to the reader, however, that despite—indeed because of—his newly found creative energies, his narrator is on a journey more terrible than he knows.

You may have noticed how naturally I have spoken of the crimes of the

Holocaust. I could have spoken of the crimes of the Hitler years, or the Third Reich. But to think of that period as defined by the crimes of the Holocaust is now second nature to us. It wasn't always so; indeed, as Tony Judt, among others, pointed out, when the genocide against the Jews and the gipsies was carried out, and for some years after, it mattered only to its victims (*Post War*, 2005). The dawning realisation in the 1960s, in Germany and elsewhere, of what really happened under the Third Reich had two aspects. The first could be revealed in film footage, in documents and in the facts revealed in trials and so on. I will call this knowledge of the facts, thinking of the concept of a fact as a judge does when she says to an emotional or theatrical witness, 'Stick to the facts, please.' Facts, in this workaday sense, are put in textbooks, accumulated in encyclopaedias, and can be learned in breathtaking numbers by whiz-kids.

As well as learning more of the facts, people were trying to understand the *meaning* of those facts. And, it is important to remember, we—everyone, and not only the Germans—are still trying. We still argue about how to understand the concepts of genocide and crimes against humanity. And we still argue about whether there is an aspect of the Holocaust that is different from and worse than those crimes, and which no legal or moral category can capture adequately. To understand the *meaning* of facts we turn to writers like Primo Levi, Elie Wiesel, Jean Amery and Hannah Arendt. Arendt's book *Eichmann in Jerusalem: A Report on the Banality of Evil* (1963) was one of the first, and to my mind is still one of the most profound, works to alert us to the importance—moral, legal and political—of understanding why genocide is a crime different and more serious than mass murder, even when mass murder involves more victims, and why it should be called a crime against humanity.

The distinction between a chronicle of facts and a narrative that discloses their significance, their human meaning, which, as my examples indicate, is not merely the distinction between fact and fiction, is shown to us in *Landscape of Farewell* when Max tells us of three different ways in which events may be recounted. One is orally, by a storyteller. Dougald tells Max the story that he asks him to write because he cannot. We know that Dougald has for years written reports for mining companies, so we have no reason to think he would find it difficult to write a chronology of the facts of the massacre.

But when, having read what Max writes, he exclaims with joy and gratitude that Max 'could have been there' (214), he does not mean that he reported accurately the facts of the matter as only an observer who had been there could. He means that he has written truthfully in a way that will not allow, as a chronicle of facts does, separation of form and content. Such writing can be fiction or non-fiction, but when it is non-fiction it must have the literary qualities that we find in Levi's or Amery's work.

Writing his 'fiction' liberates Max's creative energies and gives him a new understanding of the many ways one can write a truthful narrative of the past, but it does not necessarily ensure that he can now write what all his life he felt called upon to write. At the end of the novel we do not know whether he will be able to do it, but there are two things we do know: he will not steep himself in theoretical literature about the relation between history and fiction, or between fiction and non-fiction more generally; and he will write believing himself to be answerable, in imaginary conversation, to his father, his uncle and his mother, and to many people unknown, and that they are answerable to him.

When Max reflects on what he did when he wrote the story of the massacre of the missionaries, he wonders whether fictionalising it of necessity humanised the perpetrators. He imagines himself in conversation with the relatives of the slain missionaries, answerable to them for the way he portrays the perpetrators and the victims of the massacre. He tries to imagine what they would say and how he would respond. As with anything that seriously counts as conversation, no one knows how it will end.

This is a potent idea—the idea that we are answerable in imaginary conversations to people for the wrong we have done them or may contemplate doing. They may often haunt us because they belong to a general category—Germans, or Aborigines, for example—but they haunt us always as individuals, for it is only with individuals that we can seriously converse. No one in this circumstance can claim to be, impersonally, the voice of reason, or law or morality or truth. To make them strongly individuated presences is, of course, the novelist's art. Miller was, I am sure, like all fine novelists, surprised by his characters as they took on a life of their own. Nonetheless, it remains true that no matter how imaginative or empathic Max's rendering of the voice of the relatives of the missionaries is, they are not real voices, and so there is no real conversation, nothing that counts as really making oneself answerable to the individuated voice of another human being.

That may become clearer if we think of memoirs rather than novels. No matter how justly it is said of a memoirist that he brought his subject to life, if we wonder what his subject would say about this or that matter, we come across the stubborn fact that often we will not know, and that our failure is not a failure of any of our epistemic capacities, as though beings with far superior minds to ours could accurately predict what we can only guess at. That is what it means to possess the kind of individuality that we think is essential to our humanity and thereby to our sense of a common humanity. We express it when we say that all human beings are irreplaceable or when we exclaim with joy that at last we have found someone 'really to talk to', someone who, to put it as Kierkegaard did, reveals in her conversation that she has lived her own life and no one else's. But imagining a conversation cannot, even in a beautifully wrought novel, bring one into an encounter with a living individual. Martin Buber tells us why:

> Every attempt to understand monologue as fully valid conversation, which leaves unclear whether it, or dialogue, is the more original, must run aground on the fact that the ontologically basic presupposition of conversation is missing from it, the otherness, or more concretely, the moment of surprise. The human person is not in his own mind unpredictable to himself as he is to anyone of his partners; therefore he cannot be a genuine partner to himself, he can be no real questioner and no real answerer. (*The Knowledge of Man*, 113)

In one of the most moving passages in *Landscape of Farewell*, Gnapun tells his messengers that the leader of the people they will soon kill is his brother. They are puzzled—they have only 'a vague poetic sense of what Gnapun might mean' (199)—but we are told that they are confident that one day they will understand and that when they do they will assent to it. They trust his words to be wise words. It is essential to our concept of wisdom, as we distinguish it from knowledgeableness or expertise, that wisdom necessarily takes time to achieve and can only be achieved in living a life. It is also essential to the concept that we become wise only by living with others and learning from them, for there is no wisdom without understanding others, and we cannot understand others without being claimed in trust to them, to their deeds or their words, as the messengers are to Gnapun. We are claimed in trust to them because, like the messengers, we often do not understand everything that others say at the time they say it, and, like the messengers, we must allow what they say to enter our lives, to find, in its own time, ways to engage with what we already know and with our capacities—emotional, intellectual spiritual—for understanding.

For many people the Holocaust undermined—for some it destroyed entirely—the belief that all human beings and everything they do can be brought into the space of a common understanding that underpins our faith that we share with all people a common humanity. That, at any rate, is what people often seem to mean when they say that the Holocaust is mysterious, and that it will always defeat our attempts to understand it. They mean that the reason we cannot understand it is not a function of our ignorance, or our lack of imagination, that it is not something that could be remedied by an increase in whatever is needed to understand human beings and what they do—facts, psychology, history, sociology, imagination, empathy and so on. For people who think this way their bewilderment is not captured in the idea that the Holocaust severely stretched our sense of the conditions of a common humanity because it has stretched our knowledge of the terrible things that human beings can do to one another. For to say that it has stretched our understanding of human beings is to keep it within an enlarged sense of what belongs to our common understanding.

The reader has no difficulty, I think, in understanding that Gnapun should think of the people he will kill, mercilessly, as his brothers. Moving and inspiring though his example is, we accommodate it to our understanding of what human beings can do even as it deepens our sense of what it means to share a common humanity with them. Orwell said that in some circumstances one shows one's respect for someone by being prepared to kill them.

Landscape of Farewell does invite us to reflect on the evil that human beings can do, while at the same time showing us, in the quality of Max's dread when he realises that he may be entangled in 'evil beyond reckoning', that there are limits to our understanding, even in principle, of what they do and suffer. Thus, even when we are invited to reflect on our propensity for evil, to understand how deep it goes in us, we are never invited to take the perspective some people do when they quote Terence, the Roman dramatist, who said, 'I am man, nothing human is foreign to me.' They say that they can see in themselves all the possibilities of good and evil. I don't believe them because I never see real terror in their eyes or hear it in their voices. Of course, no one can say, 'I could never do such things.' But that is different from thinking that one can see in oneself, now, something from which such evil could issue.

There is a scene in *Landscape of Farewell* in which Max's father offers to help him with his mathematics homework. Max does not need help but he allows his father, as he has many times before, to believe that he does. Afterwards, while he is still working on his homework, his mother stands behind his chair and gently places her hands on his shoulders. She is, he says, expressing her gratitude to him for continuing with that fiction, because it enables them to sustain the more important lie that they are a normal family, with no terrible secrets that they keep from one another. She nurtures the conditions of their silence and secrecy within the home as though it were part of her normal duties (as then conceived) as a wife and mother to protect the psychological and moral security of her home as a place where her family can be assured of comfort. We know that she knows something but we do not know what she knows and how much she knows. Our attention has been on what Max might learn about his father. But in that scene, in a characteristically subtle way, Miller alerts us to the fact that Max does not fully comprehend how deeply he will grieve for his mother if he learns what he fears he will about his father.

Earlier I said that the lesson many people have taken from the Holocaust—that no one can say they could not do what ordinary Germans did—does not mean that they can find in themselves, now, a disposition to it or even something from which such a disposition might grow. In his early thoughts about his father, after he has been alerted by his uncle to the possibility that his father might be engaged in terrible activities during the war, Max tries to remember whether there is anything in the character and personality of his father that could make clear that he could or could not do terrible deeds, signs of a kind that someone who is psychologically acute might detect and that would reveal that his father had it in him to commit terrible crimes, at least in the circumstances of war. And we the readers are inclined to say that there *must* be something that will explain why a person was able to commit the terrible deeds that define the Holocaust, and that a novelist should try to reveal it. We feel that we must be able to say of such people, as Max is sometimes inclined to say about his father, and to a lesser degree about his mother, when he fears the worst, that we were mistaken about them when they engaged our sympathies, not merely because we did not know that they had committed terrible crimes, but because we did not know the aspects of their character and personality that enabled them to commit them.

The most terrible lesson of *Landscape of Farewell* is, I believe, that we are mistaken in our sense of how things must be. It's not just that we may not find anything: there may be nothing to find that would enable us to say justifiably that we were mistaken about such people. Those who love or admire them, ignorant of what they did or failed to do, are, of course, ignorant of something morally terrible, but not necessarily of anything substantive about their moral or psychological natures. There need be no facts of the kind we normally adduce to justify the claim that we had been mistaken to love or to admire someone.

Max is conscious of, and troubled by, the fact that he belongs to the generation of Germans that was confronted with terrible answers to the questions that had been forced on it by the revelations of the 1960s. His acknowledgement that he belongs to that generation is fundamental to his identity and to his sense of an obligation to write and to speak truthfully about what that means, an obligation to the past and to the future. But because the generality of the fact that he is a member of a generation defines his identity, his sense of the responsibility that developed from it is individuated. Thus, although he speaks as someone whose understanding of who he is has been constituted by the traumas of his generation, he speaks, necessarily, only for himself rather than for his generation.

When the facts about the Holocaust became known, many people, especially outside Germany, demanded indignantly that German children interrogate their parents about what they did or failed to do, or what they knew and didn't know. Though literally millions of people demanded this, it is astonishing that they thought they had the right to do it. No one, including German citizens, I believe, could justifiably say to a young German, in the name of a new Germany, in the name of the community of nations, or simply in the name of humanity, 'You must ask your parents and other beloved elders what they did, what they failed to do and what they knew.' Only someone with no understanding of how terrible the answer might be could do it.

In my abstract for the conference I said that because 'I am not a literary critic ... I won't comment in any detail on what strikes me as very fine writing—some of Miller's best, perhaps. I will discuss instead what I believe to be his great moral achievement in *Landscape of Farewell*: to have brought together in the one book a dramatic, fictional meditation on an Aboriginal massacre of whites and aspects of the Holocaust, each illuminating the other, but without doing anything that could properly be called comparing them, or weighing the gravity of one against the other. To do that requires, of course, great moral tact, but also much more.' In this essay, I have been trying to elaborate what I had in mind when I said 'much more'.

In the years since I first read *Landscape of Farewell*, I have done what Gnapun's messengers did: I have trusted Miller and his words, knowing them to be wise words, words that came from a deep understanding and love of humanity. I did not interrogate them. I allowed them to enter in their own way and time into my own feelings and thoughts about the Holocaust, about Australia's Indigenous peoples and about what it can mean to be terrified by the suspicion that someone one loves might be guilty of terrible crimes, by deed or by omission. It was, as I always knew it would be, trust rewarded.

WORKS CITED

Arendt, Hannah. *Eichmann in Jerusalem: A Report on the Banality of Evil.* London: Faber, 1963.

Buber, Martin. *The Knowledge of Man.* London: George Allen & Unwin, 1965.

Grenville, Kate. *The Secret River.* Melbourne: Text, 2005.

Judt, Tony. *Postwar: A History of Europe Since 1945*. London: Penguin Press, 2005.
Miller, Alex. *Landscape of Farewell*. Sydney: Allen & Unwin, 2007.
Schlink, Bernhard. *The Reader*. New York: Pantheon Press, 1997.

- 16 -

'BRIGHT TREASURES of PERCEPTION':
Writing Art and Painting Words in *Autumn Laing*

GEORDIE WILLIAMSON

One cool evening in 1938, Arthur Laing, a well-heeled Melbourne solicitor of artistic bent, arrives at his country home with a painter named Pat Donlon in tow. His wife, Autumn, has prepared rabbit pie and crème caramels in expectation of what she presumes will be a sophisticated, older guest. At first she is annoyed by the 'interesting bloke' her husband has phoned ahead to announce: he is young, working class, of Irish extraction, and his evident gracelessness makes him an awkward fit in the couple's cultured, patrician world.

It isn't long before Autumn Laing intuits the helplessness and doubt that lie beneath the young man's aggressive self-assertion, and changes her mind. He awakens maternal feeling in her and later—once she sees his portfolio, a series of nude studies of a butcher's fleshy daughter—a connoisseur's excitement at the discovery of an untutored yet original talent.

Scattered among the drawings, Autumn finds pages of poetry, pale imitations of Rimbaud. In a characteristically bold gesture she demands of Pat Donlon that he decide between poetry and art. When the young artist, taken aback, asks why he can't do both, her reply is so passionate that it may as well be a declaration of love: 'We can only give ourselves fully to any one thing. Art demands everything. Art is a woman, Pat. She is not kind to those who only give a part of themselves. She wants everything or nothing. She sees everything else as a betrayal' (212).

Those familiar with the story of Sidney Nolan's affair with Sunday Reed will know that something like this took place in reality. According to Reed's biographer, Janine Burke, Sunday sat Nolan down and read Rimbaud to him in the original French, requesting that he either write or paint in response to the words. By the end of a week it was apparently evident: Nolan was a painter not a poet (*The Heart Garden*, 190–1).

Alex Miller's tenth novel, *Autumn Laing* (2011), may follow the contours of real-life events, but its wider geography belongs to fiction. Yes, the author has kept the dynamic of this notorious relationship—Reed's superior social status balanced against Nolan's classless genius; her feminine ardour versus his masculine drive—and he has gifted the charmed circle of writers and artists at Heide (to give the bucolic home of the Reeds its proper name) the same earnest intensity it undoubtedly possessed. But history has been streamlined in the name of literature. Gone are the complicated ménages-à-trois and serial acts of adultery that characterised the Heide circle. Gone too are the war years during which Nolan, an army deserter, painted his Ned Kelly sequence while living with the Reeds. Characters and events have been rearranged, elided or expunged without compunction. The result is an appropriation of vulgar if high-toned gossip for the purposes of unrepentant art.

And Rimbaud? For much of the last century he was acknowledged as an apostle of symbolism, a destroyer of bourgeois pieties: a paradigmatic instance of the artist as Romantic genius. Most significantly for Miller's undertaking, he was also the young Sidney Nolan's hero and exemplar. It was his example the Australian painter followed in life and art. Rimbaud operates in *Autumn Laing* as a clasp between biographical fact and literary invention. That same copy of *Une saison en enfer* Reed used with Nolan sits on the shelves of the Laings' library. It is the book Autumn reads while awaiting the meeting that will change her life. Rimbaud survives the transposition of true life into fiction because the poet has something to offer beyond the rehearsal of fact: he is intertextual shorthand for the dangerous energy released by Pat Donlon and Autumn Laing's meeting and subsequent affair.

'Can one go into ecstasies over destruction and by cruelty be rejuvenated!' quotes Burke in *The Heart Garden*, her biography of Sunday Reed and Heide, in an attempt to locate a line of Rimbaud's that communicates the essence of his attraction for Nolan. Phrased as a question yet punctuated as an imperative, the fragment could easily serve as an epigraph for *Autumn Laing*. It captures the ambivalence of the story the author seeks to tell about a love affair that ennobles and damages those whom it touches. But it also clarifies the novel's thematic substance. For here is a fiction that explores nascent Australian modernism—a period of iconoclasm presented as a moment of artistic renewal—and asks whether a new art can be founded on violent acts of decreation, or if an avowedly extraterritorial artistic movement can be wedded to a specific instance of cultural nationalism.

None of this is new, of course. Alex Miller has spent the last twenty-five years pondering the relationship between art and life, often in an antipodean context. Never before, though, has he achieved a synthesis of the personal, political and aesthetic like that in *Autumn Laing*. Never before has Miller held in such perfect equipoise the mundane and the metaphysical aspects of his fictional project. Central to this achievement is the figure of Autumn Laing. It is her voice that controls the narrative—she ventriloquises her husband Arthur, lover Pat and his wife Edith, allowing them to speak in counterpoint—and it is her need to jettison the past in the final months of her life that grants the narrative urgency. Miller has written of his novel's genesis in terms of an aural hallucination, claiming that Autumn literally spoke into his ear (449). Her clarity and presence in these pages suggest the author was indeed captured for a time by his character's request. 'Your honour,' Autumn begs early on, 'I ask no more than to find the courage to tell his story and mine truthfully and in my own words. For this, imagination will be required. It is not fiction and truth that oppose each another. Fiction is the landscape beyond reality and has its own truth, the truth of our intimate lives. The place of empathy' (85–6).

Autumn will gain credibility as a character not via biographical means (her ontological proximity to the historical Sunday Reed), but through fictive vigour. When readers first meet her in the opening days of 1991, Autumn is eighty-five years old and the sole survivor of her milieu. She lives a twilight existence at the homestead of Old Farm (a suitably vague name for the real-world Heide) with an aged cat, piles of mouldering sketches and a cast of ghosts. She smokes when she can get away with it and lives on a diet of cabbages and gin.

Indeed, we discover her at a physical and emotional nadir: weary, brittle, imperious and still immured in grief. She mourns her oldest friend, Barnaby Green, dead by his own hand; Arthur, her long-suffering husband; and Pat Donlon, the painter whom she took as her lover soon after their first meeting and who eventually spurned her. And yet the shuttling back and forth of the narrative, between the twelve months of 1991 and the events of 1938 described above, allows the reader a larger view.

We see that Autumn's stubborn cantankerousness is in fact the residue of an earlier vivacity, and that the beautiful and wilfully bohemian daughter of Melbourne's aristocracy retains some inborn sense of entitlement and self-command. She will go on to describe a childhood and youth that occurs at a historical moment—the early decades of the twentieth century—when obedience to social proprieties (for women, at least) was unquestioned. We soon sense how formidable her powers of attack must have been to resist those antique prerogatives of class and gender.

Autumn, we understand, is a feral debutante: a woman once destined for a lifetime of childbearing and social adornment whose intelligence, instinctive aesthetic sense and (perhaps most significantly) intermittent mental instability have turned her against the world of her upbringing. As a young woman touring Europe, she contracted a sexually transmitted disease from a Roman psychiatrist employed to help her. It left her unable to conceive. Her procreative urges were instead channelled into the arts. Marriage to her kind and gentle partner allowed her to escape the strong pull of family and class. But the couple's wealth freed them to support emerging modernist artists of the era and, in doing so, strike a blow against the narrow philistinism of her caste.

However, that same impulse that leads her to become a muse and help-meet to these artists has other, harder and unsentimental aspects. That there is a ruthlessness in Autumn also, a sense that art's higher claims free one from the obligations of bourgeois morality, is brought home from the start. On a shopping trip to town described in the opening pages, Autumn glimpses Edith, a now-aged version of the innocent wife Pat Donlon abandoned in the midst of a pregnancy half a century previously to be with her.

That Edith should be the only other survivor of this time makes her both an *aide-mémoire* and a standing rebuke to Autumn's past actions. Certainly, this near-encounter stuns her into recollections whose roots are at once selfless and egotistic. 'There were those who never recovered from their encounter with him,' Autumn writes of Pat Donlon. 'And those who never understood him. And perhaps my deepest and hidden motive in writing this is not to deal with my guilt about the wrong I did to Edith but to discover if I am one of the ones who never recovered from him. The permanently damaged. Am I? (84)

Autumn Laing is the long answer to this question, and the story it tells is one that recalls Rimbaud in another, more specific way: his fiery relationship with the older poet Paul Verlaine. Their notorious liaison only lasted several years, but its effects were lifelong. For Rimbaud, it was a dynamic interlude that inspired *Une saison en enfer* and *Illuminations*, the poetry for which he is best remembered; for Verlaine, it led to madness and a prison term. Such was the terrible imbalance occasioned by such outsized passions described by Rimbaud's poetic father, Charles Baudelaire: 'Even though two lovers are deeply smitten and filled with reciprocal desire, one of the two will always be more calm, or less enraptured than the other. He or she is the surgeon, or the hangman; the other is the patient, the victim' (Baudelaire, 212).

The narrative of *Autumn Laing* proceeds as though this gloomy *fusée* were gospel truth. Indeed, it unfolds as a dramatic monologue on the nature of passion, in which the surviving partner of the affair has been shaped so profoundly by her experience that the rediscovery of her original form has taken a lifetime to achieve.

Hence the intermittently retrospective character of the novel. Only now, in the recent present, are the crucial events of her affair with Pat Donlon distant enough that Autumn's recounting of them has the requisite objectivity (though as with any trauma, time clarifies and isolates, but never diminishes the memory). It is a melancholy paradox that Autumn's sense of wounding should grow, even as her understanding of past events sharpens: 'There are certain moments in our lives when chance and mischance conspire either to elevate us to a new state of being, or which beat us down and leave us without hope of achieving our heart's desire' (382).

Autumn's account, from her first meeting with Donlon to the cruelly abrupt end of their affair, takes the form of a secular confession. 'Without him in whom I do not believe,' says Autumn, 'to write our story is the only hope of redemption left to me' (121). In this also, Autumn follows in the footsteps of those splenetic nineteenth-century poets, using words to negotiate the anxiety and guilt of a sinful self in a world without divine presence.

Such undertakings are by their nature heroic. And though the narrator takes some pleasure in presenting herself as a difficult and even rebarbative woman, Autumn's resolute narrative of self-disclosure eventually elicits our admiration; that, and a certain sympathy generated by the humiliations she suffers at the hands of the callow young doctor who treats her, a bossy hired nurse and, later, a live-in American biographer and art historian, Professor Adeli Heartstone, who cares for Autumn while hovering with apparently vulpine enthusiasm over the works that Donlon abandoned at Old Farm.

It is Adeli, though, who breaks the frame of the novel, allowing us to step outside of the narrative presented by Autumn and to judge its veracity. 'It is the plain truth only, I'm afraid, that Adeli looks for in her researches and not the poetry of a life' (215–16), warns Autumn, as though in pre-emptive anticipation of the 'Editor's Note' the Californian academic will furnish at the novel's conclusion: a brief statement that calls into question much of what Autumn has said in the hundreds of preceding pages. In the note, Adeli asserts that she was fictionalised and distorted by Autumn Laing in the pages of her memoir. She further explains that, contrary to Autumn's suggestion, the two women cooperated closely on the academic's researches into Pat Donlon's surviving artworks at Old Farm, and that Autumn did not in fact burn her diaries and day-books as she claimed, but gifted them to Adeli.

What purpose does it serve the author to include an afterword that muddies the clarity of the novel as a whole? As with the fictions of Vladimir Nabokov[1]—a touchstone author for Miller and the one who provides *Autumn Laing* with its epigraph[2]—such exercises in deception augment the narrator's legitimacy, not undermine it. To flag the fictive nature of the old woman's enterprise from a point of presumed objectivity has the effect of bolstering Autumn's subjective version of events: the second lie reinforces the truth of the first.

Indeed, *Autumn Laing* is a novel in which facts are forever being bent to larger metaphysical service. Pat Donlon, to take a central example, is described in warm and vivid terms; his inner life is informed by the same combination of arrogance and uncertainty that surely characterised his real-life model, and the rich texture of his lived experience is relayed in corresponding detail. Readers are appraised of the character's emotional states, the intricate involutions of his thought, and the quotidian data from which his daily round is constructed—all of it in a manner that we think of as typically realist.

In Miller's hands, however, mimesis is continually placed at the disposal of metaphor. When Arthur Laing attempts to identify the historical and aesthetic forces at work in Pat Donlon's art, as in the following passage, he blends personality with archetype: '"The new is always a little frenzied. A little afraid of itself. The new is driven by chance, by risk and by uncertainty. In seeking to establish itself, the new seeks to disestablish the old order. The new is apocalyptic and is forever exulting in the courage to court failure"' . . . (260).

Yet palpable presence is never subordinated to symbolic function in *Autumn Laing*. However tempting it may be to view Pat Donlon as modernism embodied or Autumn as mother to Donlon's wayward child—or to link Arthur's passivity and complaisance in the face of his wife and friend's illicit affair with a lack of artistic ambition and imagination—each figure's more expansive meaning is suggested through strictly realist means.

In other words, while representing a rich social history, characters are not severed from their distinct human traits. Throughout the long lunches and convivial weekend parties at Old Farm, during which a version of the Heide circle gathers together, didactic commentary is placed with deceptive casualness in the mouths of speechifying inebriates. Ideas are drunk like wine and exhaled like cigarette smoke in a philosophical questing indistinguishable from bohemian excess.[3]

A typical example, worth quoting at length, comes when Louis, an artist and member of the Laings' circle who is defiantly Eurocentric in his aesthetic views, rounds on Pat Donlon during a weekend party at Old Farm:

> 'You've rejected the conventional training of the artist not from some high disciplined principle, as you seem to claim . . . but from the commonplace need of youth to effect some kind of revolt against the elders. What you are doing is utterly traditional. That is what it is. That is all your wonderful revolt is, Patrick. It's commonplace. You know?

Ordinary. You have nothing to replace that which you've rejected. If you had, then what you say might be interesting. Either you'll soon see the error of your ways and re-enrol at the Gallery School, or you'll stop doing art altogether... Full stop! Your ideas, if I may say so, amount to very little. It takes enormous skill and heroic persistence to make something new in art. Either we follow Europe in this, or we Australians will fall by the wayside and remain a pointless backwater forever'. (301–2)

Louis, we understand, is drunk. The narrative alludes to his physical state ('Drink didn't suit him'), and other characters interrupt or offer ironic rejoinders to his speech in a manner that suggests the seriousness of his criticisms is being undermined by the nature of their delivery. The monologue is characterised by the repetitions and overly insistent manner we typically identify with drunken speech.

And yet Miller's authorial cunning works here by slipping into the narrative what in another context might be seen as an instance of didacticism, at a moment and in a manner that permits its disavowal as a well-lubricated rant. Throughout *Autumn Laing*—using conversations such as these, internal monologues, letters and journal entries—Miller conveys instruction and information without seeming to. He addresses matters of politics, art and metaphysics on the sly.

Whether discussions are concerned with a specific cultural moment (Meldrum-school tonalism, say, versus European modernism in Melbourne in the late 1930s), or the more abstract tensions existing between aesthetics and ethics, they operate simultaneously as embedded enunciations—relevant only to the revelation of character (mainly waspish and contentious when it comes to the Old Farm circle; in brutal earnest when it comes to Autumn and Pat)—and as explicit commentaries on world and idea. Indeed, Edith Donlon simultaneously operates as a distinct character, granted chapters of first-person narration (albeit in Autumn's imagination) and a walk-on role at the novel's conclusion, and as a walking exemplar for the kind of art that Pat, Autumn, and the entire Old Farm circle hold in contempt. It is her technically assured yet conservative landscape painting, gifted to the Laings, that serves a narrative function (working as a time capsule or *aide-mémoir* when recovered from the outbuilding where it has lain for decades) and as a point of aesthetic contention. Autumn's altered aesthetic response (one more generous in retrospect) is of a piece with her changed perspective on past events. It is a tribute to the author's economies that a character could be employed so variously.

So it is that arguments outlined in *Autumn Laing*, between nationalism and cosmopolitanism, established class structures and creative aristocracy, the sometimes incommensurable virtues of literature and the visual arts, and so on, represent orphaned opinions: summoned into being by the creative imagination of an author, who subsequently disclaims paternity. The novel as didactic vessel that Vladimir Nabokov decried as a 'baggy monster' is here embraced in such a way as to maintain the stylistic purity and personal intimacy of the work. The faithful picture of reality captured by *Autumn Laing* just happens to contain fragments that edify and inform.

This reticence in regard to placing the novel too obviously at the service of the socio-political actualities of the day has its roots in Miller's personal aesthetic. For him, story emerges first and foremost from the meeting of imagination with the world of the senses. If history is the objective recording of facts in the world, then the novel operates at the margin of existence as it is and a vision of the world as it could be. This truism may be old as the inauguration of the Romantic project, but it remains problematic today. Miller has written elsewhere of the complex interdependence between an artwork and its historical moment ('John Masefield's Attic', 260–72).

Just as Autumn sees herself obliged to perform at some imagined midpoint between outer life and inner emotional landscape ('There is a cruel symmetry in this. My life the skipping rope swung by these two thieves [biographer Adeli and lover Pat] at either end of it keeping me dancing to their tune in the middle' (231)), so too does Miller's novel position itself between the pure, writerly desire to *tell a story* with the necessity of plundering sullied reality for narrative material.

Viewed from this angle, *Autumn Laing* could be regarded as the love letter of a writer to the less messy, tangled, compromised endeavour of the visual arts (at least in its painterly, modernist tradition). In this telling, Pat Donlon holds in his hands a potential for transcendence unavailable to the novelist, tied as he or she is to the ground by words: incorrigibly referential, hopelessly concrete, cleaving always to the life of the tribe.[4]

Paradoxically, this is the point where Autumn's testimony most closely approximates the stated beliefs of her maker. She apologises on several occasions for the febrile prose from which her memoir is constructed, claiming in her defence that such a hectic, unpolished style is obedient to Pat Donlon's aesthetic diktats: 'I write with a pen. A fine felt-tip. And no rewriting. You're getting this just as it comes out, like toothpaste from the tube ... Rewriting is erasure. Like repainting. The thing gets muddy. Pat never repainted. He never refined a line. All Pat's works are first drafts' (82).

Autumn's recollections of this aspect of Pat Donlon's genius have an air of unfeigned humility. Her memories simply genuflect. 'He wasn't striving like the rest of them to get something fine and finished,' she recalls: 'He wasn't striving at all ... Pat was heeding his imagination without questioning the direction it offered him, following the prompts ... That is how he worked: dashing things off, to catch the fierce and true while it shone for him' (82–3).

And here is Miller in 'John Masefield's Attic', an essay written during the composition of *Autumn Laing*: 'Writing a novel is rewriting; it is a revisiting a familiar place time and time again and seeing it anew each time. Beginning the writing of a novel is entering a puzzle, a maze whose centre is unknown to the author' (263).

So how are we to square this essential position of Miller's with his painter's provocative words? 'Our unconscious motive in rewriting and repainting, he claimed, is always to conceal ourselves. The unbidden truth that stares at us, ugly and blemished. So we erase and rework in the name of art, in the name of refinement and perfection. And we do this not to reveal the reality of the thing, but to distract ourselves from the problems of depicting its reality. Art is the expert lie, he said' (84).

While the irony of Miller taking pains to shape such statements for the mouth of his creation is self-evident, the author's final position on such matters remains complicated, to say the least. Autumn lacks Pat Donlon's genius—all she possesses is what her beloved Uncle Mathew describes as 'the gift of recognition' (15)—and she distrusts the ability of language to encompass experience: 'Language is useful for a few restricted realities. But for the rest, for the life of the gods, language has nothing to say . . . Our blood, not our words, carries the message that compels us to submit . . .' (274).

However the notebooks from which the novel is constructed tell a different story. Whether Autumn's recollections are a series of spiritual meditations, or the secular psychoanalytic circling of a traumatic event—a contemporary instance of Tennyson's 'sad mechanic exercise'—the effort involved in providing testimony nonetheless grants her words a dimension missing from Pat Donlon's intuitive art, a dimension necessary to bringing an aspect of the artist's creation to light: 'I and he together made this country visible. To make my claim on his art and compose the testament of our truth. A testament without which his pictures must remain forever incomplete. Forever mute. Deaf and dumb to the posterity they inhabit' (8).

There is an abounding richness in the series of interrelations established by Miller in *Autumn Laing*. The bond between Laing and Donlon is characterised in terms of sexual passion, parental love, class struggle, gender roles: a whole panoply of human compacts, designed to reinforce the idea of a duality in which each party recognises some lack in the other and sets out to supply it.

These various interdependencies work dynamically within the novel, granting the narrative drama and drawing thematic connections between the lovers' earthy passions and the metaphysical underpinnings of art. But Autumn and Pat also enact the covenant between the author, imagination and reality that Miller explores in 'John Masefield's Attic', an essay in which the external world and the writer's inner life mysteriously combine with inchoate imagination to bring stories forth. It is only in the relation between these, Miller argues, that hidden facets of our existence are yielded up: 'Fiction bows to the imagination and bends the truth in order to get closer to it, and in bending the truth it creates distortions and transgressions, but it also arrives at perspectives on ourselves not otherwise available' (271).

Autumn stakes her claim on Pat Donlon and his art in *Autumn Laing*. She uses words and the necromancy of memory to bind the absent figure to her. That Alex Miller should be so polished and insightful in his realisation of her character only confirms how close his own experience has lain to hers.

Of course, any author must at some point lay claim over their local reality, the storehouse of their personal experience, if they are to produce authentic works of fiction. It is Miller's own biography, however—the uniqueness of his personal journey—that brings this process into sharper relief.

Which is to say: Alex Miller is unhomed. Where the Trinidadian-born Indian author VS Naipaul explores the alienation of those uprooted by the after-effects of colonialism, Miller uses his writings more positively, as a means of re-establishing a sense of *Heimat* (that untranslatable German word which refers at once to a site of geographic origin and to a metaphysical connection with place) in a new environment. This is not merely a 'literary' undertaking but a knitting together of lived experience, memory, people and place using the artwork as a ontological frame. The philosopher Martin Heidegger suggested that the work of art performs three functions: it *manifests*, *articulates* and *reconfigures* the style of a culture from within that culture. Miller's fictions may be seen as a series of contextualising texts in which the equipment, roles and practices that delineate the world in which the author discovers himself, are rendered intelligible—and thus habitable. His upbringing in London as the child of an Irish mother and Scottish father, his arrival in Australia as a teenager without his family in 1952, his subsequent years as a stockman and rural labourer, his relatively late turn to tertiary education in preparation for becoming a novelist: all these experiences served to separate the future author from unconscious or easily assumed affiliations, whether towards class, nation or intellectual caste. Where a self is aligned closely with a particular environment and milieu from its earliest beginnings—as in pre-modern rural England or Aboriginal Australia—culture (in its widest sense) may be seamlessly inculcated. But where an individual has suffered dislocation of some kind, an exile's more agonised, provisional attitude towards people and place may be discerned.

The particular difficulties faced by émigré writers in the postwar era have been outlined by Naipaul with singular, melancholy eloquence. Miller approvingly refers to Naipaul's biographical writings and has borrowed key expressions from the older writer—such as 'finding the centre'—to describe his fictional method ('John Masefield's Attic', 262–3). What Miller does not share is Naipaul's notorious disdain for the geographic, cultural and racial periphery of the Anglosphere, and his concomitant valorisation of the Imperial centre.

Miller has instead concentrated on using language to discover the world anew. Culture for him is not only the vast accretion of preceding texts that describe reality at second-hand (though his prose style is consciously informed by earlier writers and admired coevals); rather, it emerges from the individual effort of the author to apprehend the world as it is, with an unblemished eye.

To a degree rare in contemporary fiction, Miller's novels have been shaped by an elemental vision of nature and our place in it. From the atavism of the hunt in *The Tivington Nott* to the maternal imperative that drives *Lovesong*, it is Miller's attentiveness to the material, physical and literal grounds of existence that sets his fiction apart. The envisioning of Australia undertaken by Miller (whether directly or indirectly) throughout his fictions is not diminished by the continent's relatively slender cultural productions; it is challenged and enlivened by the freedoms such open ground offers to the clever and the industrious.

The figure of Pat Donlon is only partly emblematic of Miller's particular fictional project—his efforts to write a distinct Australian culture into being without allowing the deep, specific history of the language he uses to deform those efforts. Rather he serves as an ideal extension of that project: a hound able to hunt where his master may not. Donlon's peculiar genius is to create independently of the rules established by older, more prominent cultures. His intuitive eye and improvisational skills are perfectly designed to bring a fresh world into being through the paintbrush or the pen. That the author's vivid portrait of the artist is reliant on more dogged and pedestrian effects, that Miller's words should necessarily be spoken by the more earthbound (by gender, by fidelity to local culture and place) Autumn Laing only reinforces the complex interrelations that shape Miller's novel. For the writer and the artists, like the painter and muse, writer and artist all have their part to play in the act of creation: 'For we must go on in our search for truth and justice; collecting a bit of this and a bit of that, each morsel connected in some way to the invisible circuit from which the expression of our sense of ourselves and our culture is slowly (and painfully) fitted together' (427).

NOTES

1. *Lolita* (1955), Nabokov's best-known novel, opens with a faux-forward by Humbert Humbert's psychologist John Ray, who presents the main body of the narrative as the case study of a pervert.
2. 'The most enchanting things in nature and art are based on deception.' From *The Gift*.
3. The circle of artists and writers who make up the Old Farm group are more faithful reflections of their real-world counterparts than *Autumn Laing*'s central figures. Barnaby, for instance—Autumn's boon companion—closely approximates Barrett Reid, the Queensland-born poet and editor who was closely associated with the Reeds and Heide from 1947 until his death at the property in 1985. Cameos by Albert Tucker, Joy Hester, and the Australian-Israeli artist Yosl Bergner, along with other notable figures, appear with only a light fictional overlay. Miller evidently enjoys recreating the vibrancy of their group discussions. But Autumn herself is not illusioned as to their potential to operate as a closed, clannish and self-regarding clique. In her recollection, the circle consisted of those 'trapped in an invisible web of disdain for the rest of humankind, bewitched by their own way of talking and their vain egotism' (329).
4. Stephane Mallarmé wrote of the poet's undertaking as cleansing the words of the tribe: 'Donner un sens plus pur *aux mots de la* tribu.'

WORKS CITED

Baudelaire, Charles. *Baudelaire: His Poetry and Prose*. New York: Modern Library, 1919.

Burke, Janine. *The Heart Garden: Sunday Reed and Heide*. Sydney: Random House, 2004.

Miller, Alex. *Autumn Laing*. Sydney: Allen & Unwin, 2011.

——. 'John Masefield's Attic'. In Robert Drewe, ed. *The Best Australian Essays 2010*. Melbourne: Black Inc., 2010.

FURTHER READING

WORKS BY ALEX MILLER

The Novels

Miller, Alex. *Autumn Laing*. Sydney: Allen & Unwin, 2011.

——. *Lovesong*. Sydney: Allen & Unwin, 2009.

——. *Landscape of Farewell*. Sydney: Allen & Unwin, 2007.

——. *Prochownik's Dream*. Sydney: Allen & Unwin, 2005.

——. *Journey to the Stone Country*. Sydney: Allen & Unwin, 2002.

——. *Conditions of Faith*. Sydney: Allen & Unwin, 2000.

——. *The Sitters*. Ringwood, Vic.: Viking, 1995.

——. *The Ancestor Game*. Ringwood, Vic.: Penguin, 1992.

——. *The Tivington Nott*. London: Robert Hale, 1989.

——. *Watching the Climbers on the Mountain*. Sydney: Pan, 1988.

Essays, Stories and Interviews

Bugeja, Tony. 'The Interview: Alex Miller'. *Wet Ink* 5 (2006): 26–8.

Caterson, Simon. 'Playing the Ancestor Game: Alex Miller Interviewed by Simon Caterson'. *Journal of Commonwealth Literature* 29.2 (1994): 5–11.

Daniel, Helen. 'An Interview with Alex Miller'. *Australian Book Review* 170 (May 1995): 44–6.

Hard, Lynn. 'Alex Miller is interviewed in his home in Port Melbourne by Lynn Hard'. *AdFlicks. Interviews with Authors.* Canberra: Australian Defence Force Academy, 1994.

Miller, Alex. 'Call of the Wild'. *Weekend Australian*, 23–24 October 2010: 22–3.

——. 'The Last Sister of Charity'. In *Heart Matters: Personal Stories About That Heart-Stopping Moment*. Peter Corris and Michael Wilding, eds. Camberwell, Victoria: Viking, 2010.
——. 'Manuka'. In *10 Short Stories You Must Read in 2010*. Maggie Alderson, ed. Surry Hills, NSW: Australia Council, 2010.
——. 'She Imagined Him Back from a Long Journey, So Long He Had Forgotten Her'. *Age*, 6 January 2010: 18.
——. 'Open Page: Alex Miller'. *Australian Book Review* 315 (2009): 64.
——. 'Waxing Wiser Than Oneself'. *Australian Literary Review* 4.9 (2009): 24–5.
——. '70s'. *Age*, 9 August 2008: 13.
——. 'In the End It Was Teaching Writing'. *Australian Literary Review* 3.2 (2008): 17.
——. 'Salem Lodge'. *Meanjin* 67.3 (2008): 151–8.
——. 'Nothing Will Silence It'. In *What Difference Does Writing Make?: Leading Writers on Writing*. Helen Sykes, ed. Albert Park, Vic.: Future Leaders, 2007.
——. 'Ashes'. In *The Best Australian Stories 2006*. Robert Drewe, ed. Melbourne: Black Inc., 2006.
——. 'Ringroad'. *Southerly* 66.2 (2006): 145–51.
——. 'Written in Our Hearts'. *Weekend Australian*, 16–17 December 2006: 8–9.
——. 'Dual Miles Franklin Award Winner Alex Miller Goes in Search of Australia's Heartland'. *Age*, 29 May 2004: 1, 4.
——. 'Prophets of the Imagination'. In *Ngara: Living in This Place Now*. John Muk Muk Burke and Martin Langford, eds. Wollongong, NSW: Five Islands Press and The Poets Union, 2004.
——. 'The Artist as Magician'. *Meanjin* 62.2 (2003): 41–7.
——. 'The Other Man (from the Other Man, a Work-in-Progress)'. *New Literatures Review* 40 (2003): 6–16.
——. 'Sweet Water'. *Bulletin*. 16 December 2003–13 January 2004: 100–04.
——. 'Travels with My Green Man'. *Weekend Australian*, 31 May–1 June 2003: 4–5.
——. 'Destiny's Child'. *Age*, 3 August 2002: 6.

——. 'A Letter to a New York Friend'. *Meanjin* 61.1 (2002): 182–5.
——. 'Speaking Terms'. *Eureka Street* 11.3 (2001): 16.
——. 'Friendships, Good Government, Free Speech and the Writer's Voice'. In *Chinese Cultures in the Diaspora: Emerging Global Perspectives on the Centre and Periphery*. Julie Hsia Chang, Zhizhang Zhang and Kee Pookong, eds. Taipei: The National Endowment For Culture and Arts (Taiwan), 1997.
——. 'Impressions of China'. *Meridian* 15.1 (May 1996): 85–9.
——. 'Why I'm Falling in Love with Madame Du Terre'. *Sydney Morning Herald*, 18 May 1996: 9s.
——. 'My First Love'. *Age*, 18 March 1995: 3–4.
——. 'Rollover'. In *Books, Death and Taxes*. DJ O'Hearn, ed., Ringwood, Vic.: Penguin, 1995.
——. 'The Limits of Democracy'. *Eureka Street* 4.4 (1994): 29–32.
——. 'Chasing My Tale'. *Kunapipi* 15.3 (1993): 1–6.
——. 'In Touch with the Displaced'. *Sydney Morning Herald*, 20 November 1993: 13A.
——. 'Not the Last Word: Training for the Afterlife'. *Age*, 4 September 1993: 7.
——. 'The Wine Merchant of Aarhus'. *Kunapipi* 15.3 (1993): 7–11.
——. 'This is How It's Going to Be Then'. *Australian Book Review* 127 (December; January 1990): 30.
——. *Exiles*. Melbourne: Australian Nouveau Theatre, 1981.
——. *Kitty Howard: A Play*. Melbourne: Melbourne Theatre Company, 1978.
——. 'How to Kill Wild Horses'. *Quadrant* 20.2 (1976): 58–62.
——. 'Comrade Pawel'. *Meanjin Quarterly* 34.1 (1975): 74–85.

WORKS ABOUT ALEX MILLER: A SELECTION OF CRITICAL ESSAYS

Brennan, Bernadette. 'Literature and the Intimate Space of Death'. *Antipodes* 22.2 (2008): 103–9.
Dixon, Robert. 'Cosmopolitan Australians and Colonial Modernity: Alex Miller's *Conditions of Faith*, Gail Jones's *Black Mirror* and A.L. McCann's *The White Body of Evening*'. *Westerly* 49 (2004): 122–37.
Dorgelo, Rebecca. 'Frontier Violence and the Power of the Sacred: Alex Miller's *Journey to the Stone Country* and *Landscape of Farewell*'. In

Frontier Skirmishes: Literary and Cultural Debates in Australia after 1992. Russell West-Pavlov and Jennifer Wawrzinek, eds. Heidelberg: Universitätsverlag Winter GmbH Heidelberg, 2010.

Huang, Yuanshen. 'The Ancestor Complex: The Theme of *The Ancestor Game*'. In *A Unique Literature: A Critical View of Australian Literary Works*. Yuanshen Huang, ed. Chongqing, China: Chongqing chu ban she, 1995.

———. 'The Ancestor Complex: A Reading of *The Ancestor Game*'. *Meridian* 15.1 (May 1996): 90–100.

Jacobs, Lyn. 'Ancestral Furies: The Fiction of Beth Yahp, Ding Xiaoqi and Alex Miller'. *New Literatures Review* 28–29 (1994): 153–64.

Jorgensen, Mette. 'Readings of Dialogue in Alex Miller's *The Ancestor Game*'. *Kunapipi* 15.3 (1993): 12–20.

Liu, Yun-qiu. 'Journey of Self-Salvation of Soul: Interpretation of Alex Miller's *Landscape of Farewell*'. *Journal of Xihua University* 29.5 (2010): 115–19.

Mullaney, Julie. '"This Is Dog Country": Reading Off Coetzee in Alex Miller's *Journey to the Stone Country*'. *Postcolonial Text* 4.3 (2008).

Pan, Zijie. 'The Chinese Man in *The Ancestor Game*'. *Southerly* 67.3 (2007): 96–110.

Pierce, Peter. 'The Solitariness of Alex Miller'. *Australian Literary Studies* 21.3 (May 2004): 299–311.

Rolfe, Patricia. 'The Lore of the Land'. *Bulletin*. 16 December 2003–13 January 2004: 100–4.

Sellick, Robert. 'Alex Miller: Games and Puzzles.' In *A Talent(Ed) Digger: Creations, Cameos, and Essays in Honour of Anna Rutherford*. Hena Maes-Jelinek, Gordon Collier and Geoffrey V. Davis. Amsterdam: Rodopi, 1996.

Stockdale, Jacqueline. '"I Dreamed of Snow Today": Impediments to Settler Belonging in Northern Queensland as Depicted in a Selection of Recent Fiction'. *Etropic: Electronic Journal of Studies in the Tropics* 9 (2010).

CONTRIBUTORS

David Brooks is a poet, novelist, short fiction writer and essayist, and Associate Professor of Australian Literature at the University of Sydney, where he is also Director of the Graduate Program in Creative Writing, and managing co-editor of *Southerly*, the premier journal of Australian writing. He is a vegan and an animal rights advocate. Amongst his current projects is a volume of essays on animal/human relations with John Kinsella. His most recent publication is *The Sons of Clovis: Ern Malley, Adoré Floupette and a Secret History of Australian Poetry* (University of Queensland Press, 2011), a comprehensive revision of the accepted story of the Ern Malley hoax.

Frank Budby is an elder of the Barada people whose traditional country is in the northern Central Highlands of Queensland. A former drover and stockman, more recently he founded a major consultancy business (Woora Consultancies) which employs Barada (and the closely allied Barna) people to manage cultural heritage on the numerous coal mines in their country. Frank lives between Mackay and Nebo in Central Queensland. He is also concerned with the current registered native title claim by Barada Barna people over their traditional country.

Adrian Caesar was Associate Professor of English at the University of New South Wales at the Australian Defence Force Academy until 2004. More recently, he has taught Creative Writing part-time at the Australian National University while concentrating on his own writing. He is the author of several books of literary criticism, including *Dividing Lines: Poetry, Class and Ideology in the 1930s* (Manchester University Press, 1991) and *Taking it Like a Man: Suffering, Sexuality and the War Poets* (Manchester University Press, 1993). His non-fiction novel, *The White* (Picador, 1999) won the Victorian Premier's Award for non-fiction and the ACT Book of the Year in 2000. He has also published four books of poetry, including his latest publication, *High Wire* (Pandanus Press, 2005).

ROBERT DIXON FAHA is Professor of Australian Literature at the University of Sydney and a judge of the Miles Franklin Literary Award (2004–2009). His most recent books are *Photography, Early Cinema and Colonial Modernity: Frank Hurley's Synchronised Lecture Entertainments* (Anthem, 2011); *The Diaries of Frank Hurley 1912–1941* (Anthem, 2011), co-edited with Christopher Lee; and *Republics of Letters: Literary Communities in Australia* (Sydney University Press, 2011), co-edited with Peter Kirkpatrick.

RAIMOND GAITA FAHA is Professorial Fellow in the Melbourne Law School and the Faculty of Arts at the University of Melbourne and Emeritus Professor of Moral Philosophy at King's College London. His books include: *Good and Evil: An Absolute Conception*, *Romulus: My Father*, *A Common Humanity: Thinking About Love and Truth and Justice*, *The Philosopher's Dog*, *After Romulus*, and as editor and contributor, *Gaza: Morality Law and Politics*, *Muslims and Multiculturalism*, and with Alex Skovron and Alex Miller, *Singing for All He's Worth: Essays in Honour of Jacob G. Rosenberg*.

ELIZABETH HATTE was born and raised on cattle stations in the Queensland Central Highlands. She holds degrees in Classics and archaeology from the University of Queensland and La Trobe University. She worked as a teacher in England and Melbourne before returning to North Queensland to teach and practise archaeology. She was one of the founders of the first archaeological survey company in Townsville. Since then she has completed hundreds of cultural surveys in association with Aboriginal traditional owners from Cape York to the Central Highlands.

ANITA HEISS is a member of the Wiradjuri nation of central New South Wales and a writer, poet, activist, social commentator and academic. She is author of *Dhuuluu-Yala: Publishing Aboriginal Literature*, *Paris Dreaming* and *Who Am I?: The Diary of Mary Talence*. She won the 2004 New South Wales Premier's History Award (audio/visual) for *Barani: The Aboriginal History of Sydney*. Anita is co-editor of the *Macquarie PEN Anthology of Aboriginal Literature*.

COL MCLENNAN is an elder of the Jangga people whose traditional country lies north of the Barada. Col was born and raised on his grandmother's cattle station near Mount Coolon township and he became a champion rodeo rider and stockman, travelling widely around Queensland. He founded Jangga Operations, which manages cultural heritage on Jangga country and negotiates agreements with mining companies on behalf of his people. He also oversees work on the registered Jangga native title claim.

ELIZABETH MCMAHON is a senior lecturer at the University of New South Wales where she teaches Australian literature and critical theory. She is also co-editor of *Southerly*, Australia's oldest literary journal, and with Brigitta Olubas edited *Remembering Patrick White: Contemporary Critical Essays* (Rodopi, 2010). Her current research on Australia's geographical imaginary is published in a range of international journals, including *Space and Culture* (2010), *Political Geography* (2011) and the *Island Studies Journal* (2011).

BRIGITTA OLUBAS is a senior lecturer in English at the University of New South Wales. She has published widely on Australian literary and visual culture and recently edited *Remembering Patrick White: Contemporary Critical Essays* (Rodopi, 2010) with Elizabeth McMahon. She is vice-president of ASAL (Association for the Study of Australian Literature) and co-editor of the Association's journal *JASAL*. Her critical study of Shirley Hazzard will be published by Cambria Press in 2012.

PETER PIERCE is Honorary Research Fellow and Professor at Monash University. From 1996–2006 he was Professor of Australian Literature at James Cook

University. He was a Chief Judge of the Prime Minister's Literary Award for Fiction from its inception in 2008 until 2011. His most recent publication—as editor—was *The Cambridge History of Australian Literature* (2009).

BRIGID ROONEY is a senior lecturer in Australian Literature at the University of Sydney. Most recently, she is the author of *Literary Activists: Writer-Intellectuals and Australian Public Life* (University of Queensland Press, 2009), and has published essays in Australian literary journals on the works of such contemporary Australian writers as Christina Stead, Patrick White, David Malouf and Helen Garner.

RONALD A SHARP is Professor of English at Vassar College, where he was Dean of the Faculty from 2003 to 2008. Before he came to Vassar he was Acting President, John Crowe Ransom Professor of English, and Provost of Kenyon College, where he was also editor of the *Kenyon Review*. Sharp is the author or editor of six books, including *Keats, Skepticism, and the Religion of Beauty*; *Friendship and Literature: Spirit and Form*; *Reading George Steiner* (with Nathan A Scott, Jr); *The Persistence of Poetry: Bicentennial Essays on John Keats* (with Robert M Ryan); and *Selected Poems of Michael S. Harper*. With the late novelist and short-story writer Eudora Welty, he edited *The Norton Book of Friendship*.

INGEBORG VAN TEESELING is a PhD candidate at the University of Wollongong, looking at the work of English-speaking migrant writers. As a journalist in the Netherlands, she wrote two Dutch non-fiction books: *Never Enough: Adult Children on Their Fathers* (Atlas, 1996) and *The Eye of the Storm: Victims in Action* (Veen, 2001).

BRENDA WALKER has written four novels, the most recent of which, *The Wing of Night*, won the 2006 Nita B Kibble Literary Award and the 2007 Asher Literary Award, and was shortlisted for the Miles Franklin Literary Award. Her memoir, *Reading by Moonlight*, in which she describes a personal connection between literature and healing, was the winner of the 2010 Victorian Premier's Literary Award for non-fiction and the 2011 Nita B Kibble Literary

Award. She is Winthrop Professor of English and Cultural Studies at the University of Western Australia.

SHIRLEY WALKER has lectured in Australian literature here and overseas (notably in Spain) for many years and is now an Honorary Research Fellow at the University of New England. Her most recent books are *Roundabout at Bangalow: An Intimate Chronicle* (University of Queensland Press, 2001), and *The Ghost at the Wedding* (Penguin, 2009). The latter was co-winner of the Asher Literary Award (2009) and winner of the Nita B Kibble Literary Award (2010).

GEORDIE WILLIAMSON is chief literary critic of the *Australian* and winner of the 2011 Pascall Prize for critical writing.

ELIZABETH WEBBY AM FAHA was Professor of Australian Literature at the University of Sydney from 1990 until her retirement in March 2007. Her publications include *Early Australian Poetry* (1982), *Colonial Voices* (1989), *Modern Australian Plays* (1990), *The Cambridge Companion to Australian Literature* (2000) and, as joint editor, *Happy Endings* (1987), *Goodbye to Romance* (1989), *The Penguin Book of Australian Ballads* (1993), *Australian Feminism: A Companion* (1998) and the Academy Edition of Rolf Boldrewood's *Robbery Under Arms* (2006). She was a contributing editor, responsible for the nineteenth-century material, for the *Macquarie PEN Anthology of Australian Literature* (2009).

LILIANA ZAVAGLIA is a PhD candidate at the University of Sydney. She is writing on ambivalent cultural desires of apology and apologia in Australian novels of reconciliation published in the years following the Australian High Court's Mabo decision of 1992.

INDEX

Adorno, Theodor 190, 213
Allen & Unwin x, 14
Amor, Rick x, 9, 12–13
Anderson, Amanda 15
Anthill Theatre Company ix, 6–7
Aplin, Morris 31, 56
apology, the (13 February 2008) 19, 26, 157, 174, 184, 193
Araluen viii–ix, 4–6, 22, 98
Arendt, Hannah 24, 223
Aristotle 90–1, 133–4
art and writing (see ekphrasis)
Ashcroft, Bill 3, 26, 204–5
Attwood, Bain 172
Augustus Downs viii, 4

Bail, Murray 21
Bao Chien-hsing 8
Barada, the x, 18, 36, 139–55
Barbara Ramsden Award x, 8
Barlow, Annette 14
Baudelaire, Charles 235
Beijing xi, 8, 119
Bhabha, Homi K 73
Bicentenary, the 19
Black, Shameem 26
Blanchot, Maurice 13, 78, 135
Blatt, Max viii, 4–6, 9, 22, 23, 30–1, 102
Blatt, Ruth, viii, 4, 9, 31
Bloch, Ernst 3, 26

Bolt, Andrew 21
Brady, Veronica 13, 92–3
Braille Award x, 39
Brennan, Bernadette 78–9
Bringing Them Home (Report) 19, 174
Broinowski, Alison 115
Brooks, David 20
Brunswick Technical School ix, 6, 8
Buber, Martin 225
Budby, Frank x, 18–20, 35–8, 139–55, 171
Burke, Janine 232

Caesar, Adrian 13–14
Carter, Paul x, 39, 69
Castlemaine x, xi, 6, 217
Clark, Lorna 180
Clark, Manning 62
Clendinnen, Inga 19–20, 23, 158
Commonwealth Writers' Prize x, 1, 8, 21, 158
Conrad, Joseph 156
Cullin-la-Ringo massacre, 18–19, 37–8, 61–4, 145–6, 162–4, 213

Damrosch, David 24
Davidson, Jim ix
Davis, Peter ix
Deleuze, Gilles 126–7
Derrida, Jacques 6, 134, 172, 188, 194

Dixon, Robert 146, 179
Donne, John 126–8

ekphrasis (writing about art) 12–14, 24, 78–88, 89–100, 101–13, 188, 231–44
Esau, Erika 116
Euchre in the Bush (painting by JCF Johnson) 12, 115–16
Evans, Raymond 146
Exmoor 3, 7, 31–2, 39, 55, 67, 209

Frankenberg, Ruth 69
Freud, Sigmund 130, 193

Gaita, Raimond 20, 24, 26–7
Gelder, Ken 204
Gillis, John 127–8
Glenroy Technical School ix, 7
Goathlands Station viii, 3
Grasby, Al 68, 75
Grenville, Kate 20–3, 158, 220
Gulf of Carpentaria viii, 7, 31–2, 55
Gunew, Sneja 68–70
Gympie viii, 3

Hamburg xi, 18, 36–7
Hangzhou ix, 8, 9
Hatte, Elizabeth (Liz) ix, x, 17–20, 35–6, 139–55, 171, 179–80
Heffernan, James 94
Heide x, 9, 13, 231–44
Heiss, Anita xi, 18–19, 36–7, 63, 139–55
Hemensley, Kris ix, 7
History Wars, the 19–23, 26–7, 146, 156–69, 170–86, 220
Hollander, Elizabeth 94
Holmesglen College of TAFE ix, 7, 17, 31
Holocaust, the 18–19, 24, 37, 106–8, 112–13, 134, 156, 168, 174–5, 190, 213, 217–30
Hornet Bank massacre, 62, 157–8
Huggan, Graham 70, 174–5

Jacobs, Jane 204
Jangga, the x, 18, 36, 139–55, 172, 179–80

Jolley, Elizabeth 71
Jones, Gail 172, 175
Jose, Nicholas 8
Judt, Tony 223

Keen, Suzanne 53
Kelly, Max viii, 4
Kristeva, Julia 188
Kundera, Milan 25

LaCapra, Dominick 21, 172, 180, 182, 184
Lawrence, DH 101
Lever, Susan 66
London viii, x, xi, 2–3, 7, 8, 18, 33, 39, 56, 66
Lynch, Sandra 134–5
Lyotard, Jean-François 127–8, 131, 134

Mabo decision, the 19
McEwan, Ian 51
McLennan, Col x, 18, 35–6, 139–55, 179–80
McMahon, Elizabeth 25
Manne, Robert 21
Marr, David 1
Meanjin ix
Melbourne viii, ix, xi, 4, 5, 6, 9–10, 16, 30–1, 36, 140–1
Melbourne Theatre Company ix, 6
Menand, Louis 46
metaphor 90–9
Mignon, Jean-Pierre ix, 6
migrancy 66–77
Miles Franklin Literary Award x, xi, 1, 8, 18, 66, 156, 203
Millar, Alexander McPhee (father) viii, ix, 2–3, 12, 33–5, 38–9, 66–7
Millar, Winifred (mother) viii, 2, 33–4
Miller, Alexander McPhee (Alex), works of
  The Ancestor Game ix, x, 1, 3, 5, 6, 8–12, 13, 14, 17, 21, 22, 23, 24, 30, 32–3, 38, 45–6, 67, 71–4, 83, 114–24, 128–36, 188, 201

255

Miller, Alexander McPhee (Alex), works of (*cont.*)
　Autumn Laing xi, 1, 2, 38–40, 231–44
　The Central Queensland novels 4, 7, 17–27, 35–8, 61–4, 139–55, 156–69, 170–86, 187–200, 201–16, 217–30
　'Chasing My Tale' 13, 89–90, 123, 129, 136
　'Comrade Pawel' ix, 5–6
　Conditions of Faith x, 14–16, 17, 22, 33–4, 38, 63, 120–2, 132–3
　The Departure 18
　Exiles ix, 7
　Jimmy Diamond 7, 18, 31–2, 36
　'John Masefield's Attic' 102, 130, 239–40, 242
　Journey to the Stone Country x, xi, 4, 8, 18–22, 25, 35–6, 46, 53, 62–3, 131–6, 139–55, 156–69, 170–86, 196–8, 201–16
　Kitty Howard ix, 6
　Landscape of Farewell x, xi, 4, 5, 8, 16, 18–20, 23, 26, 36–8, 50–1, 63, 67, 113, 131–6, 139–55, 156–69, 187–200, 201–16, 217–30
　Lovesong xi, 5, 23, 38, 39, 42–5, 64, 74–5, 122–3
　'The Mask of Fiction' 1, 3, 6, 7, 9, 11, 12, 14–15, 17, 18, 19, 22, 29–41
　'Modern, European and Novel' 23, 25
　Prochownik's Dream x, xi, 5, 12, 13–14, 23, 24, 31, 46, 101–13, 208
　The Reconciliation Trilogy 18
　The Sitters x, 5, 12–13, 14–15, 17, 23, 24, 33–5, 78–88, 89–100, 188
　'Sweet Water' 23, 25–6, 135, 170–1, 174
　'This Is How It's Going to Be Then' 7, 72
　The Tivington Nott ix, x, 7, 31–2, 38–9, 40, 44, 48–50, 55–9, 61, 64, 67, 243
　Watching the Climbers on the Mountain ix, 1, 2, 7–8, 16, 31, 35, 37, 53, 55–6, 59–62, 64, 70–1, 145

'Waxing Wiser Than Oneself' 4–6
'Written in Our Hearts' 21–2
Miller, Jane (aunt) xi
Miller, Stephanie (née Pullin) ix, x, 4, 6, 31, 36, 38, 217
Mooney, Ray ix
Moses, Dirk 174, 204–5
multiculturalism 26, 68–70, 75, 114

Nabokov, Vladimir 24, 46, 239, 244
Naipaul, VS 242
Nebo x, 18, 148
Neil, Anne viii, 4, 12
New South Wales Premier's Literary Awards x, xi, 1
New Zealand viii, 4
Nolan, Sidney, 3, 4, 13, 38–40, 56, 67, 128, 231–44
Nussbaum, Martha 6, 52–3

O'Hoy, Alan ix, 6, 8, 10, 12, 33, 72, 115
Olubas, Brigitta 13, 14
O'Rourke, Fran 90–1
Otherness 114–24, 210
Ouyang Yu ix, 9

Paris ix, x, 6
Pearson, Noel 175–7
Pierce, Peter 5, 7, 78, 205, 207
postcolonialism 26, 70, 73, 114, 129, 203–4
Praed, Rosa 62

Ranna Valley 141
Ratcliffe, Sophie 53
Reed, Sunday 39, 232–3
Reid, Barrett x, 9, 13, 39, 244
Reimer, Andrew 115
Reynolds, Henry 17, 146, 157
Richards, Jonathan 157–8, 162–3
Rilke, RM 24, 101–2
Rimbaud, Arthur 232, 235
Roberts, Tony 157
Rome x, 15
Rooney, Brigid 15, 20–1, 23

Roth, Philip 25, 42
Rowley, Hazel xi
Rudd, Kevin 19, 157, 174

Schlink, Bernhard 220
Shanghai ix, 8, 9
Sharp, Ronald 13, 21
Singer, Isaac Bashevis 195
Somerset viii, 3
Springsure viii, 4, 18, 37, 56, 63, 145
Stevens, Wallace 83
Stolen Generations, the 19, 157, 174, 178, 183–4
Stratton, Jon 68–9
Stretton, Andrea 139
Swain, Tony 204

Tolstoy, Leo 42–54
Townsville x, 17–19, 36, 38, 140–1, 145, 147
Tunisia x, 15, 33–4, 63

University of Melbourne viii, 4, 30–1
University of Sydney symposium vii, xi, 19, 139–55

Van Teeseling, Ingrid 3

Walker, Brenda 1, 7, 24–5
Walker, Shirley 18, 20, 23, 212
Webby, Elizabeth 9, 12, 23, 26, 154
Weishanhu Award xi, 157
White, Patrick 1, 3, 14, 29–30, 128
Whitehead, Anne 178
Whiteness 68–9
Wilde, Oscar 29, 84
Windschuttle, Keith 19, 157, 174
Wood, James 53
Wordsworth, William 78–9

Yehching 8

Zavaglia, Liliana 19, 20–1, 203

For Product Safety Concerns and Information please contact our EU representative GPSR@taylorandfrancis.com
Taylor & Francis Verlag GmbH, Kaufingerstraße 24, 80331 München, Germany

www.ingramcontent.com/pod-product-compliance
Lightning Source LLC
Chambersburg PA
CBHW061437300426
44114CB00014B/1721